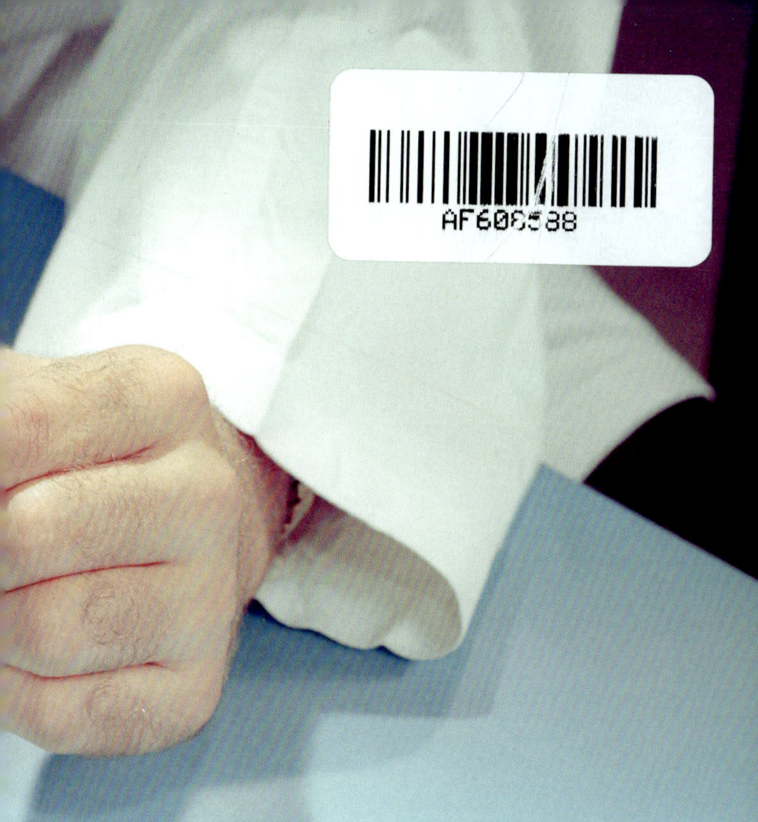

ENING

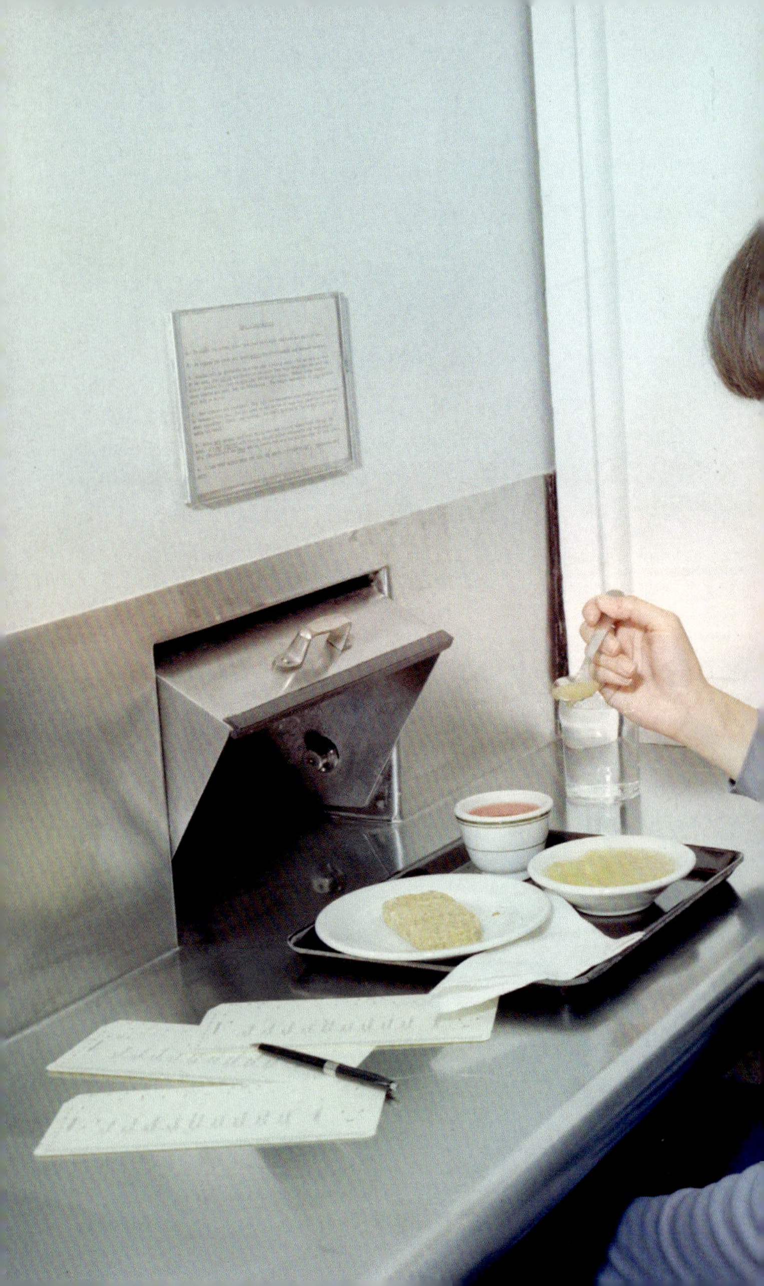

BETTER FOOD FOR OUR FIGHTING MEN

EDITED BY MATTHIEU NICOL

RVB BOOKS

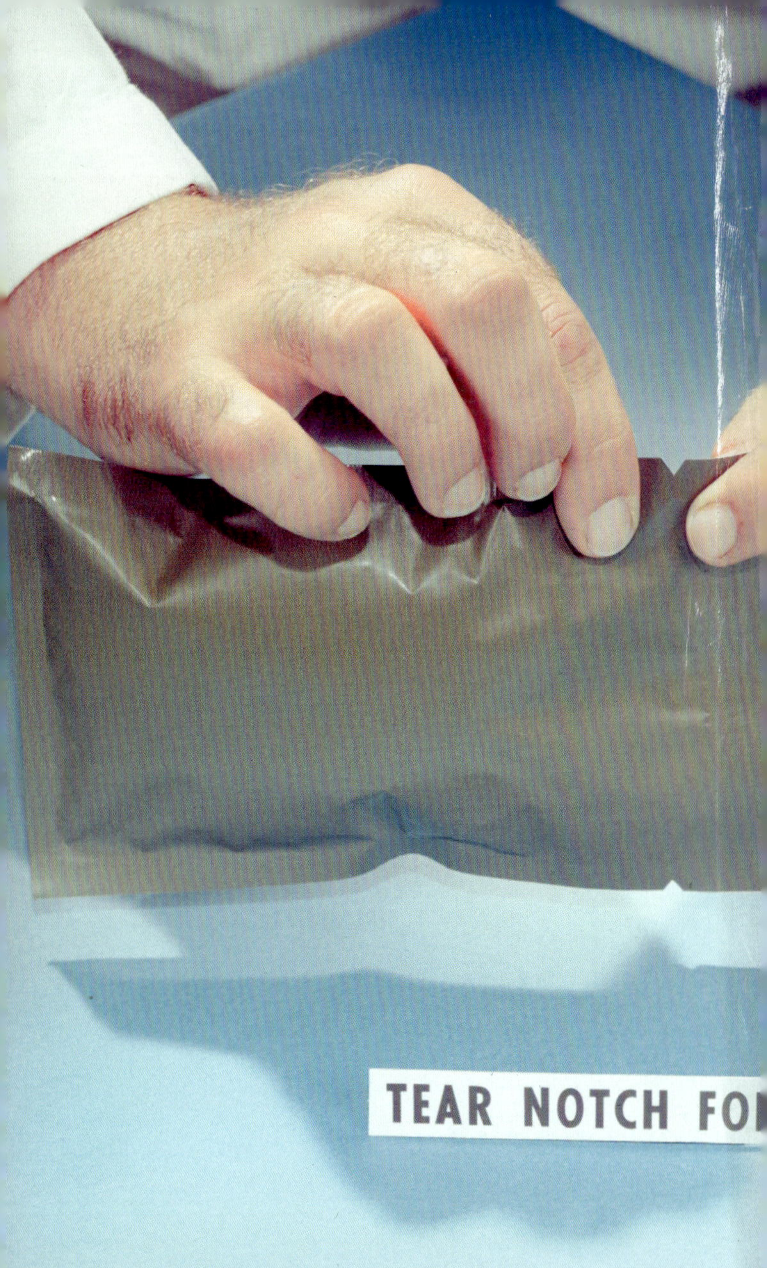
TEAR NOTCH FO

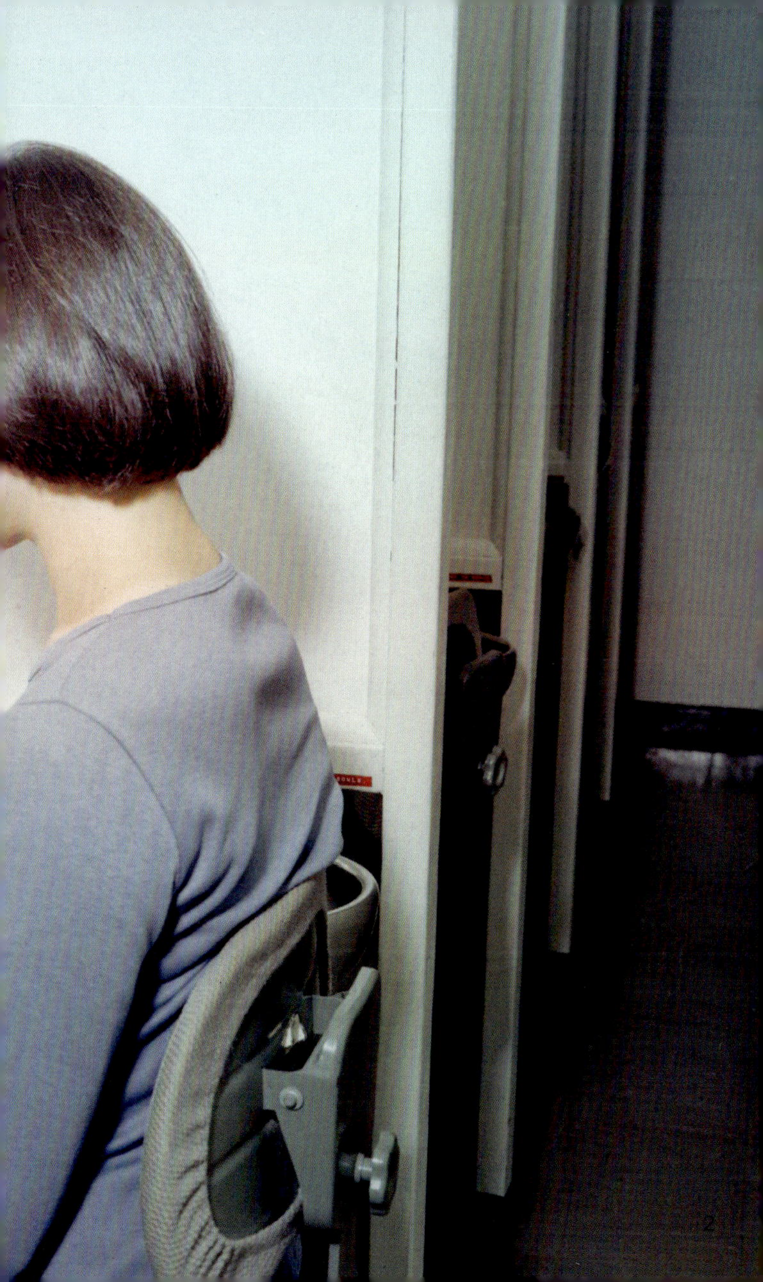

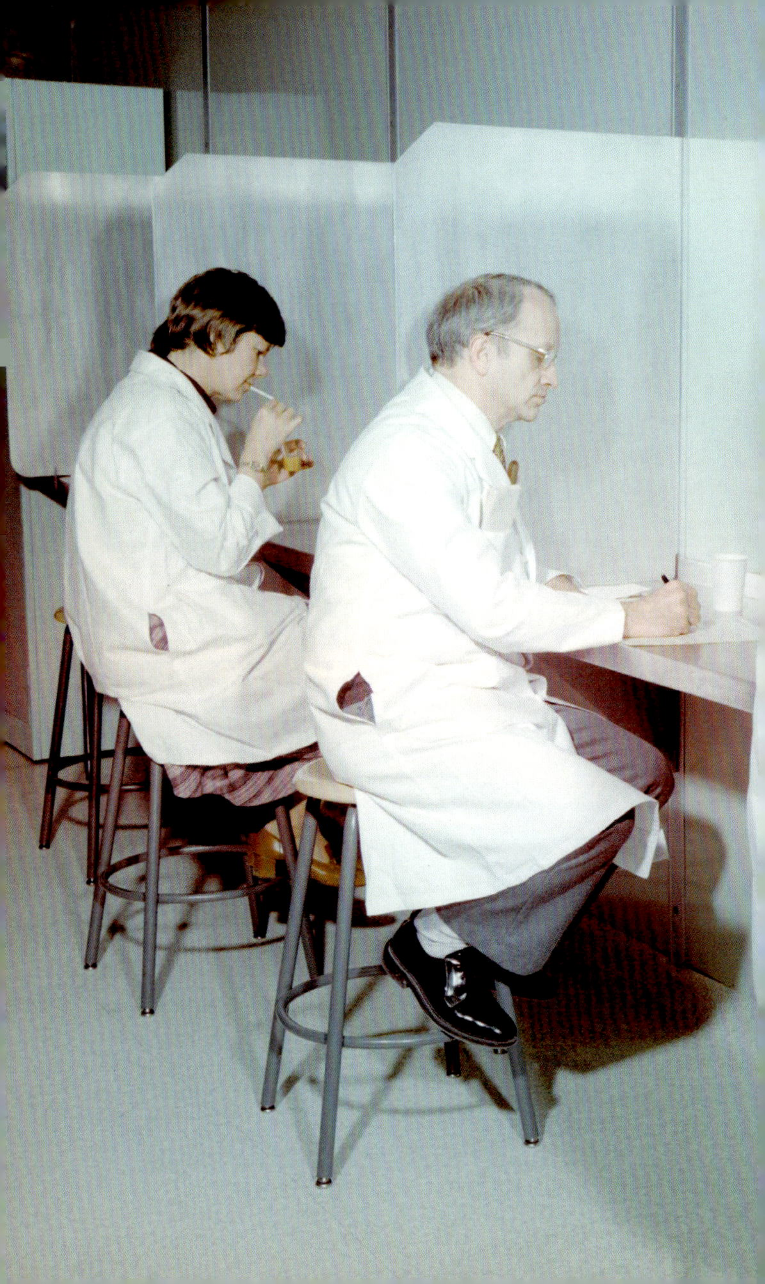

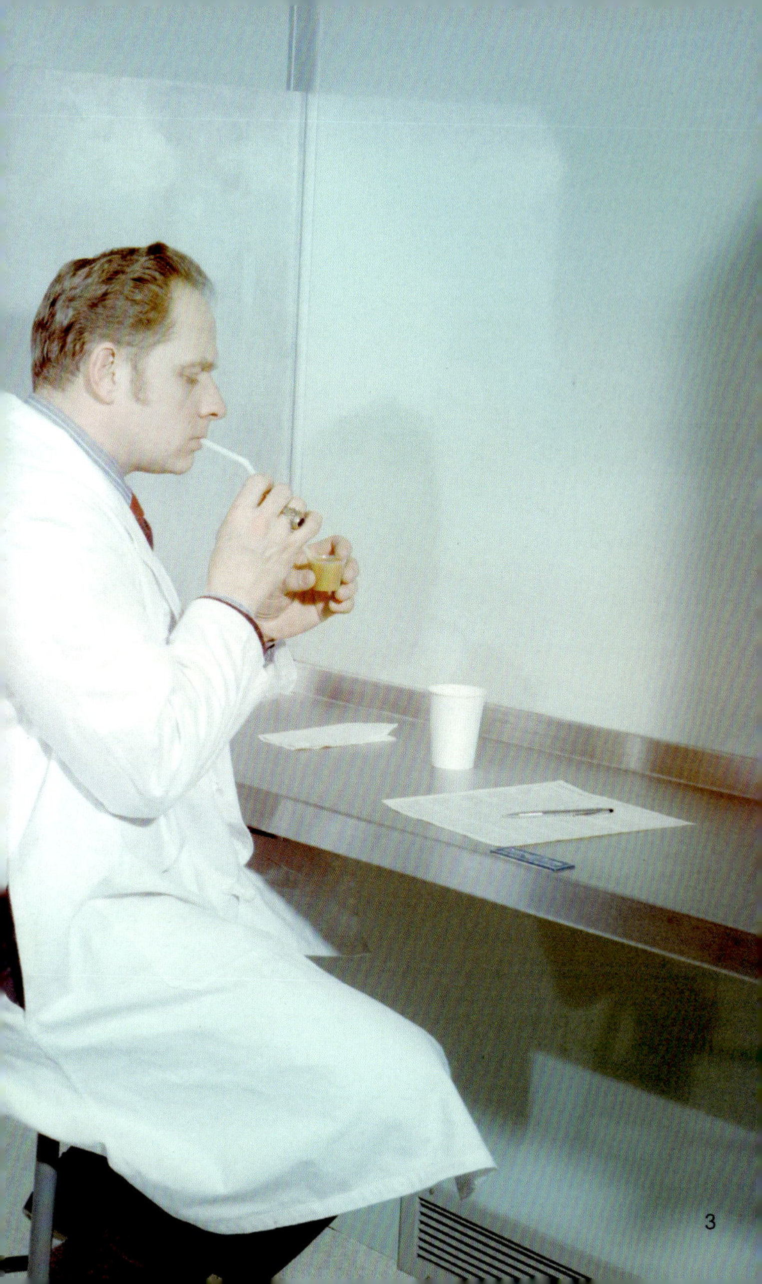

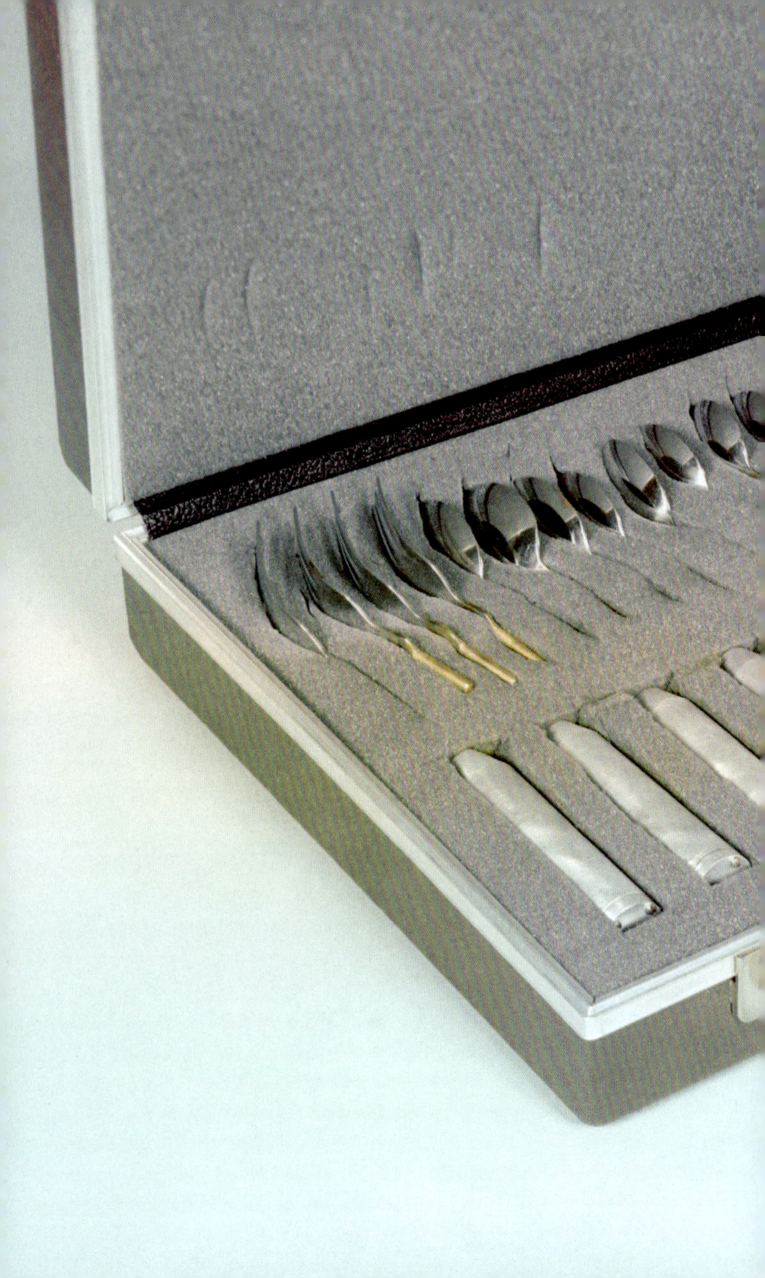

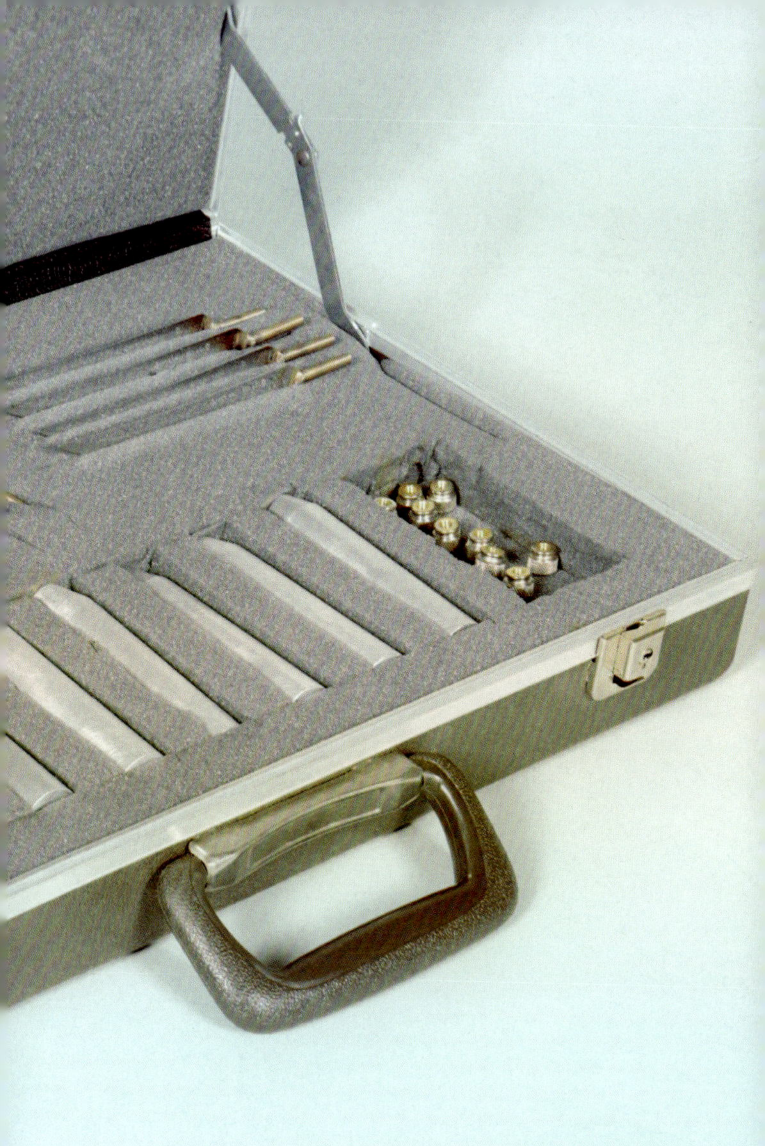

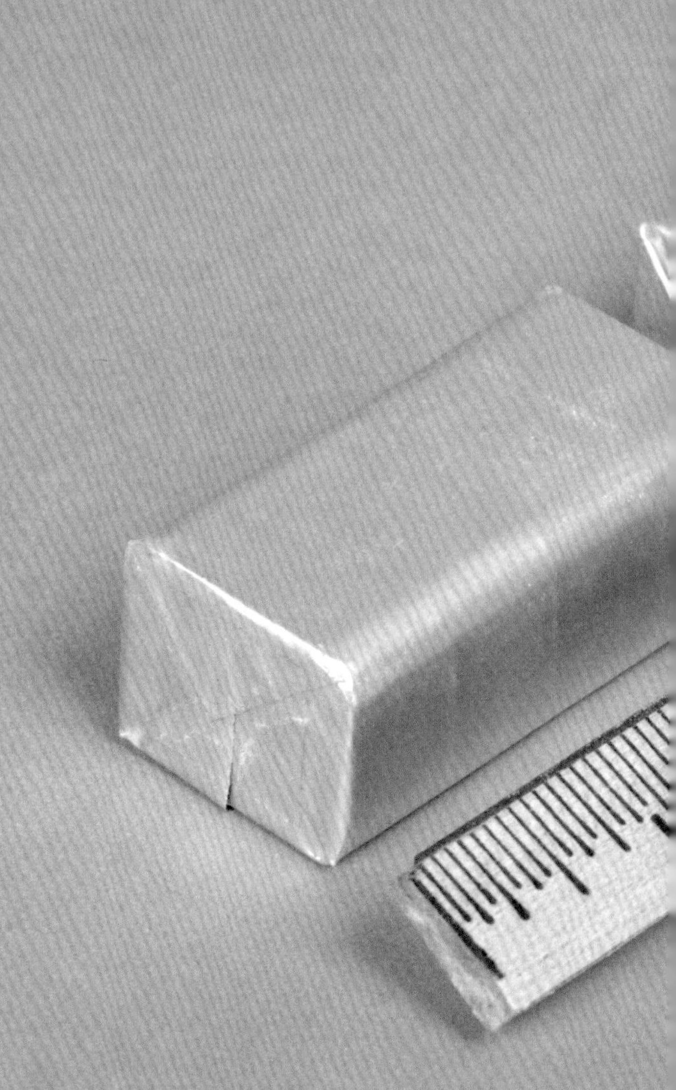

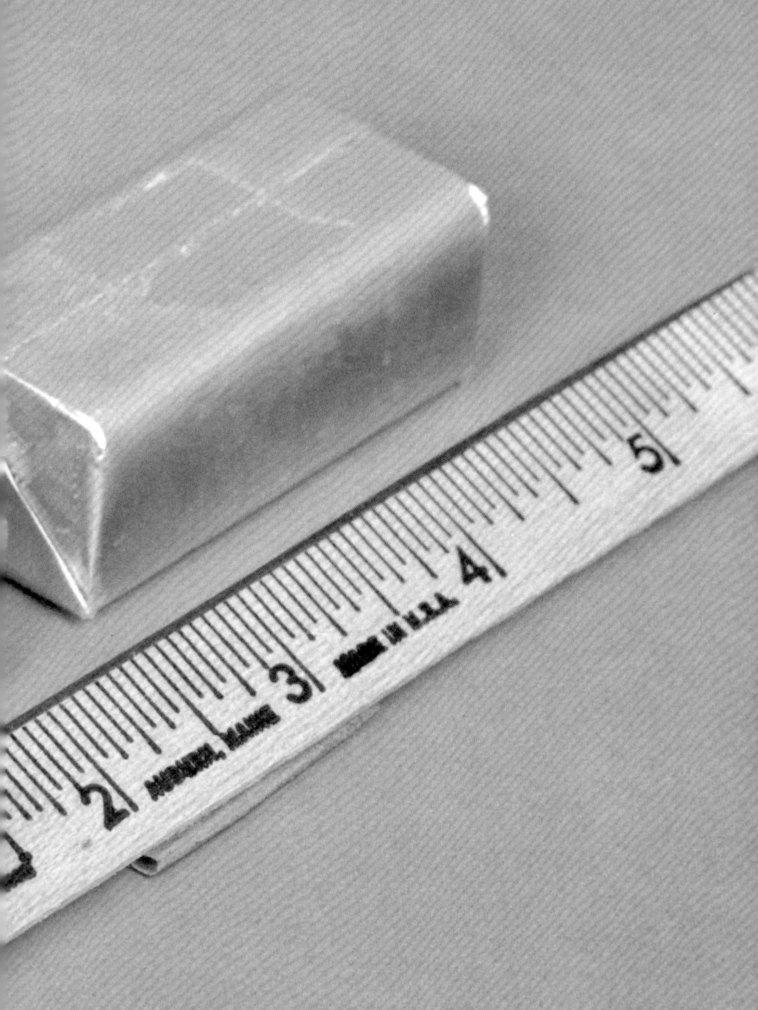
2
3
4
5

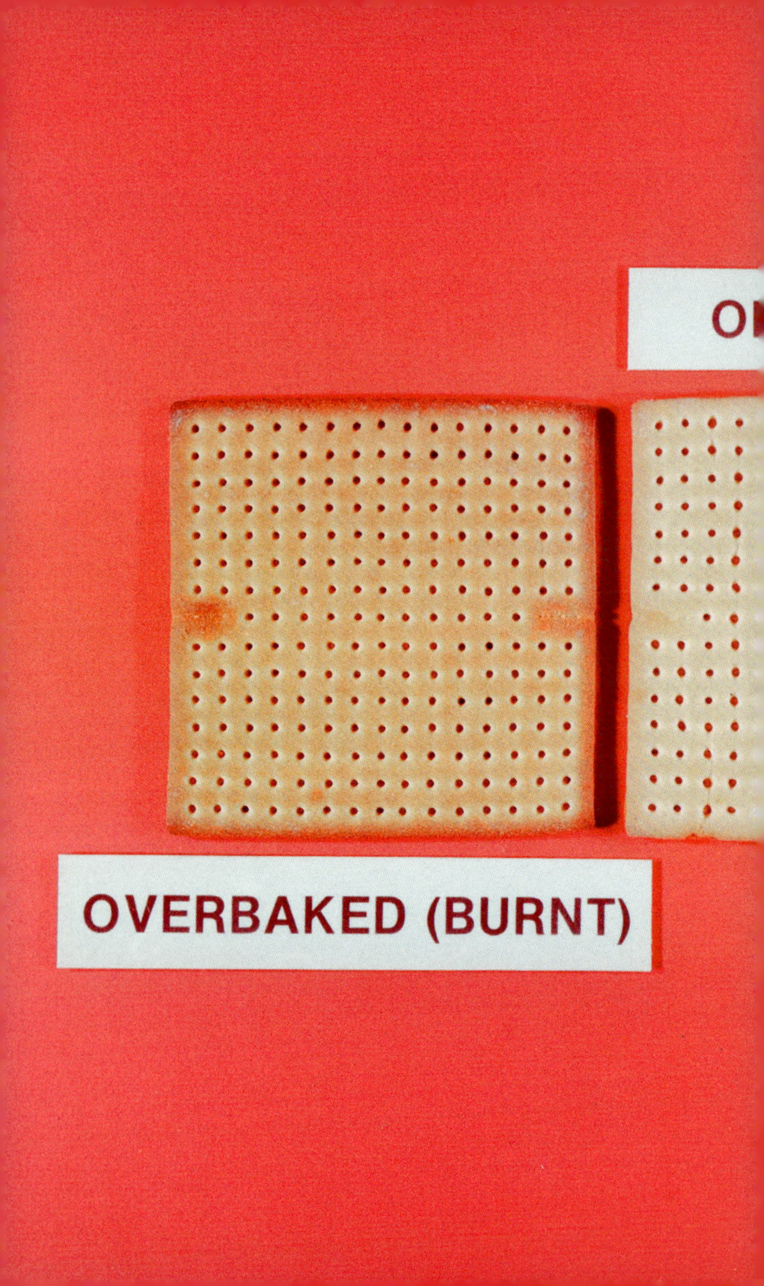

OVERBAKED (BURNT)

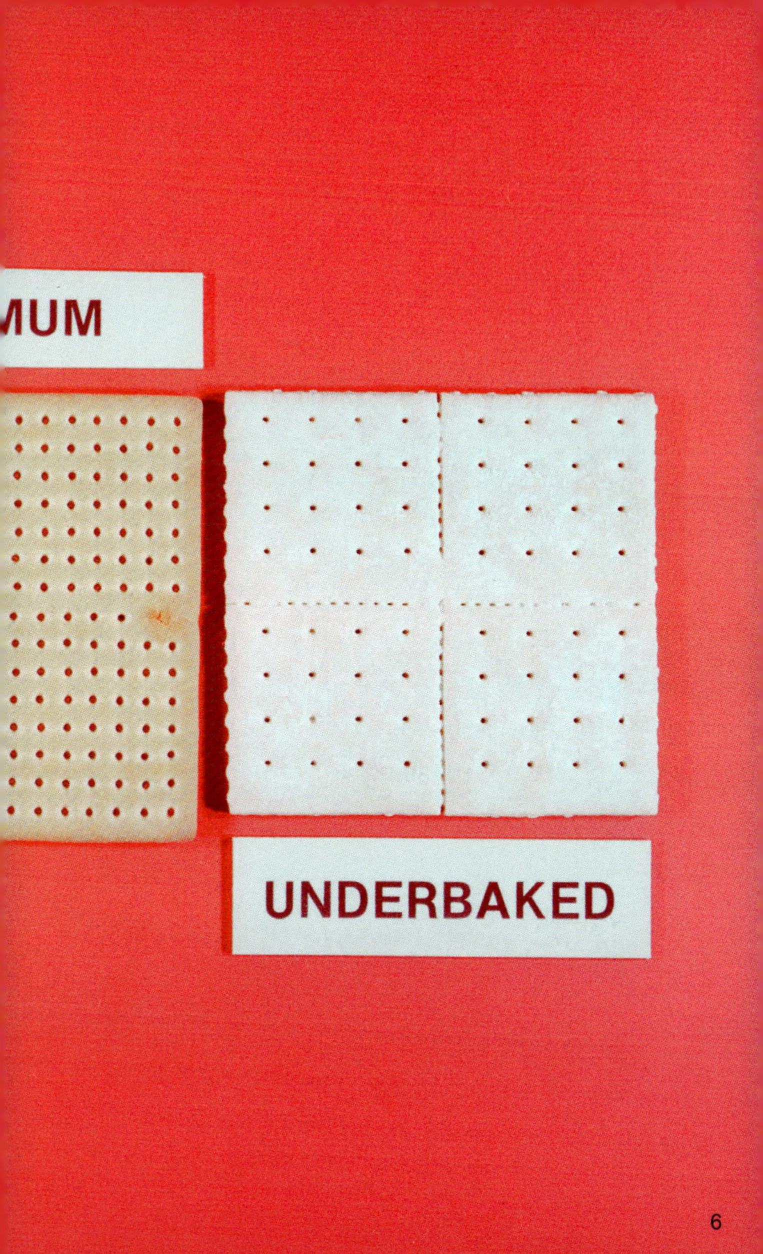

MUM

UNDERBAKED

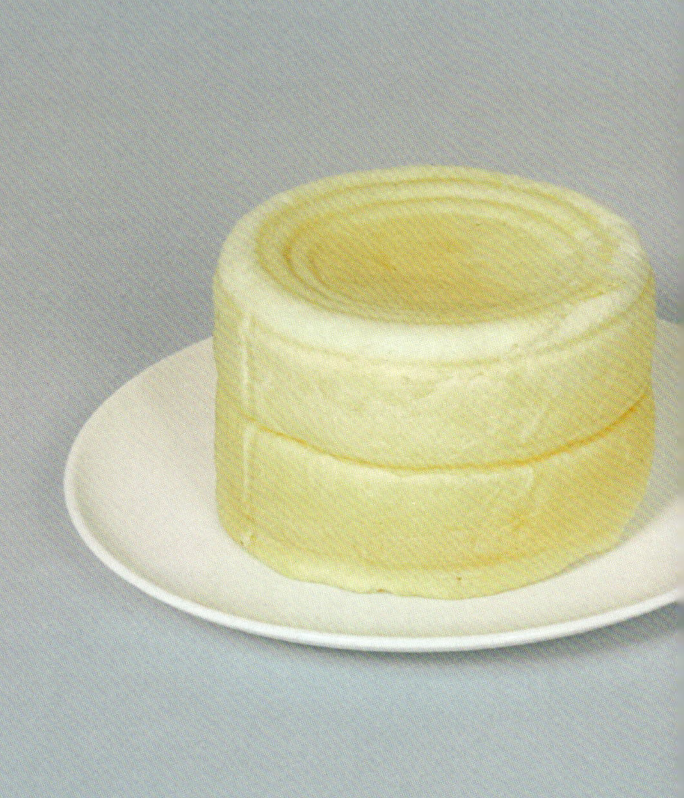

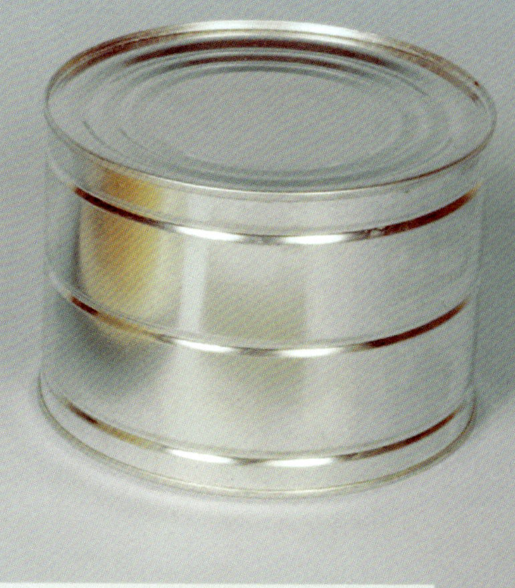

BREAD

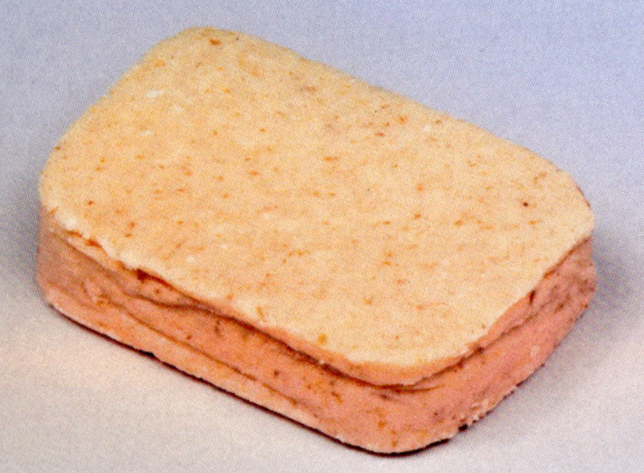

PROPOSED BREAD ALTERNATIVE
CHEESE-FLAVORED BAR

8

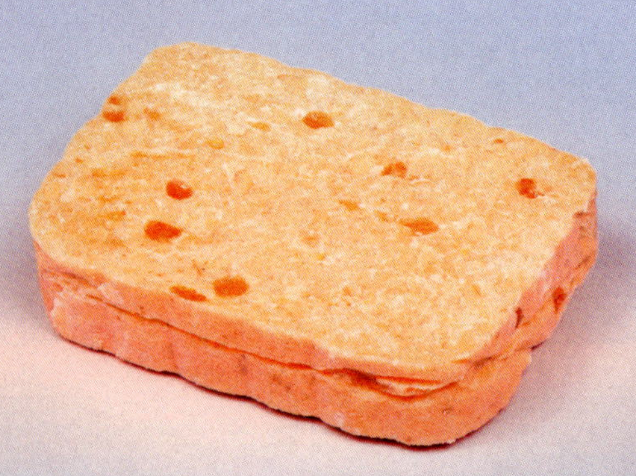

PROPOSED BREAD ALTERNATIVE
ORANGE NUT BAR

10

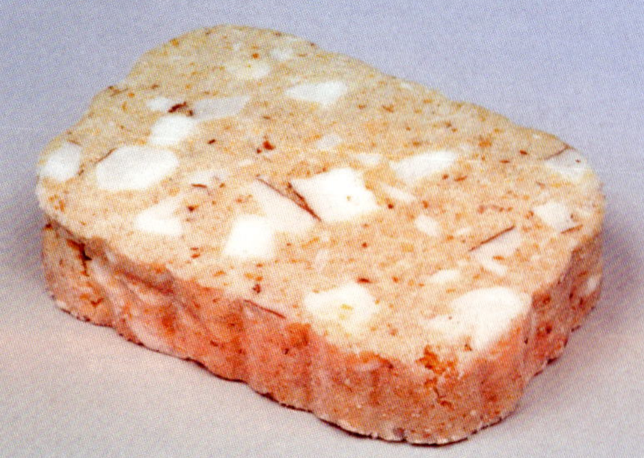

PROPOSED BREAD ALTERNATIVE
COCONUT BAR

9

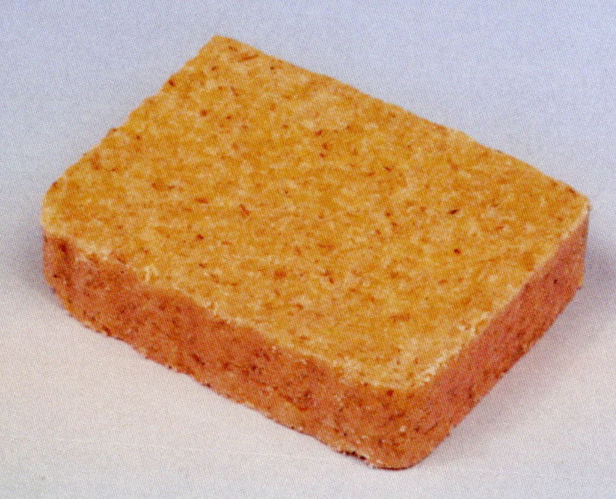

PROPOSED BREAD ALTERNATIVE
PIZZA BAR

11

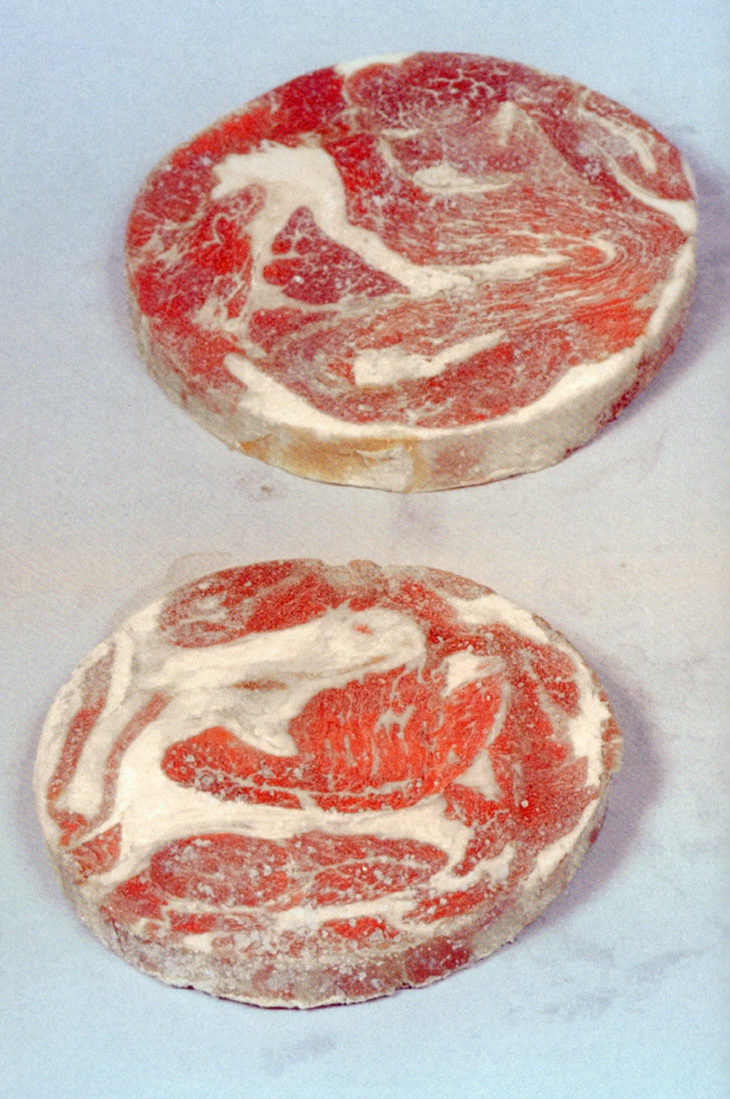

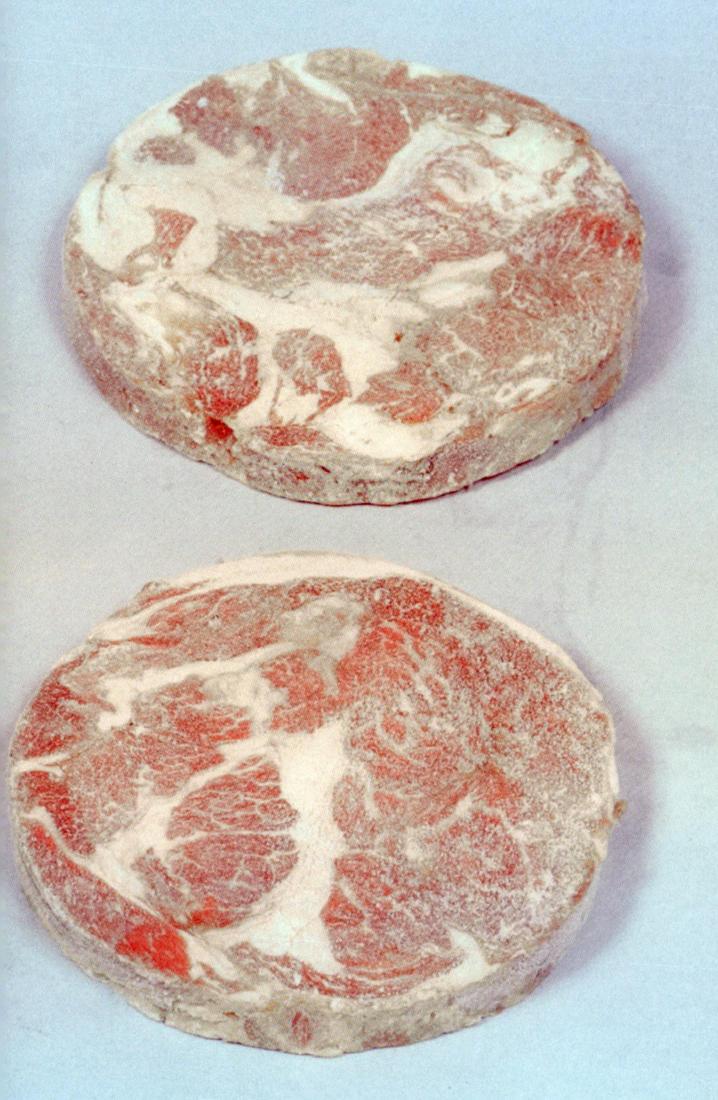

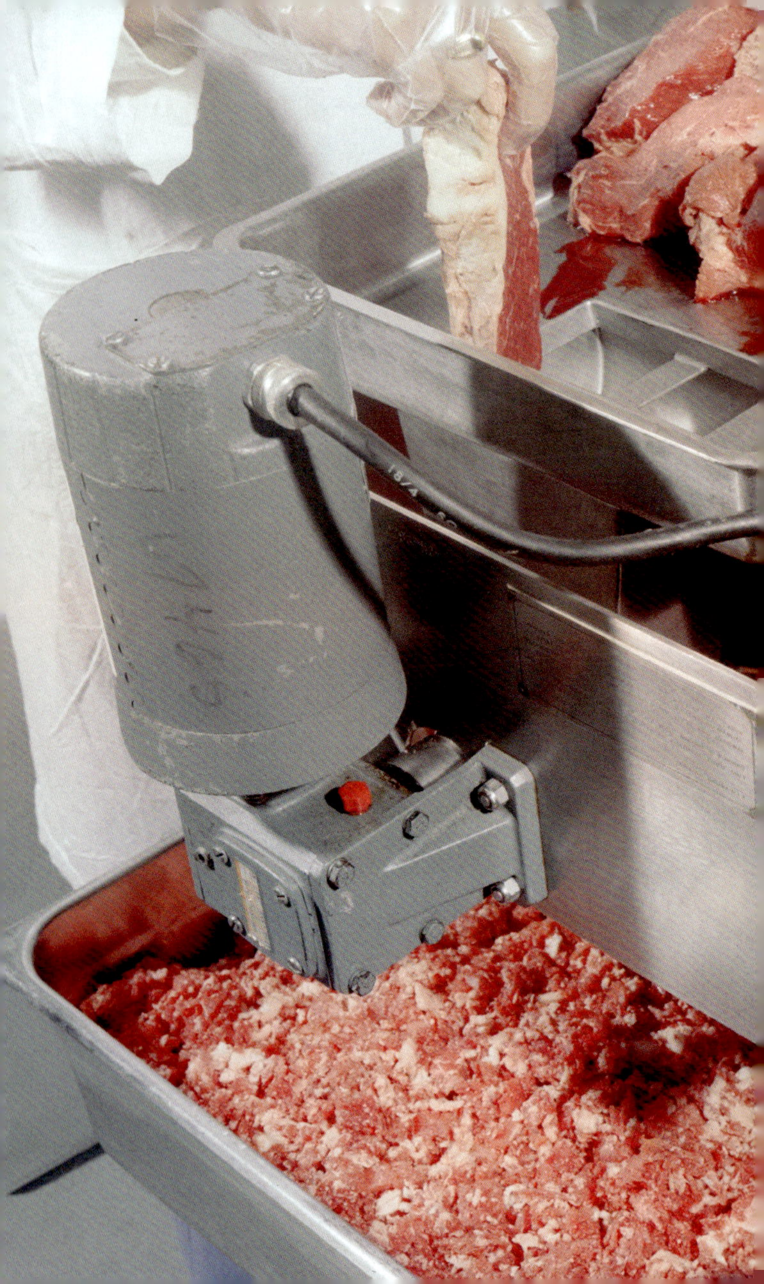

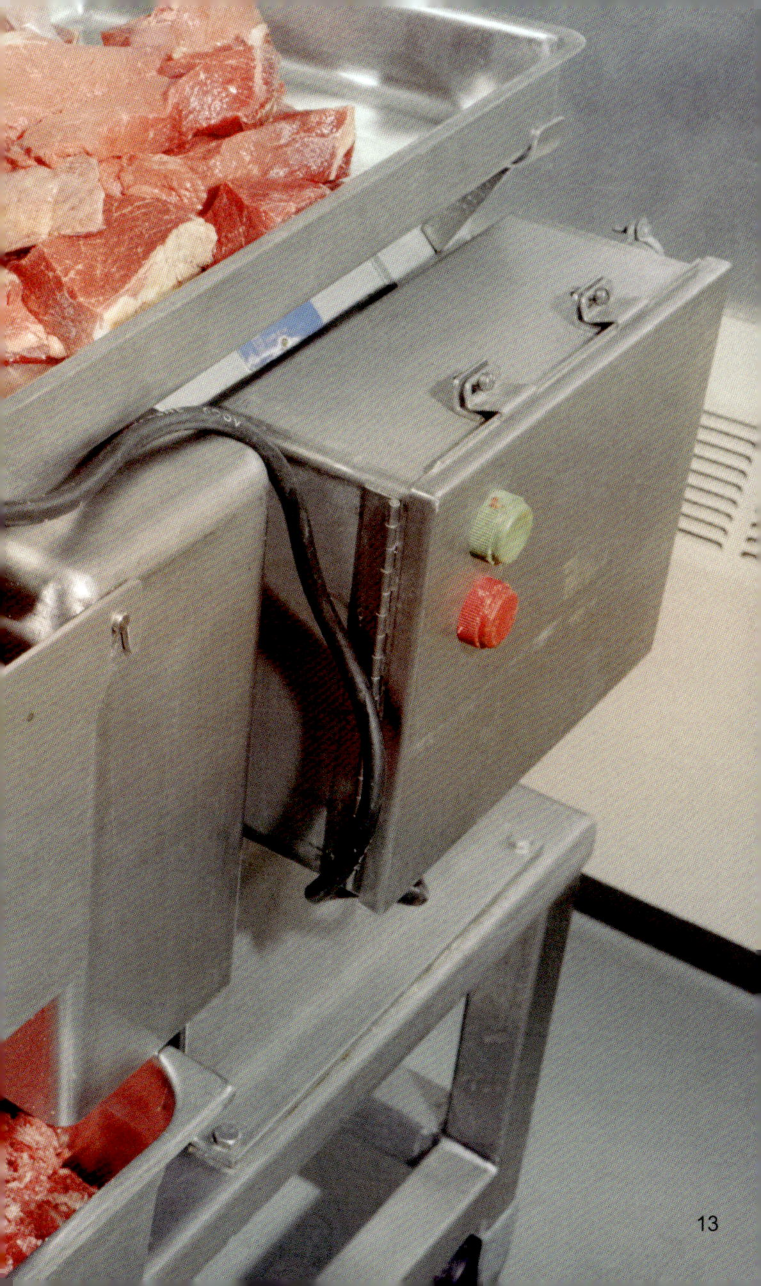

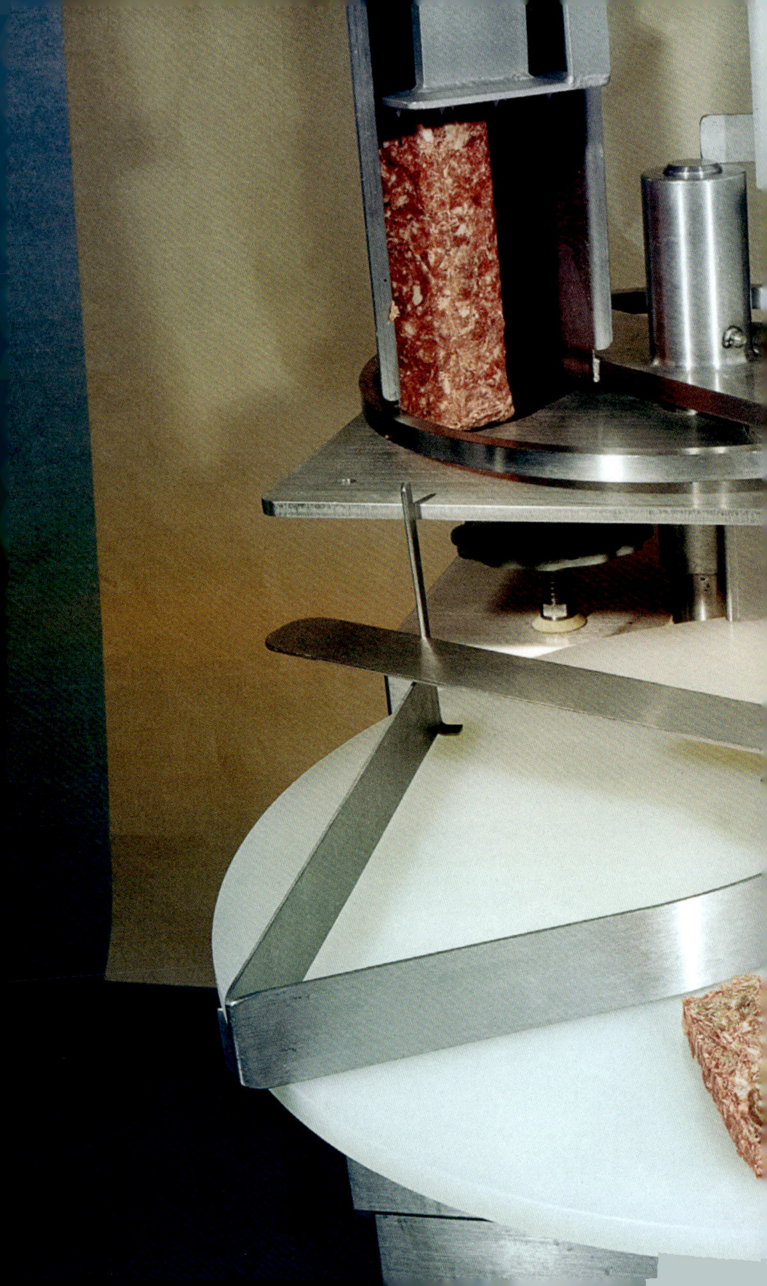

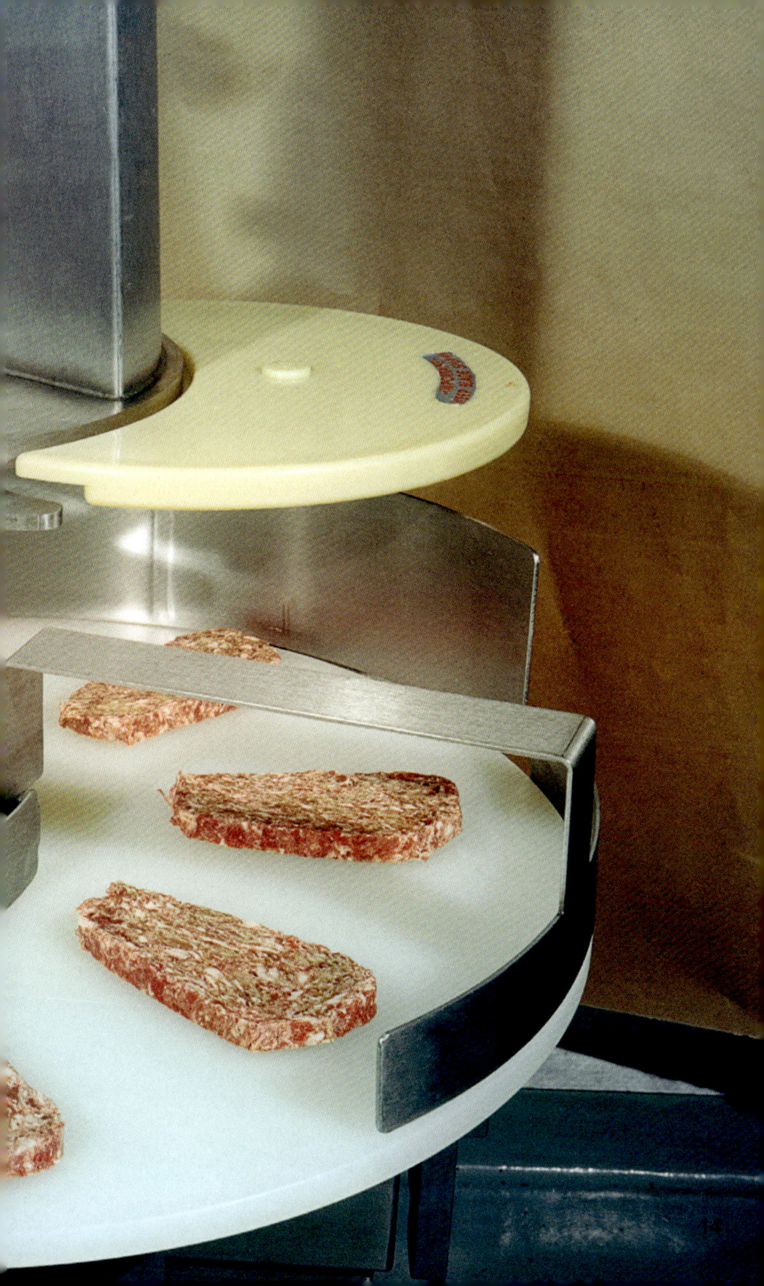

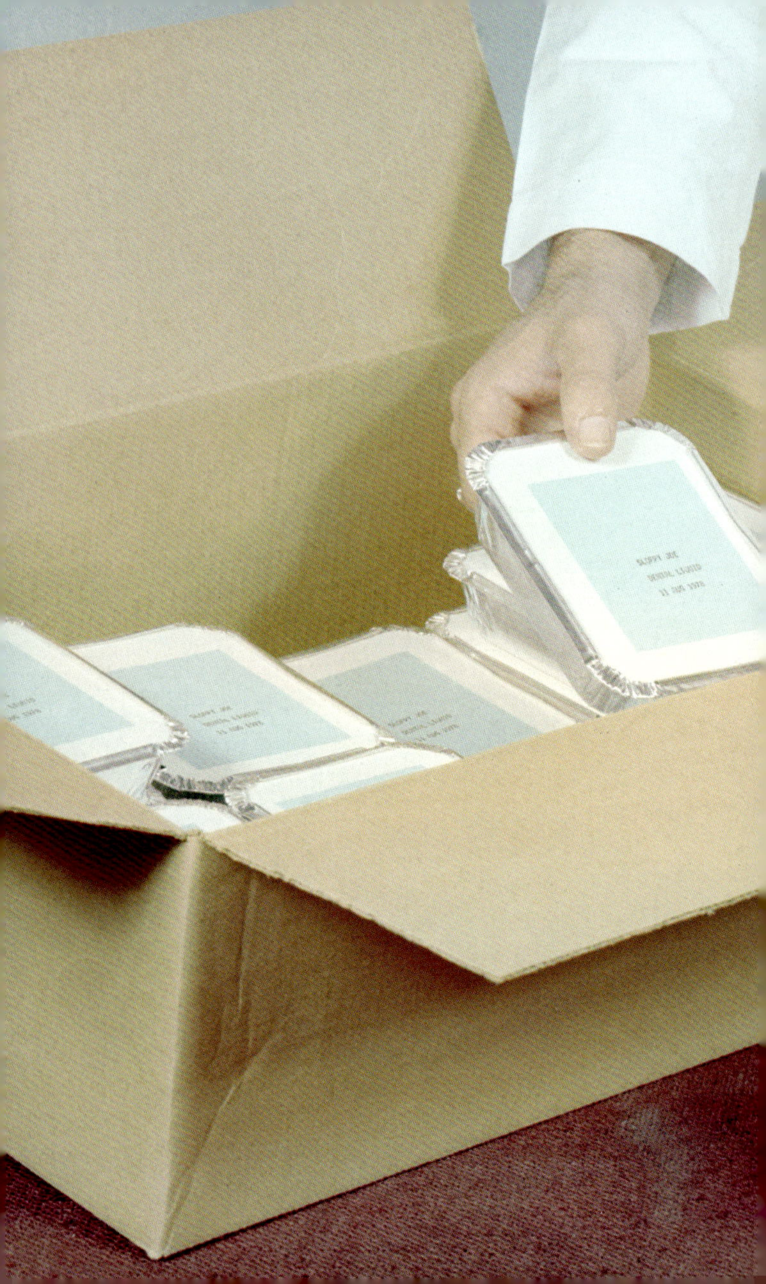

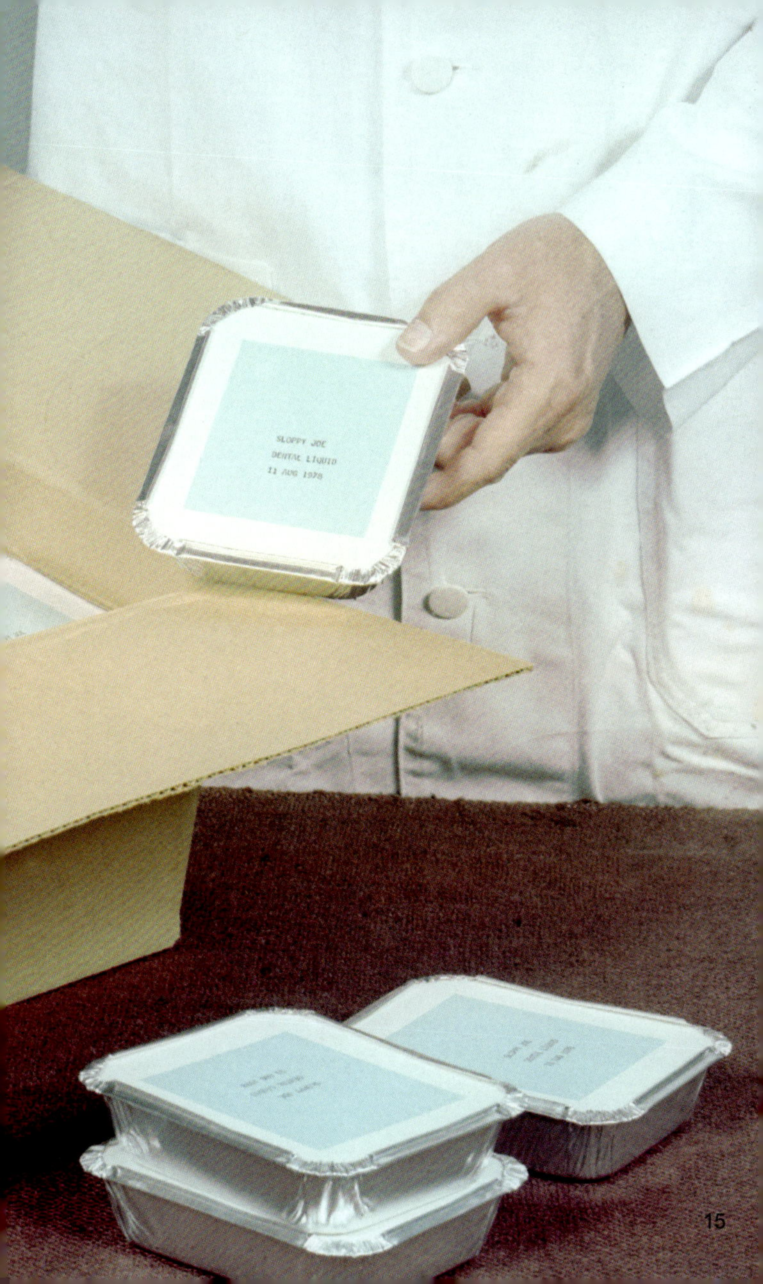
SLOPPY JOE
DENTAL LIQUID
11 AUG 1978

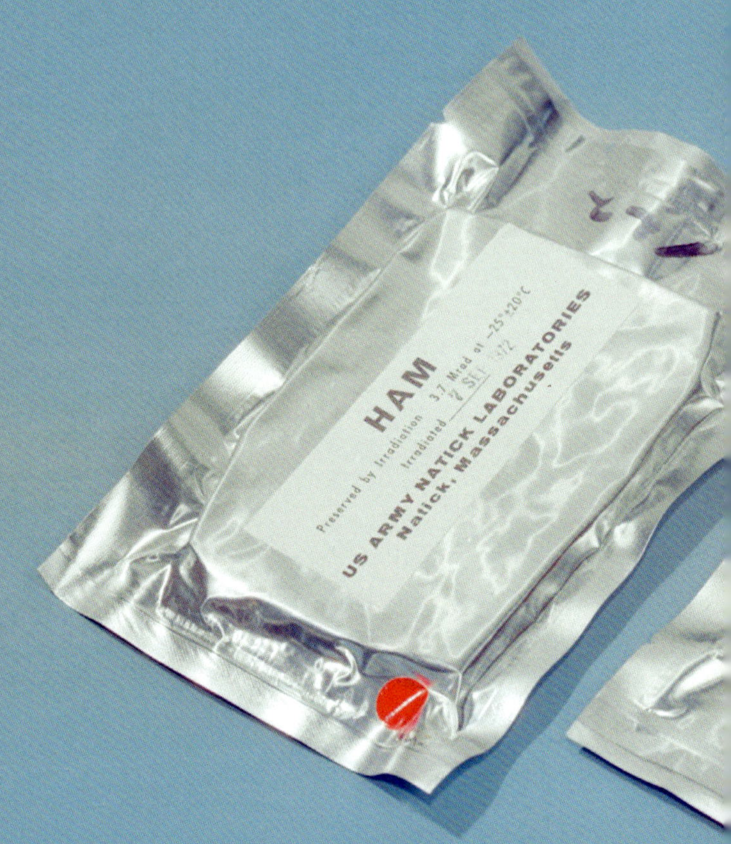

IRRADIATED HAM

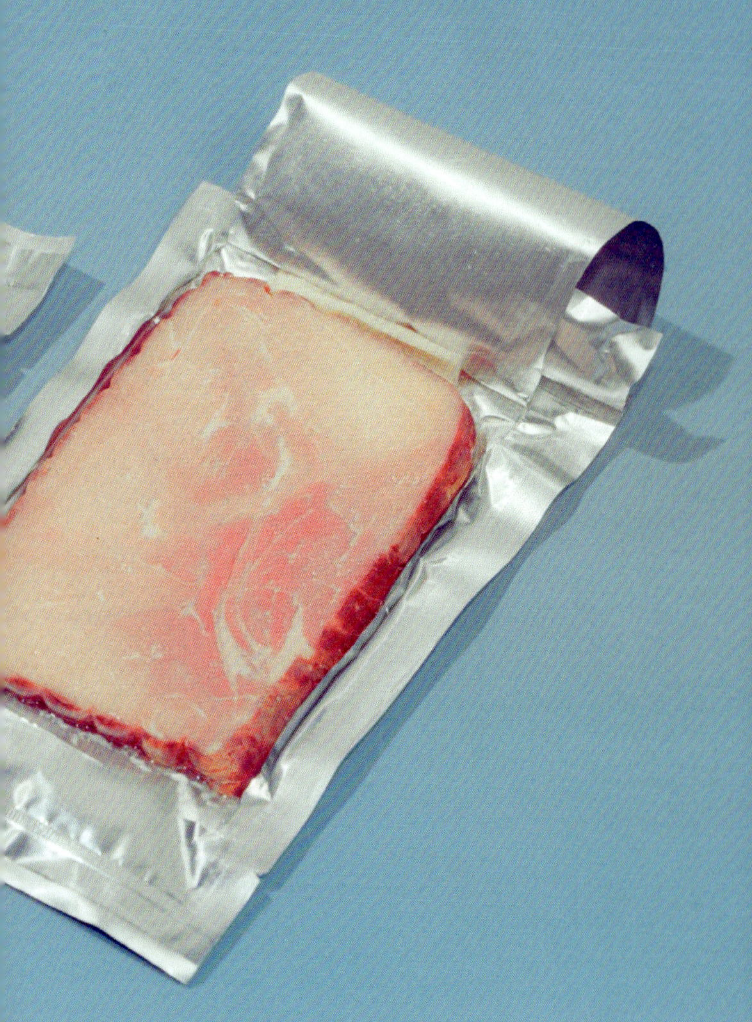

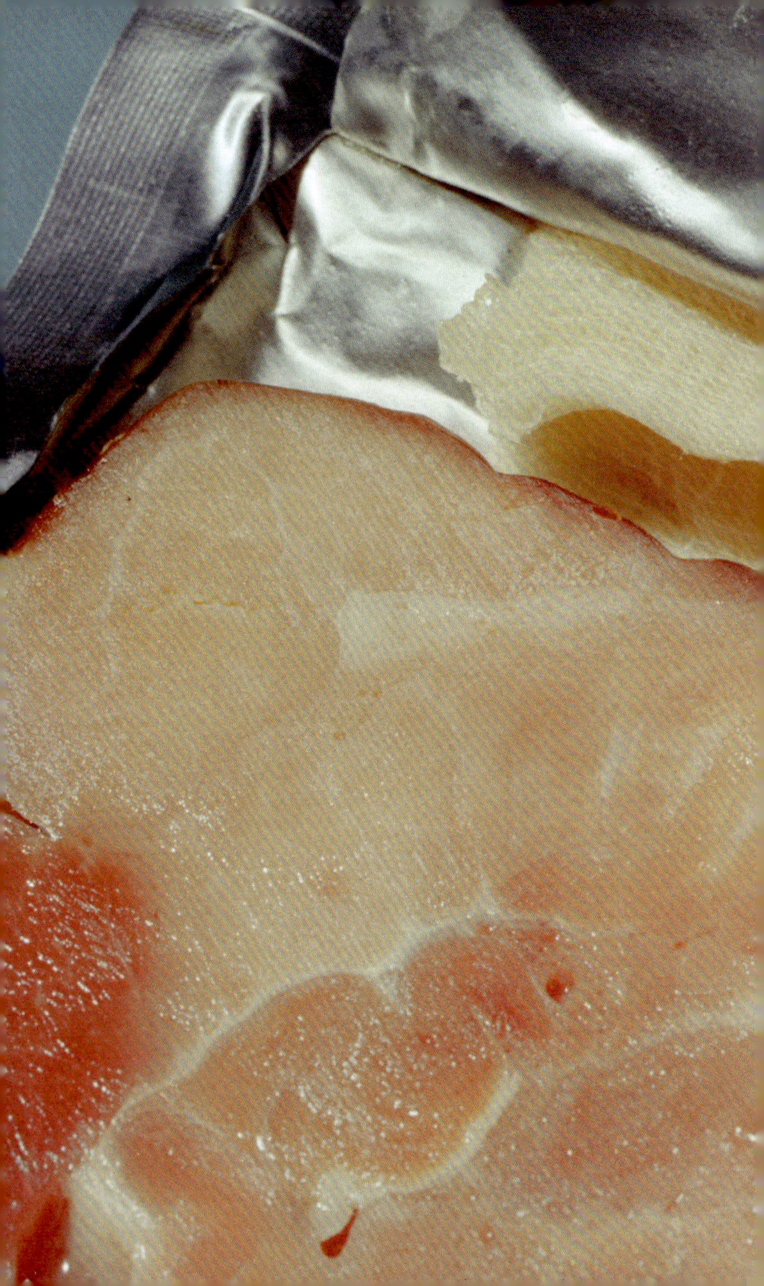

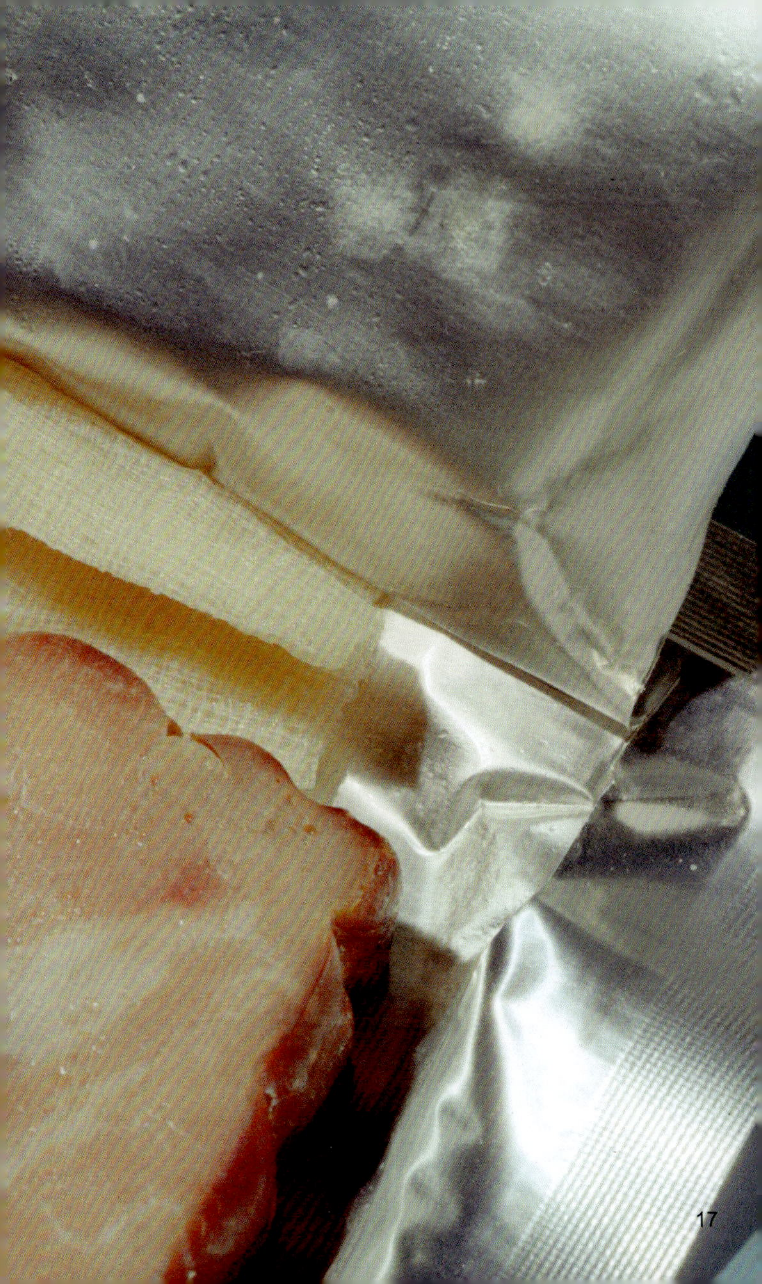

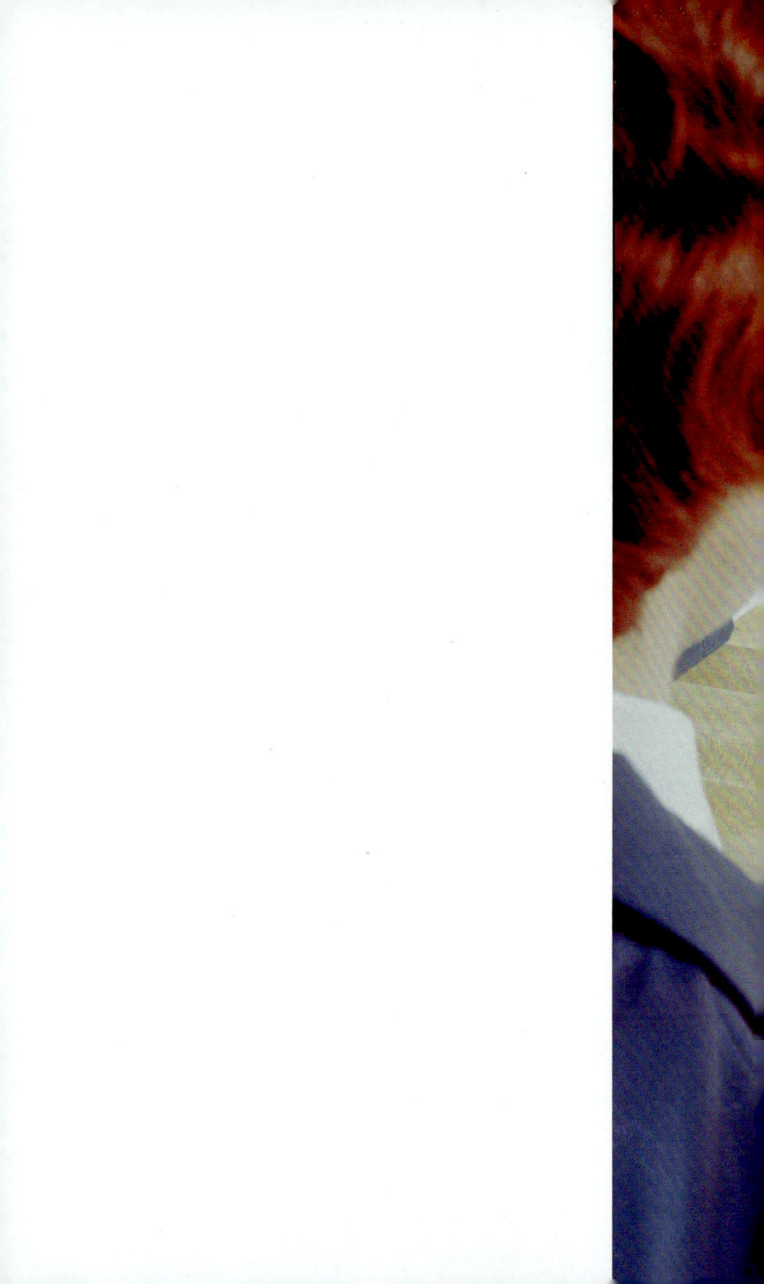

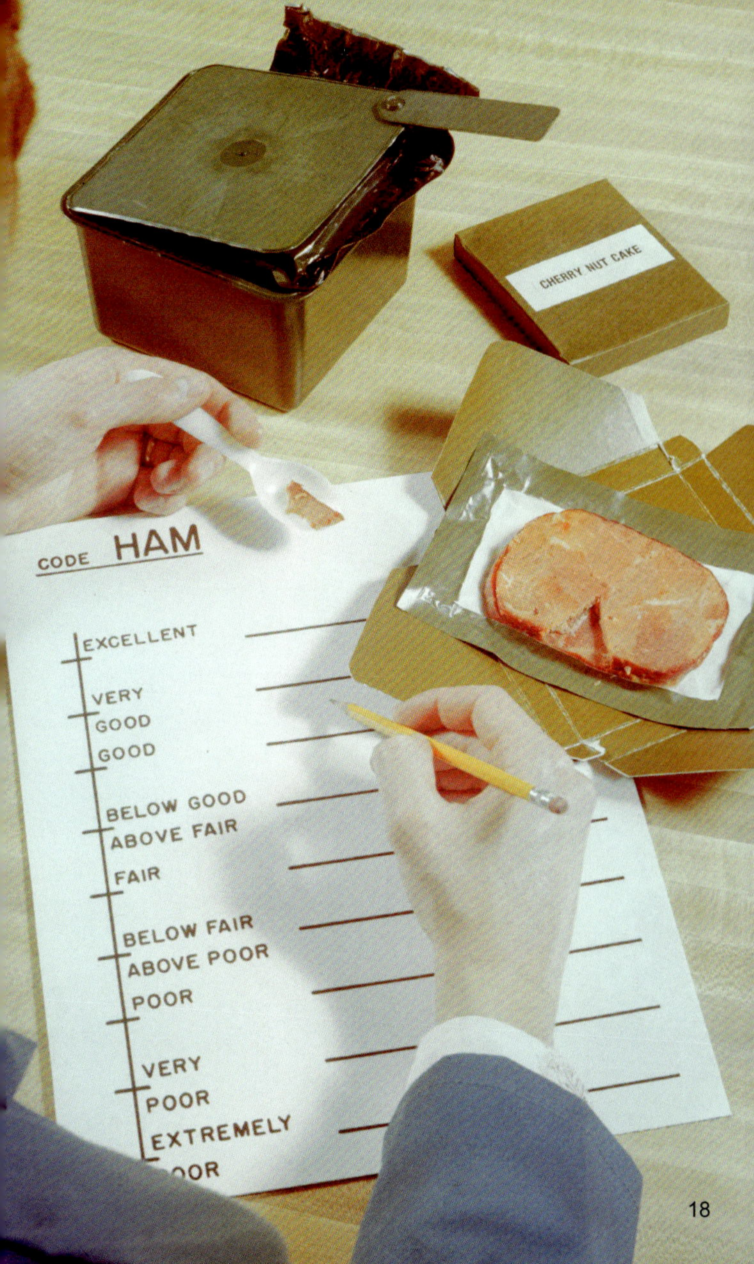
CHERRY NUT CAKE
CODE HAM
EXCELLENT
VERY
GOOD
GOOD
BELOW GOOD
ABOVE FAIR
FAIR
BELOW FAIR
ABOVE POOR
POOR
VERY
POOR
EXTREMELY

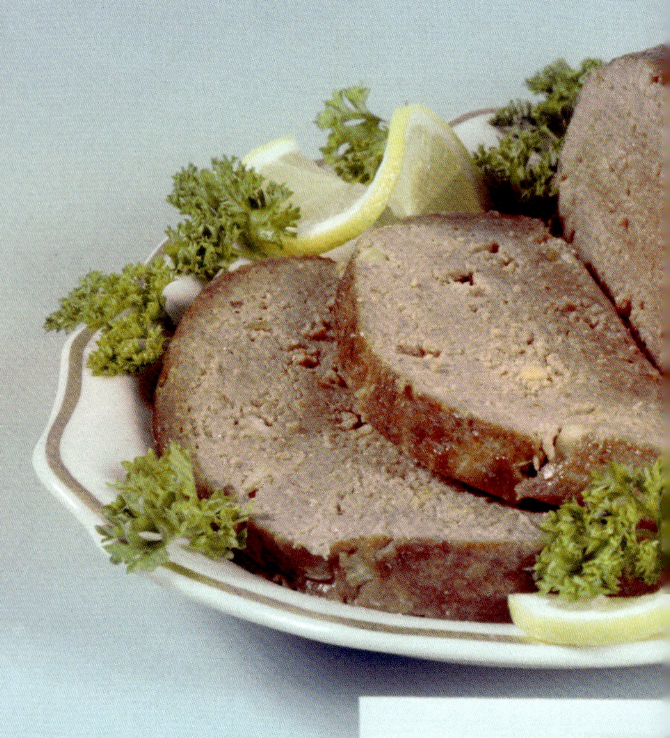
ME
SOY PR

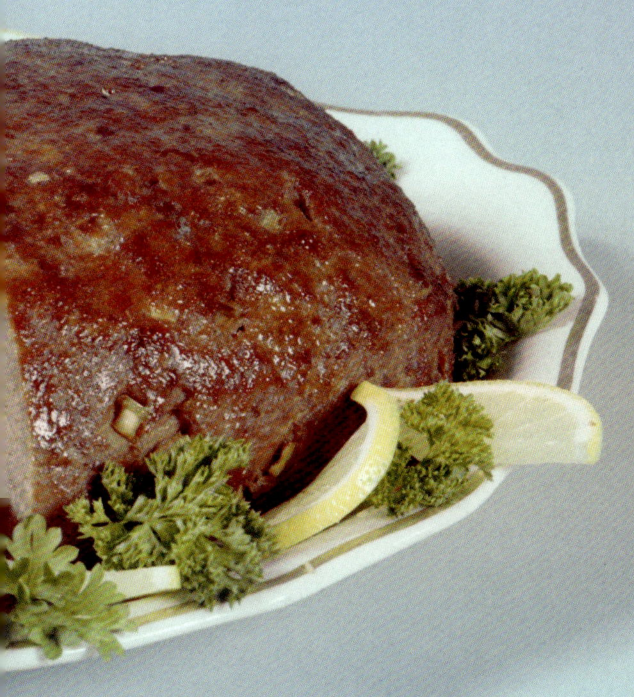

OAF
N ADDED

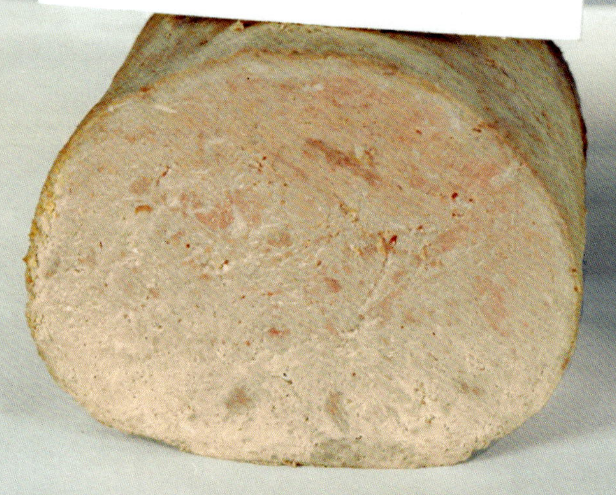
TEXTURED BEEF ROAST
OVEN COOKED

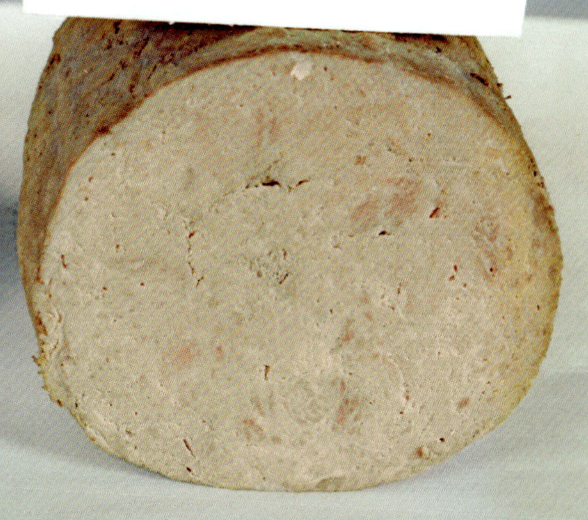
TEXTURED BEEF ROAST
WATER COOKED

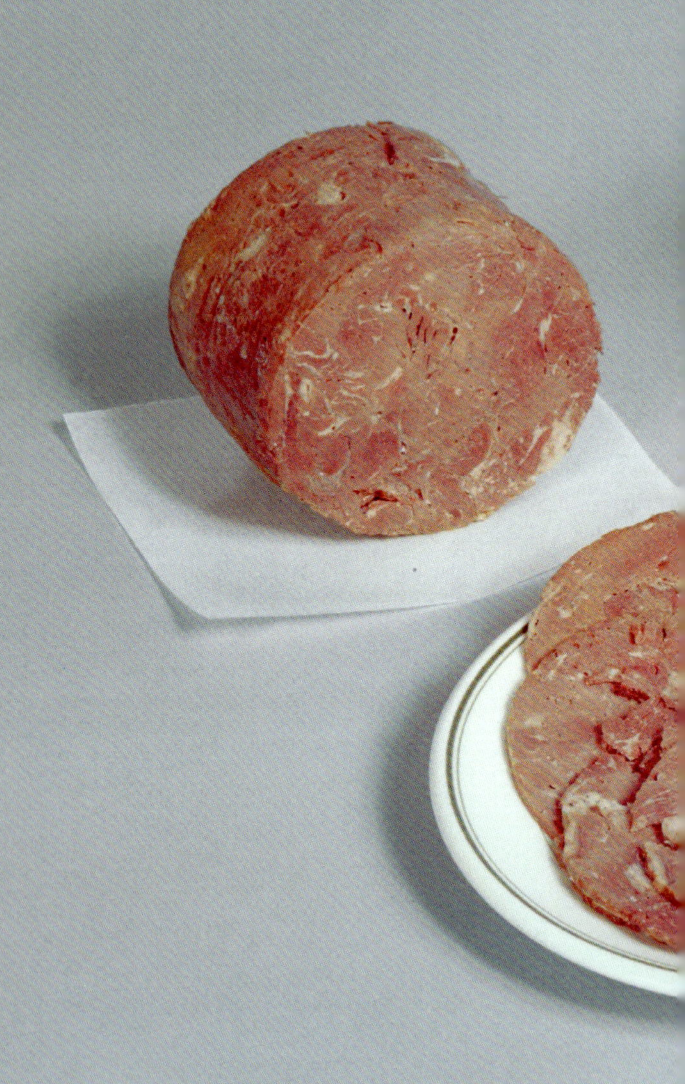

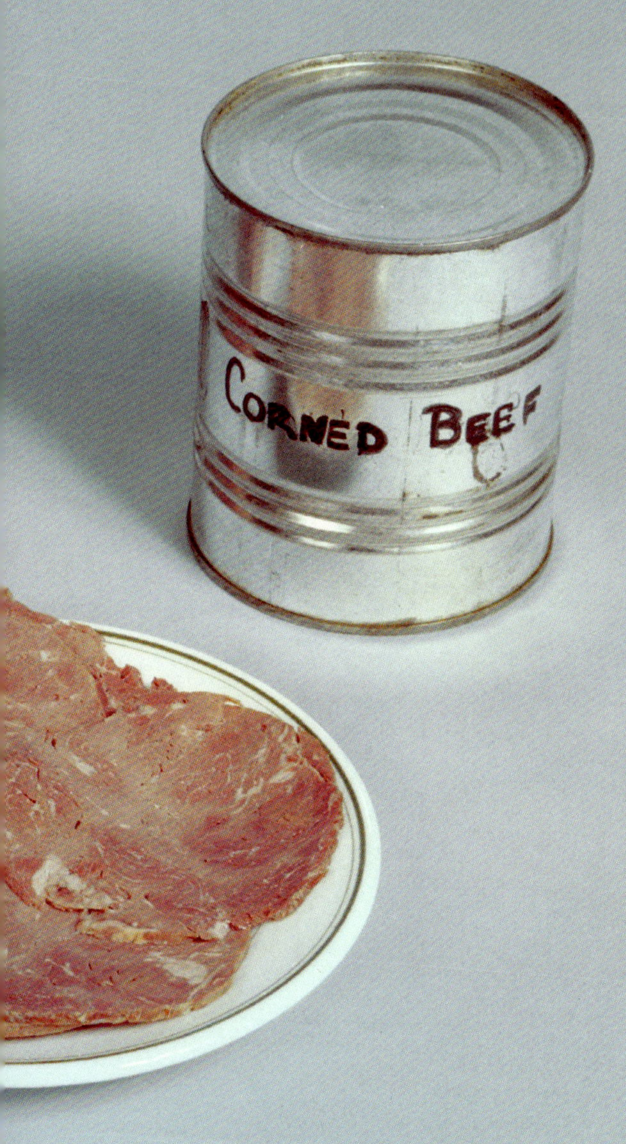
CORNED BEEF

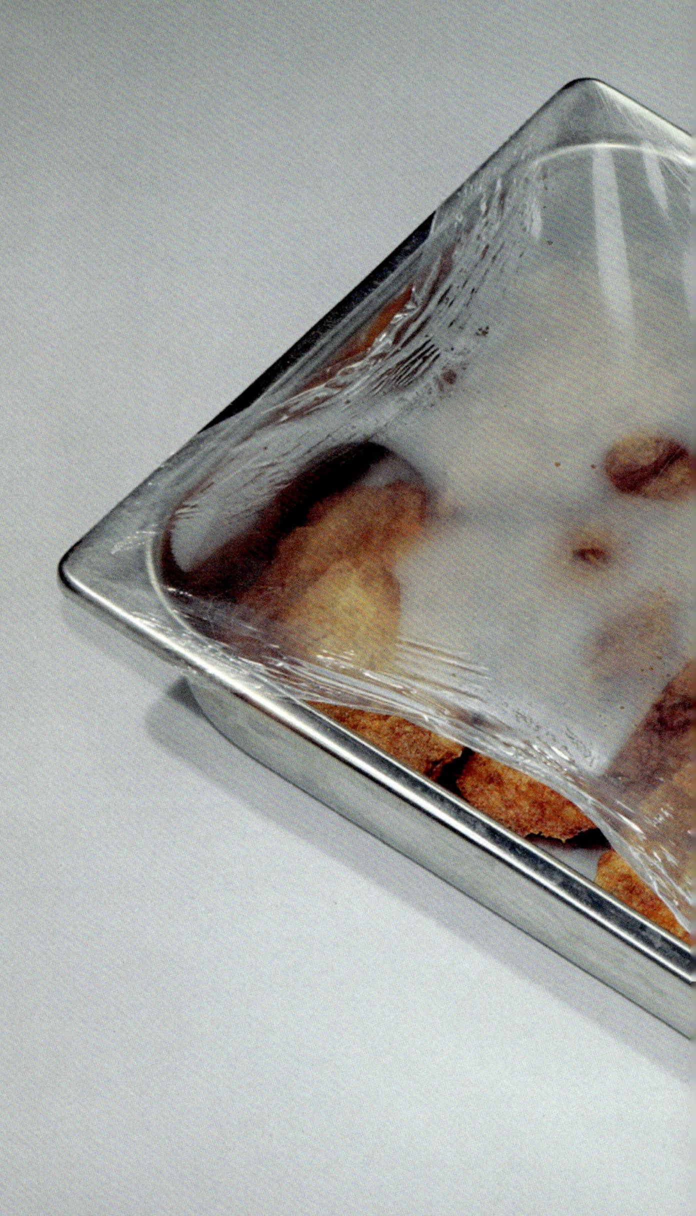

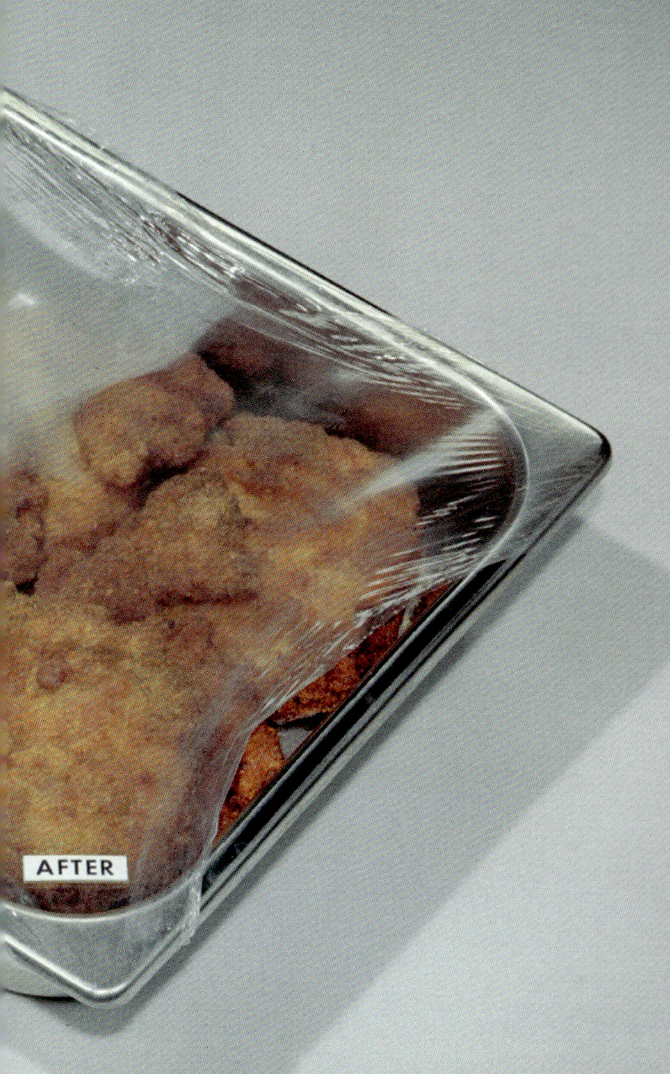
AFTER

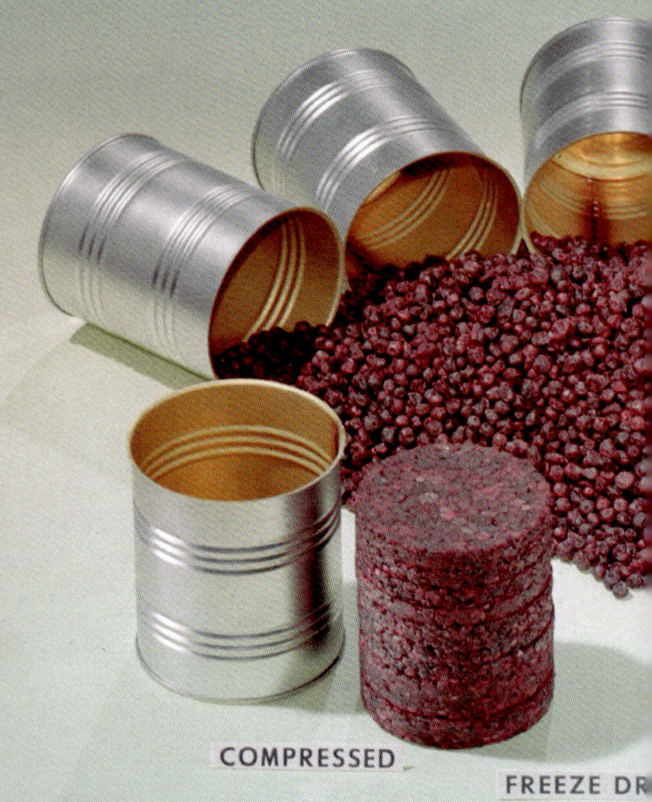
COMPRESSED
FREEZE DR

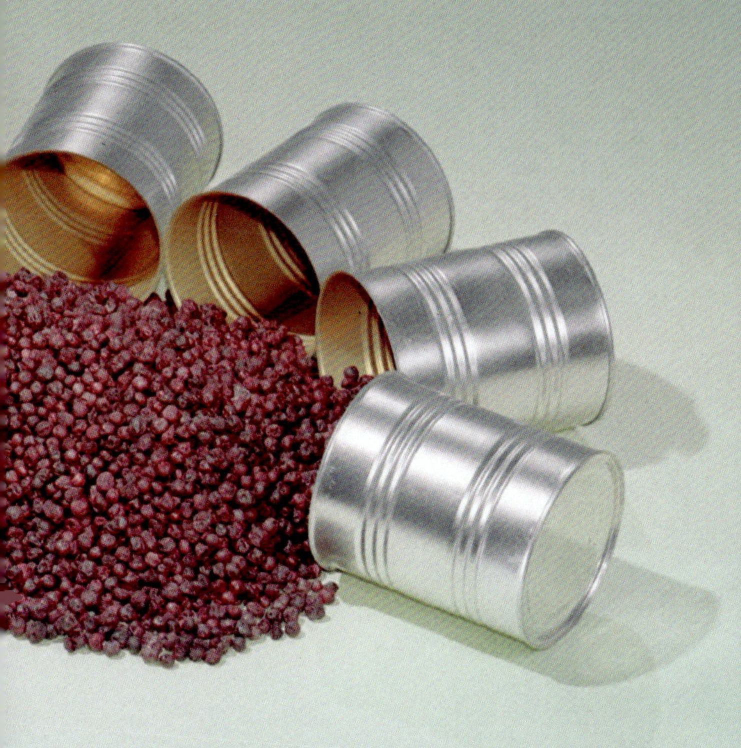

JEBERRIES

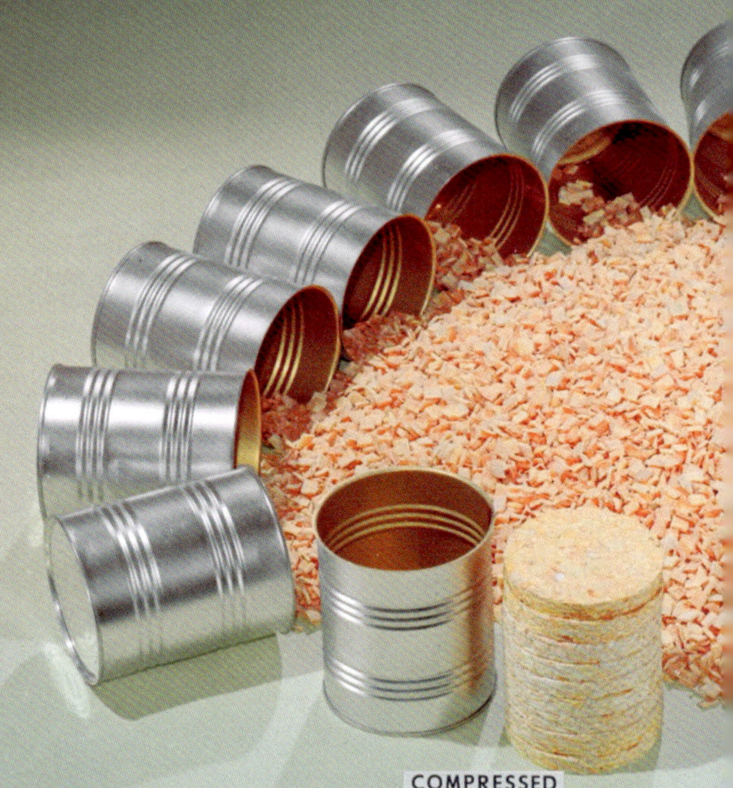

FREEZ

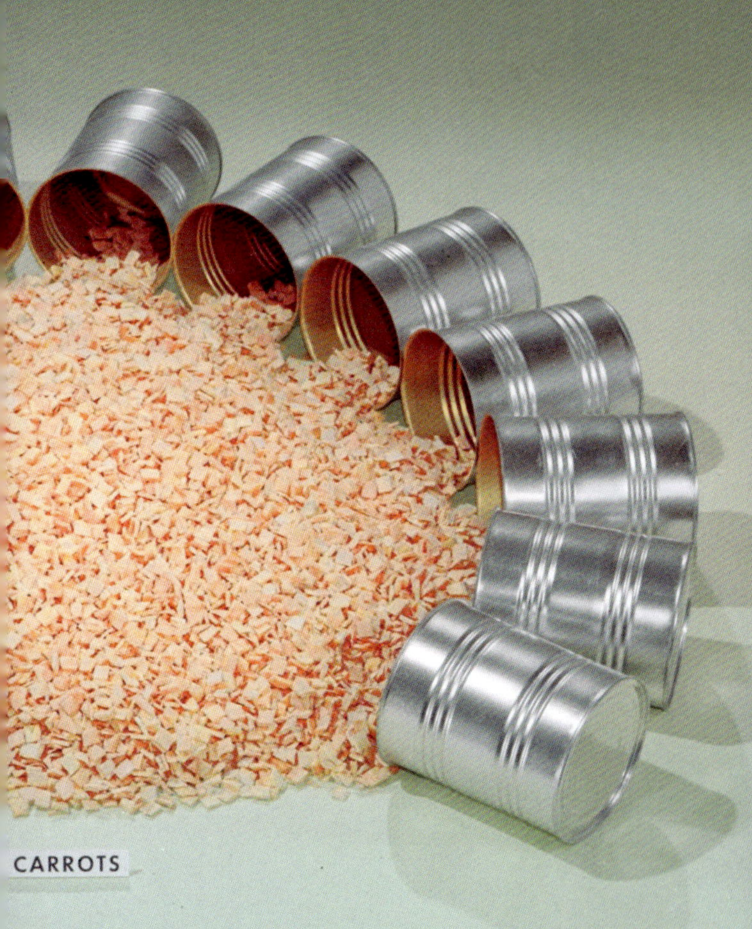

CARROTS

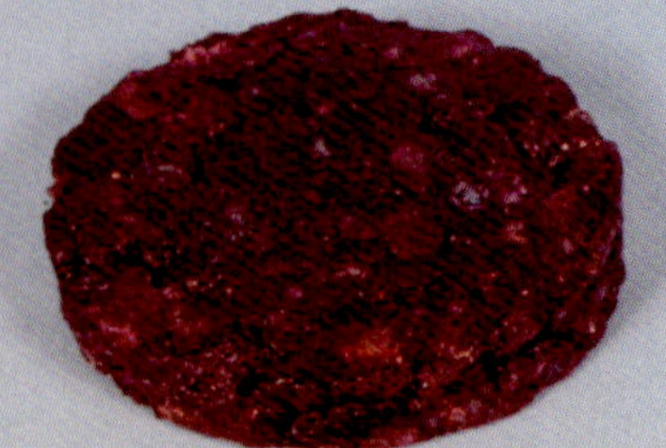
BLUEBERRIES

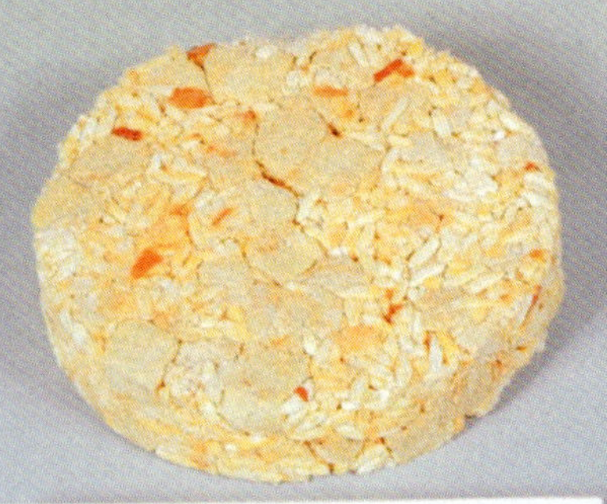
CHICKEN AND RICE

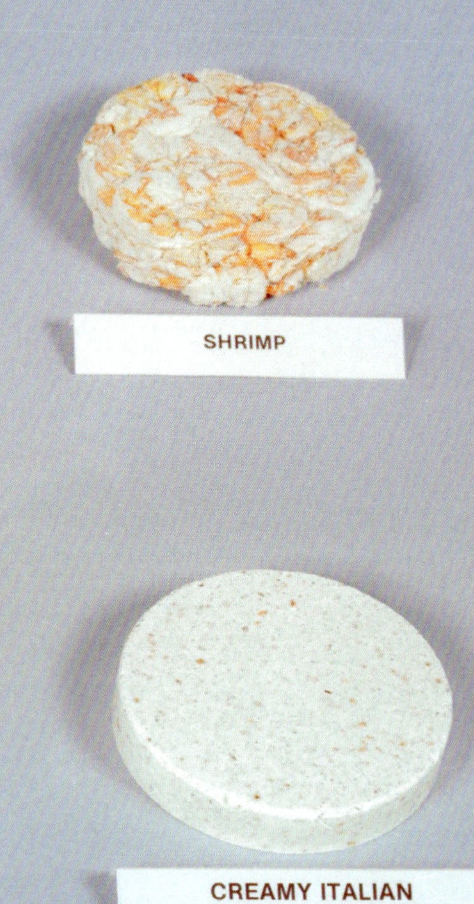
SHRIMP
CREAMY ITALIAN
SALAD DRESSING

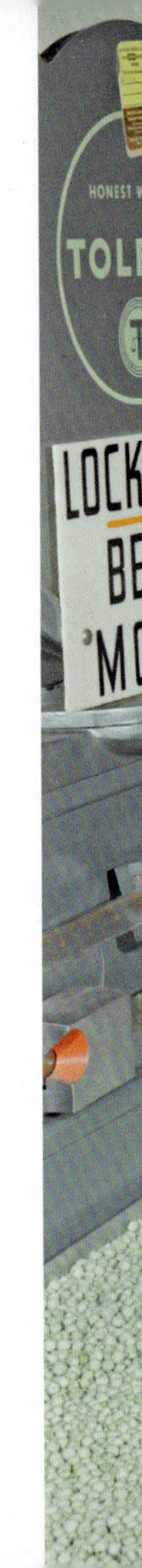
HONEST WEIGHT.
TOLEDO
LOCK SCAL
BEFORE
MOVINC

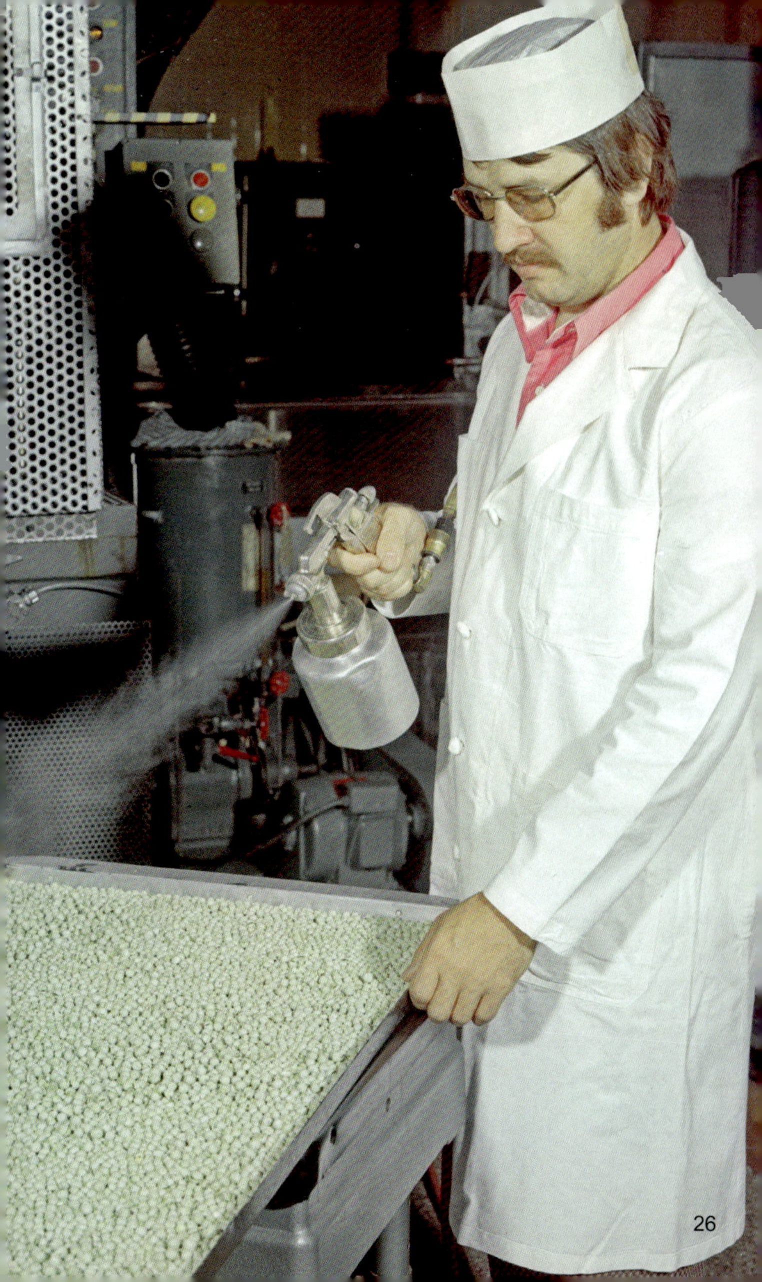

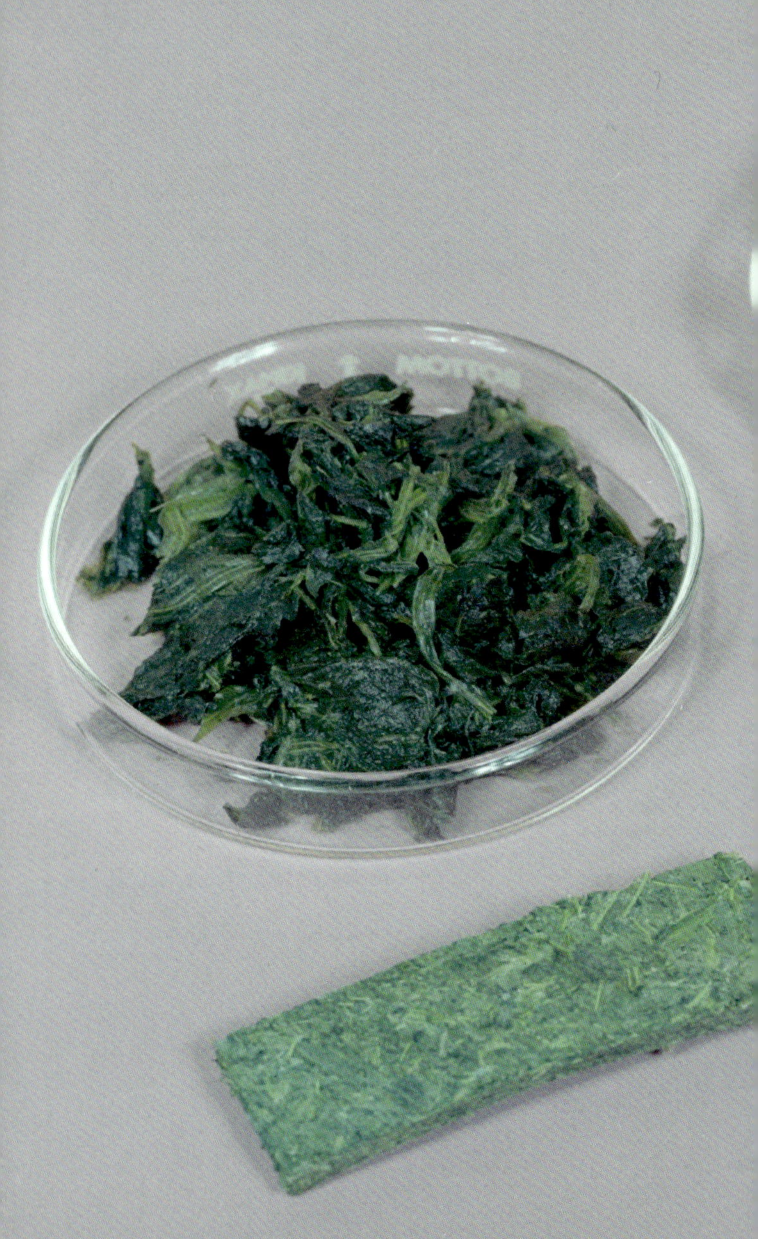

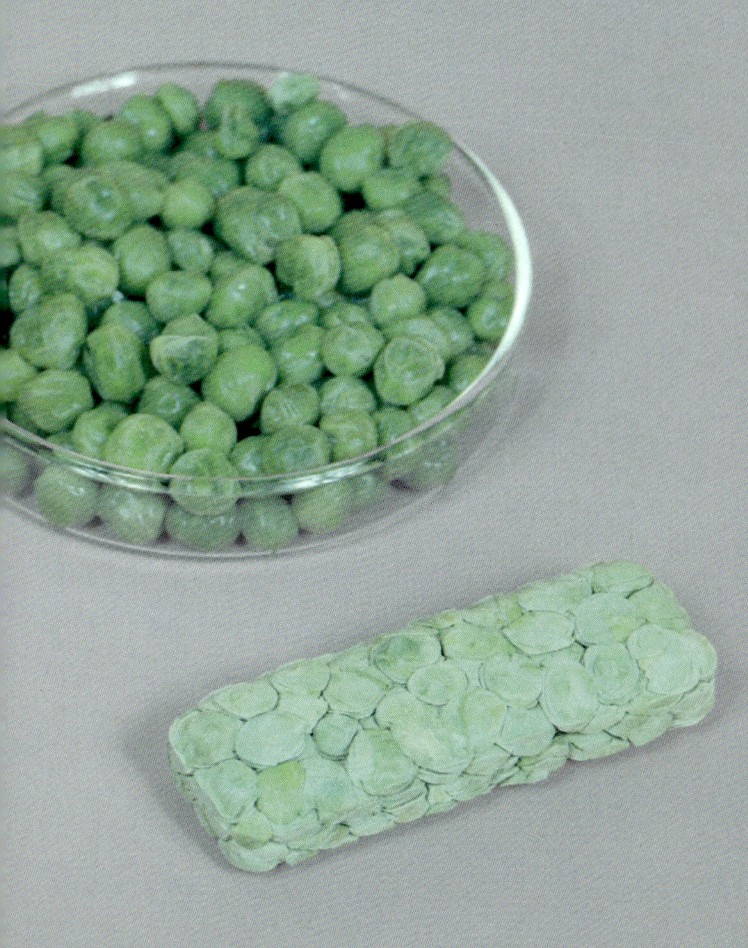

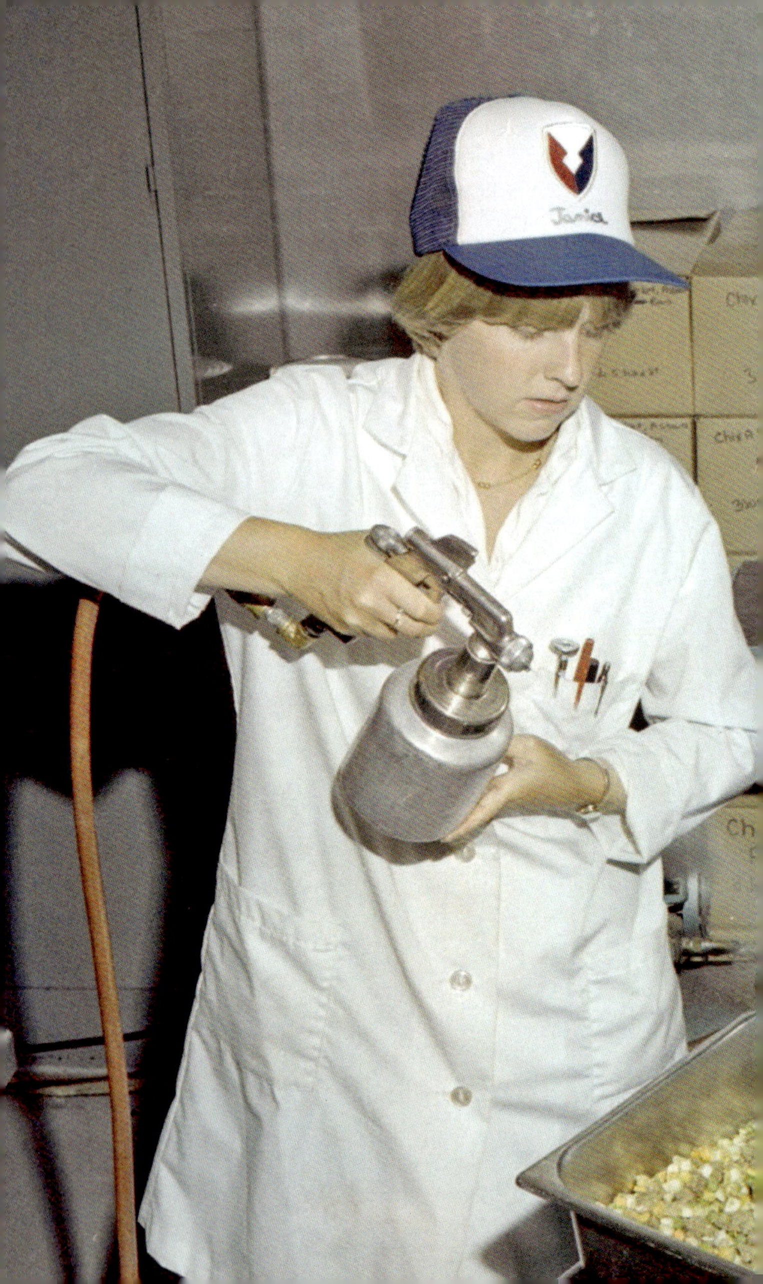
Janice

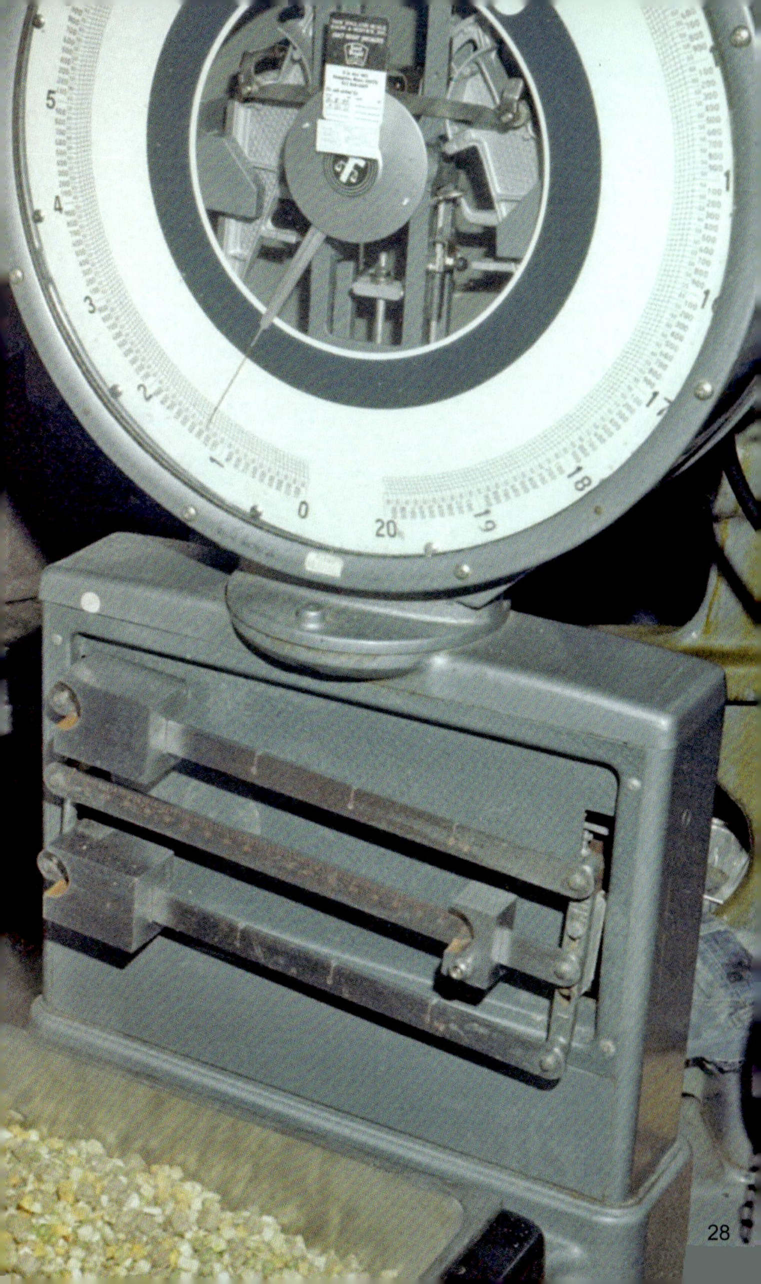

BEEF &

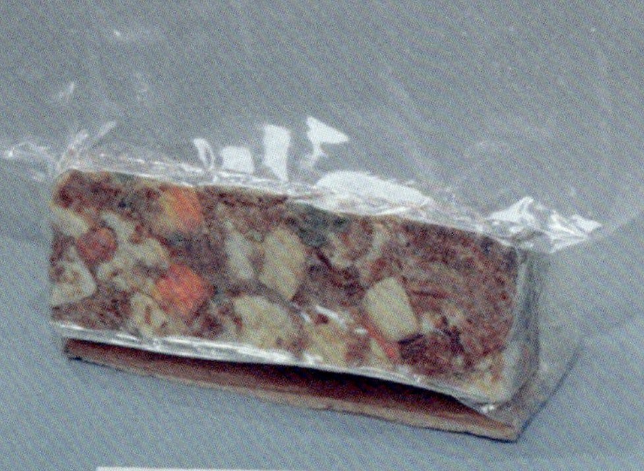

EAT AS A BAR

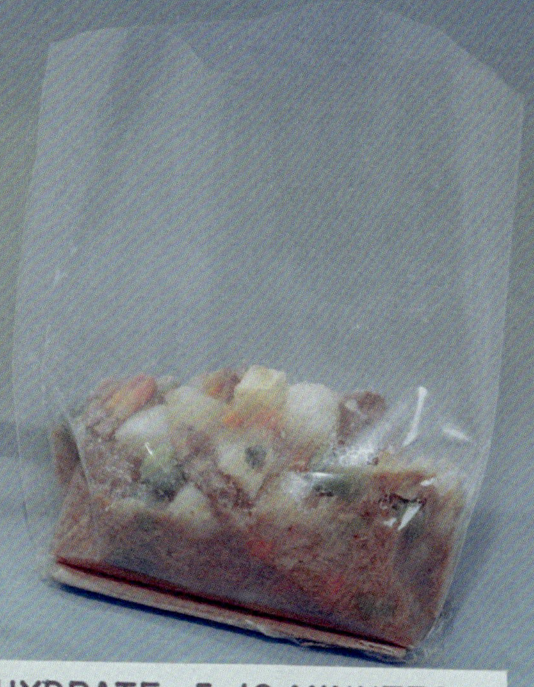
ETABLE BAR
nce)
REHYDRATE 5-10 MINUTES
TH 3 OZ. HOT OR COLD WATER

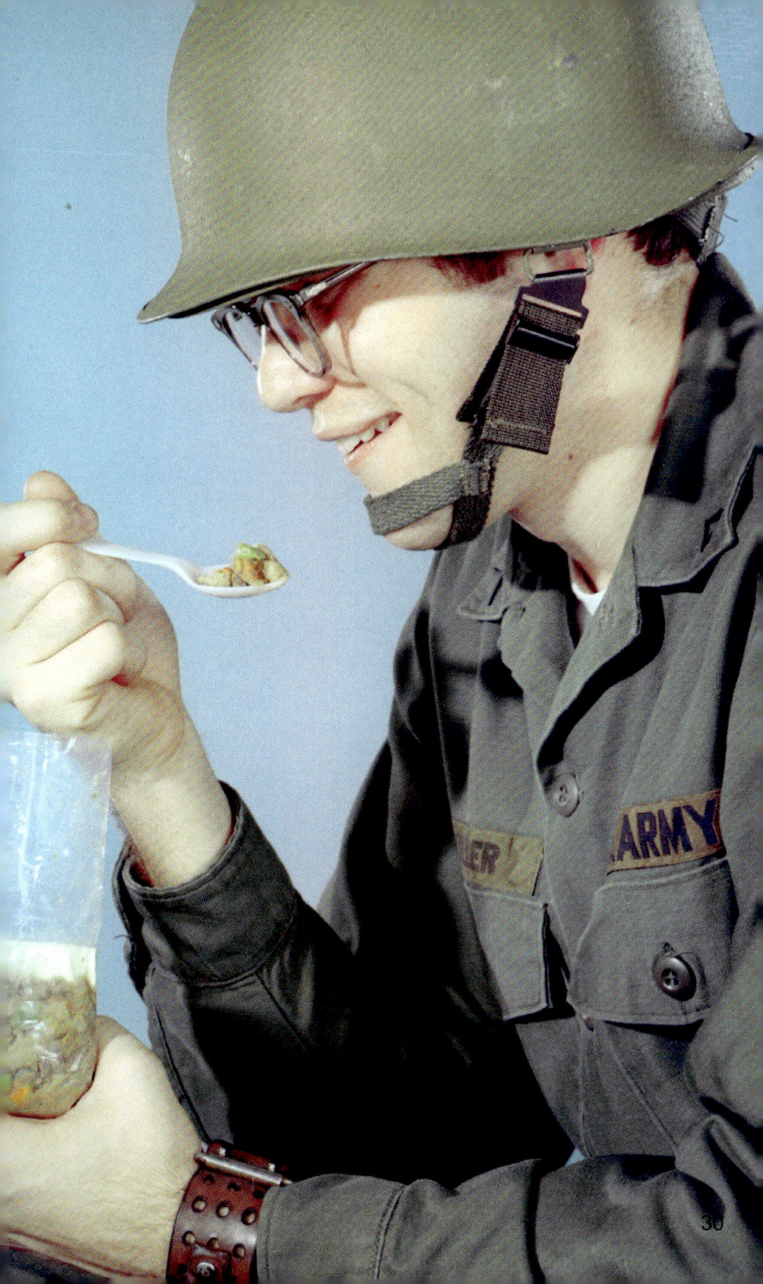
ARMY

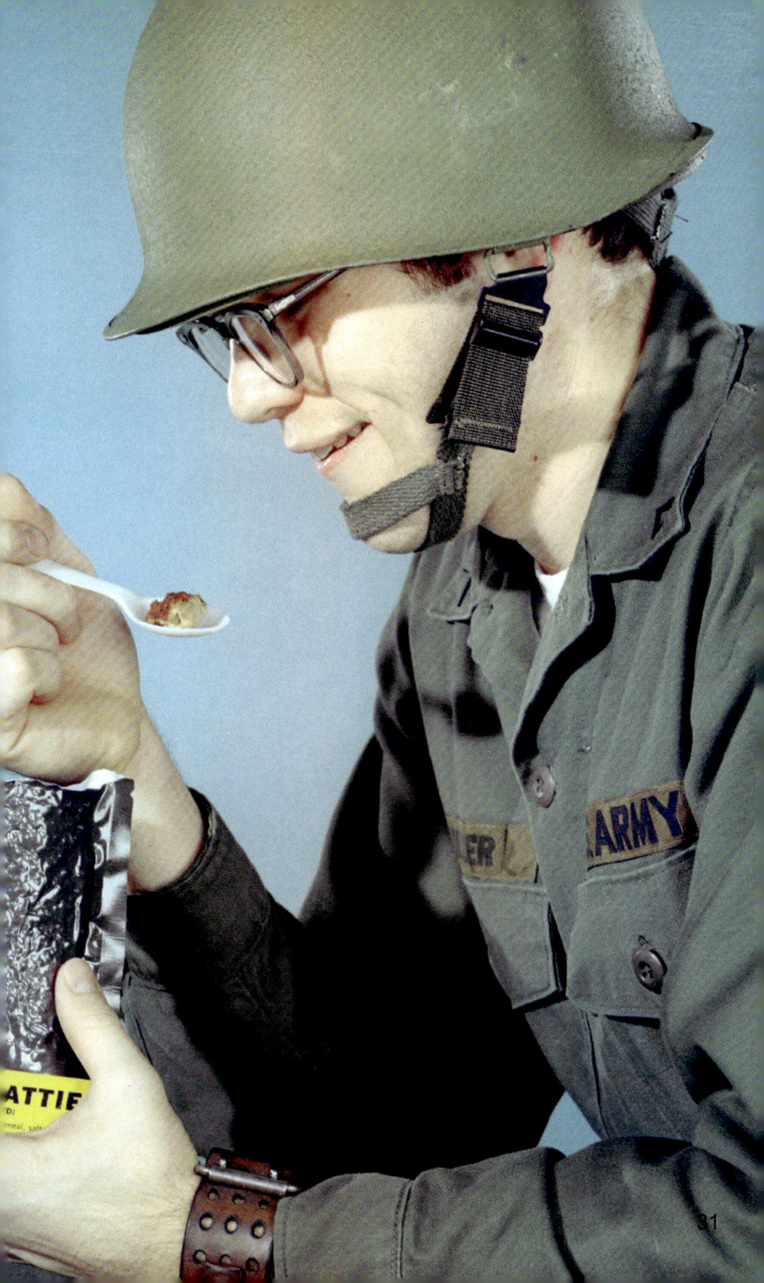
ARMY

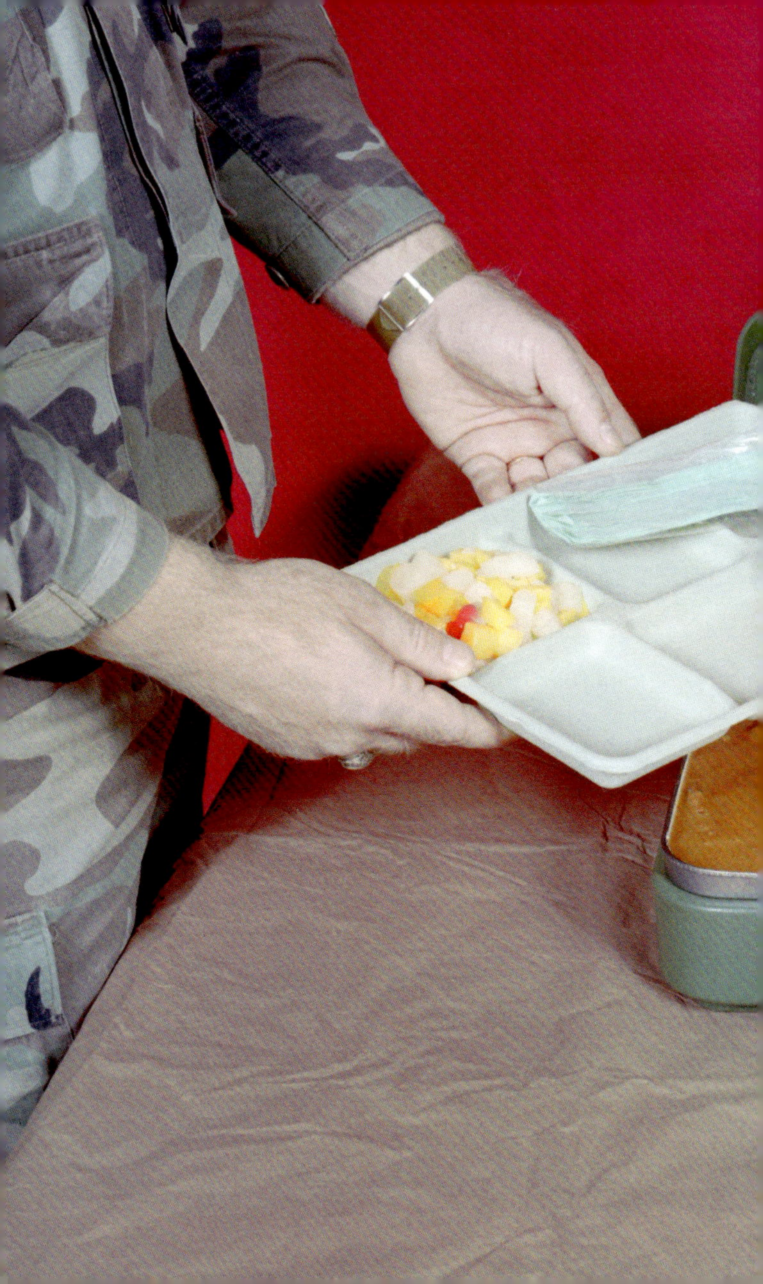

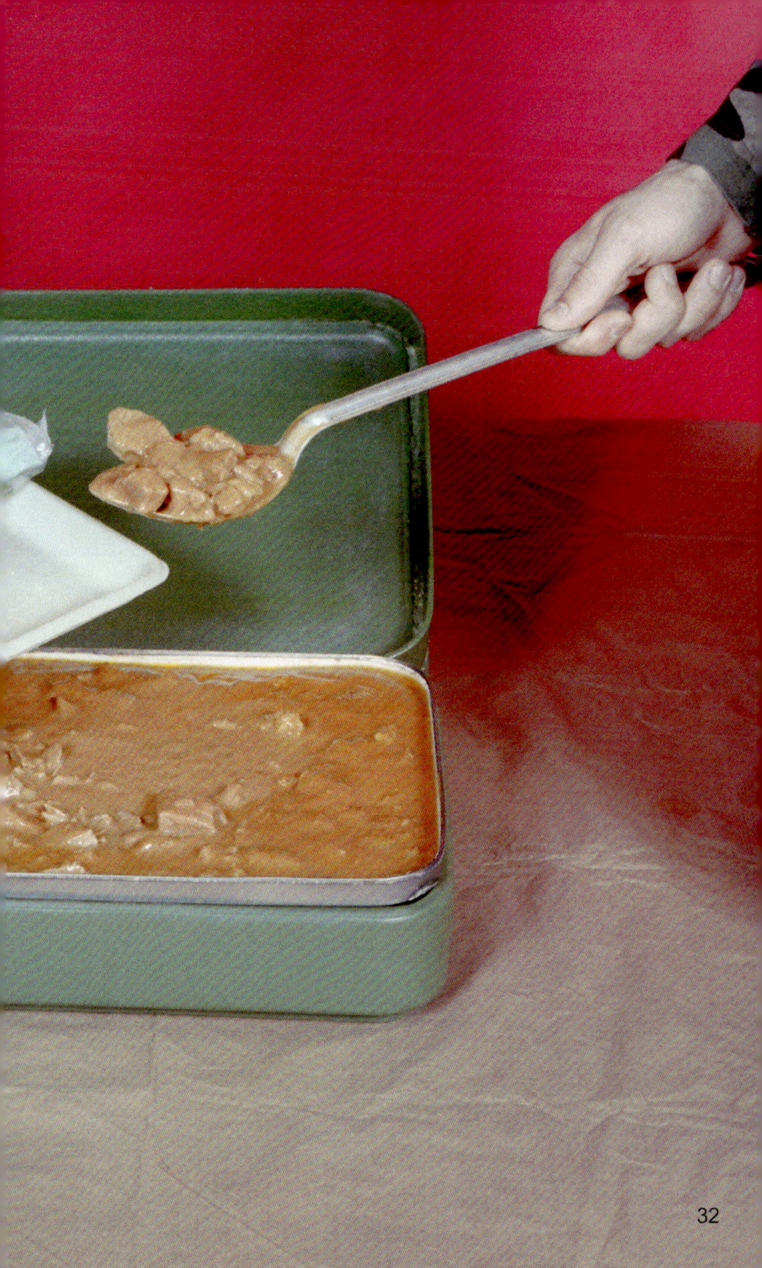

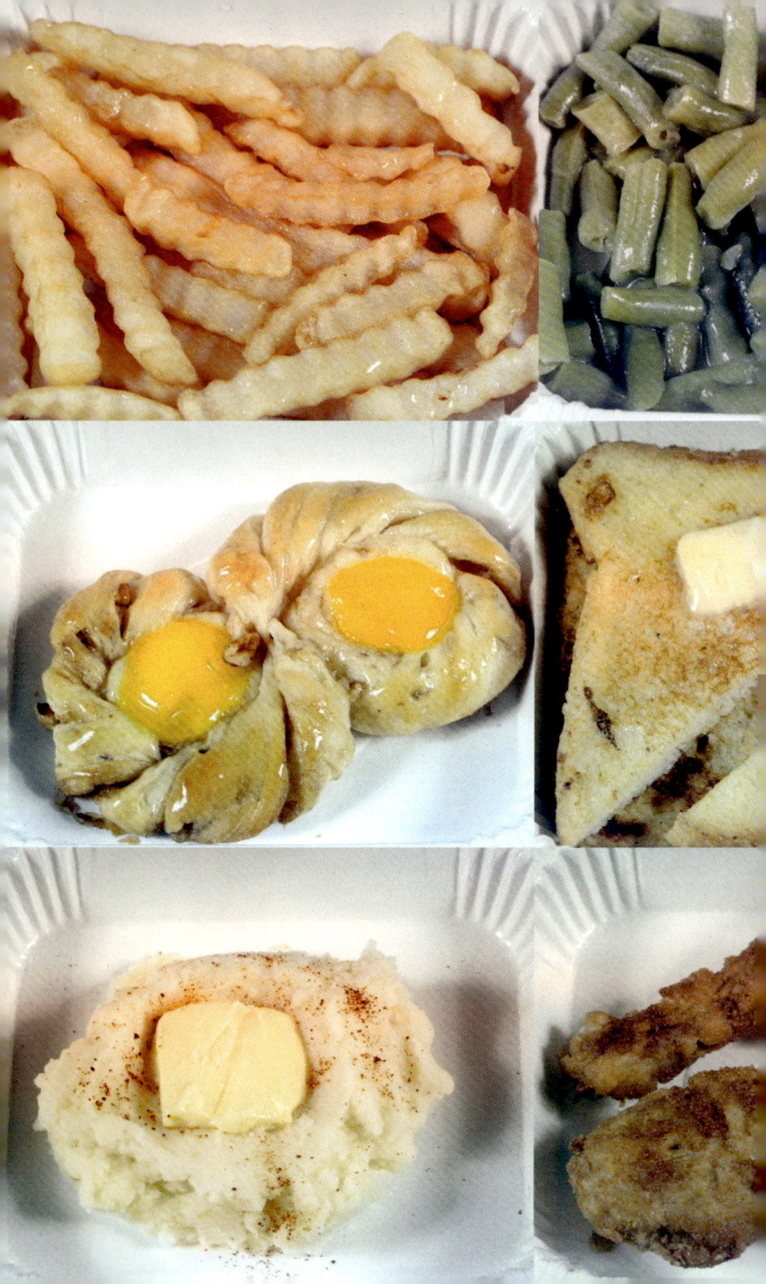

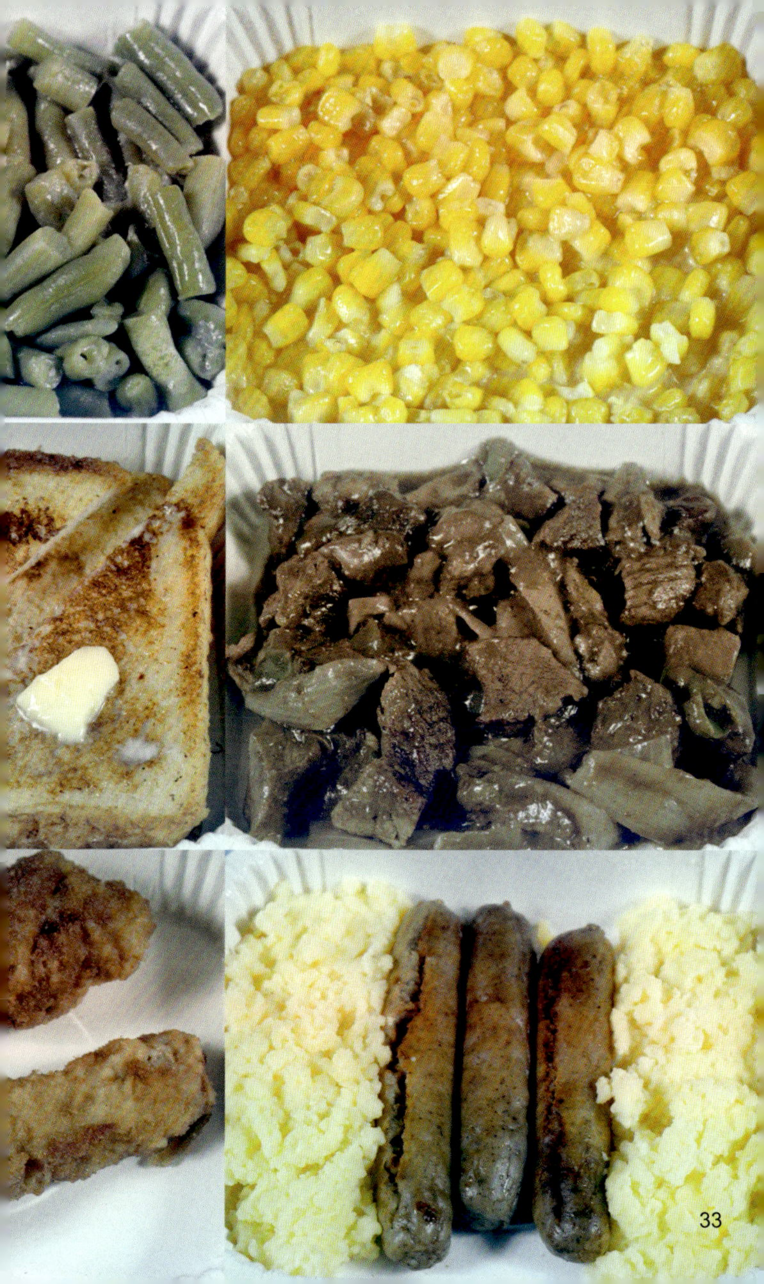

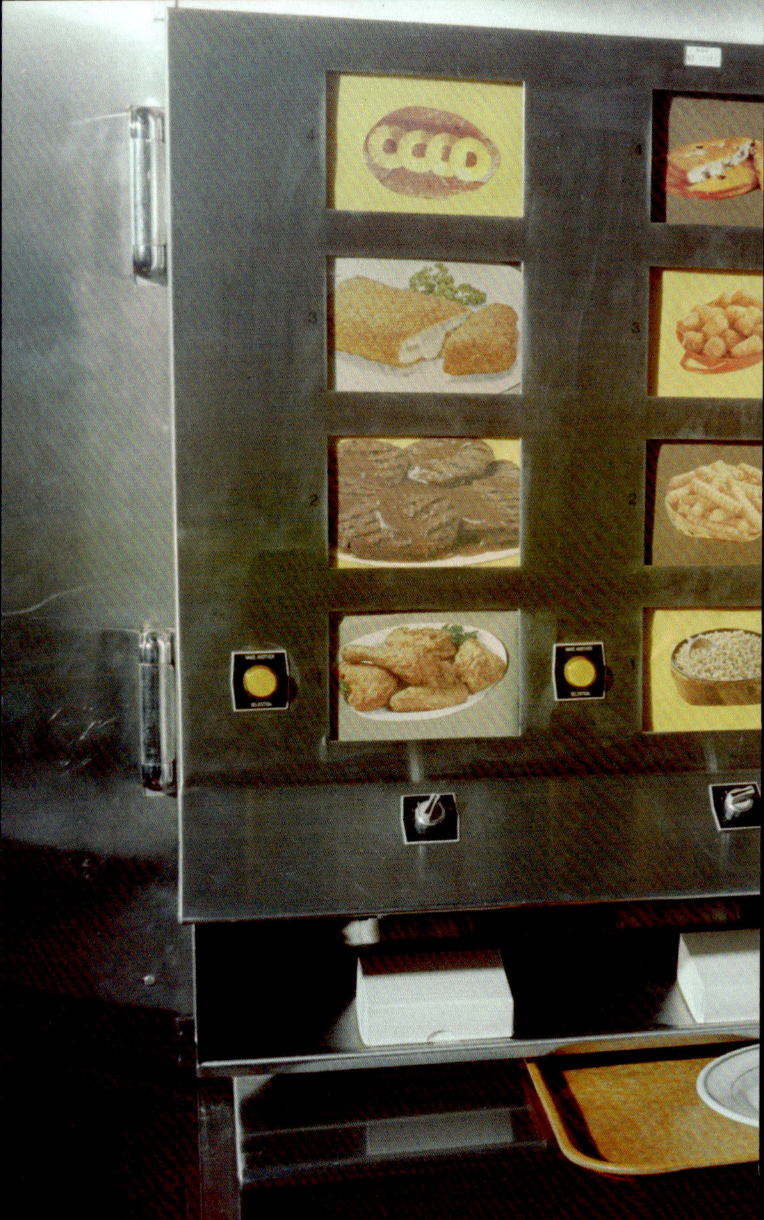

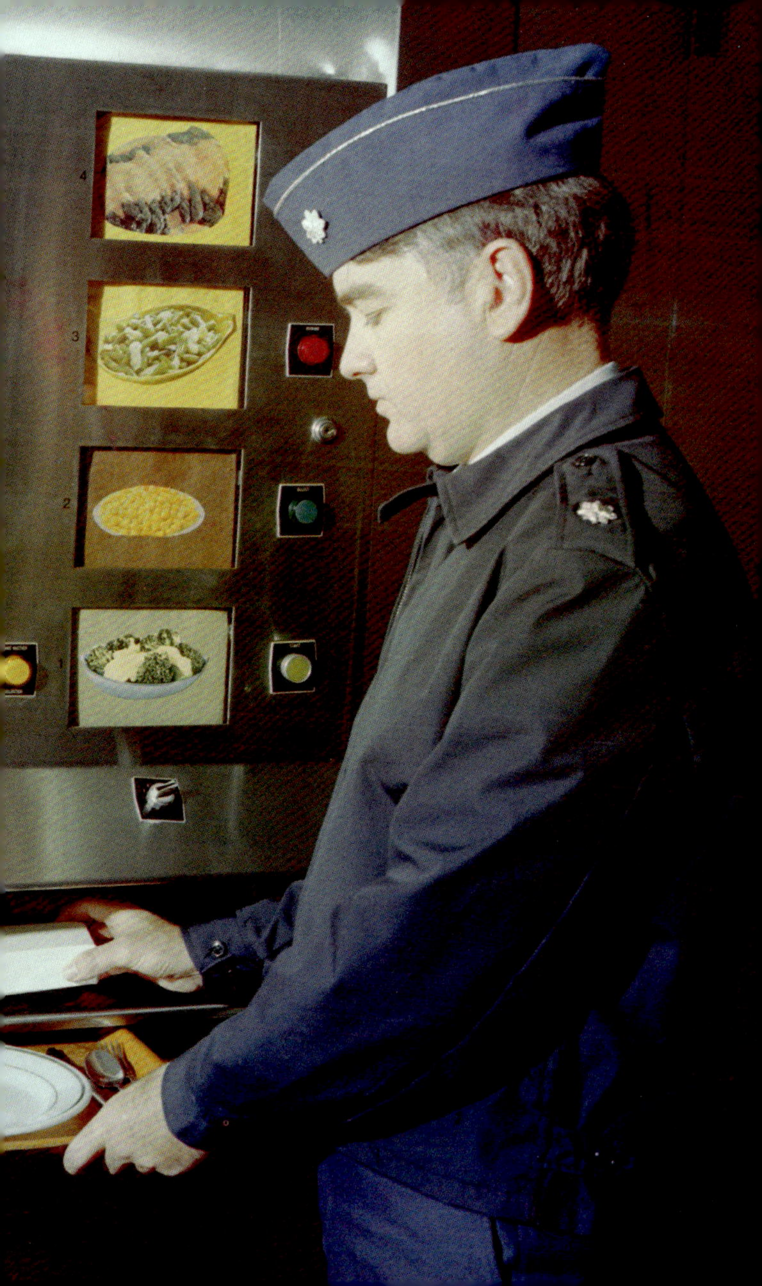
4
3
2
1

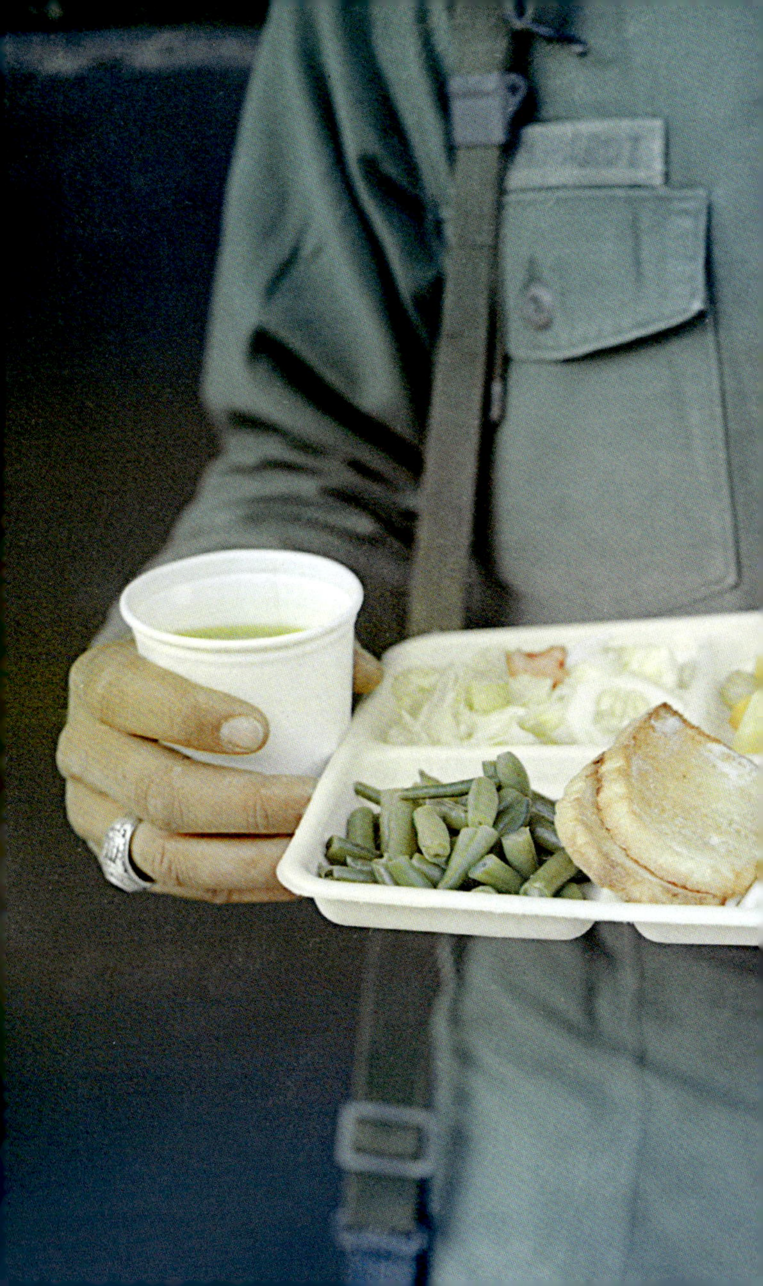

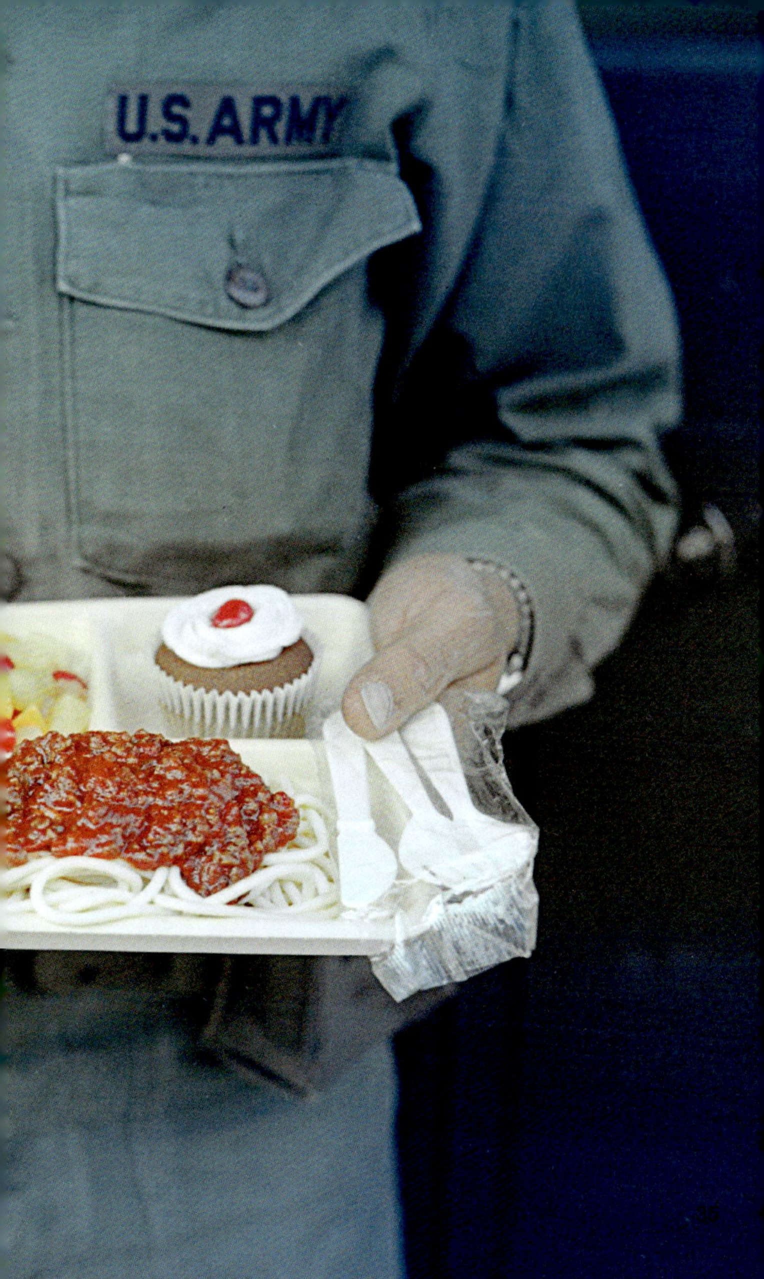
U.S. ARMY

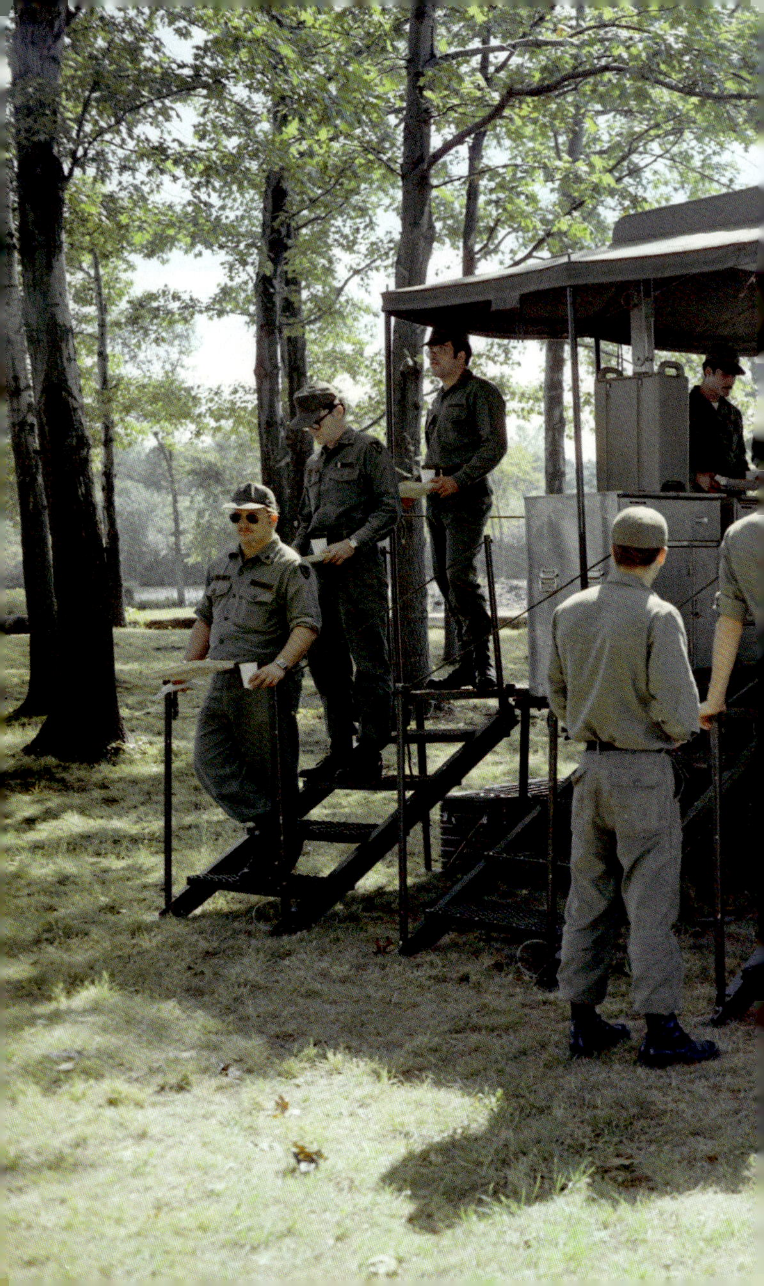

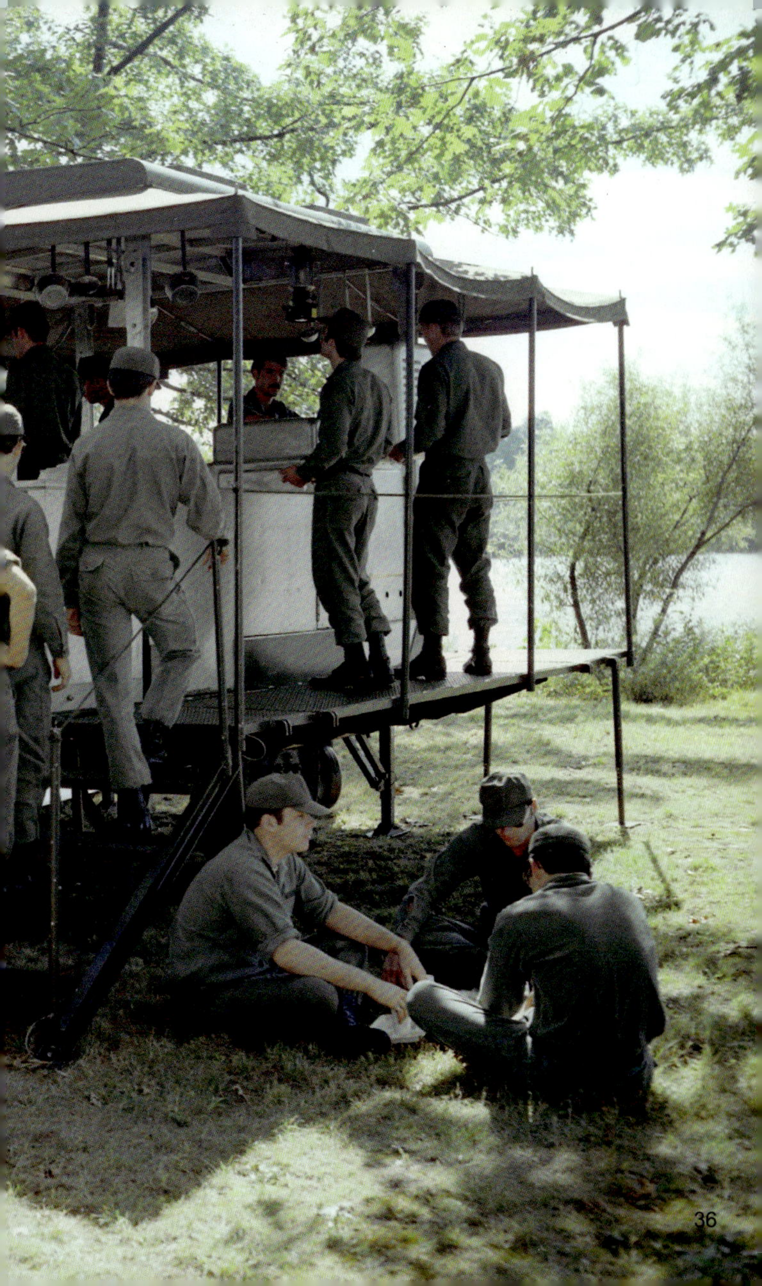

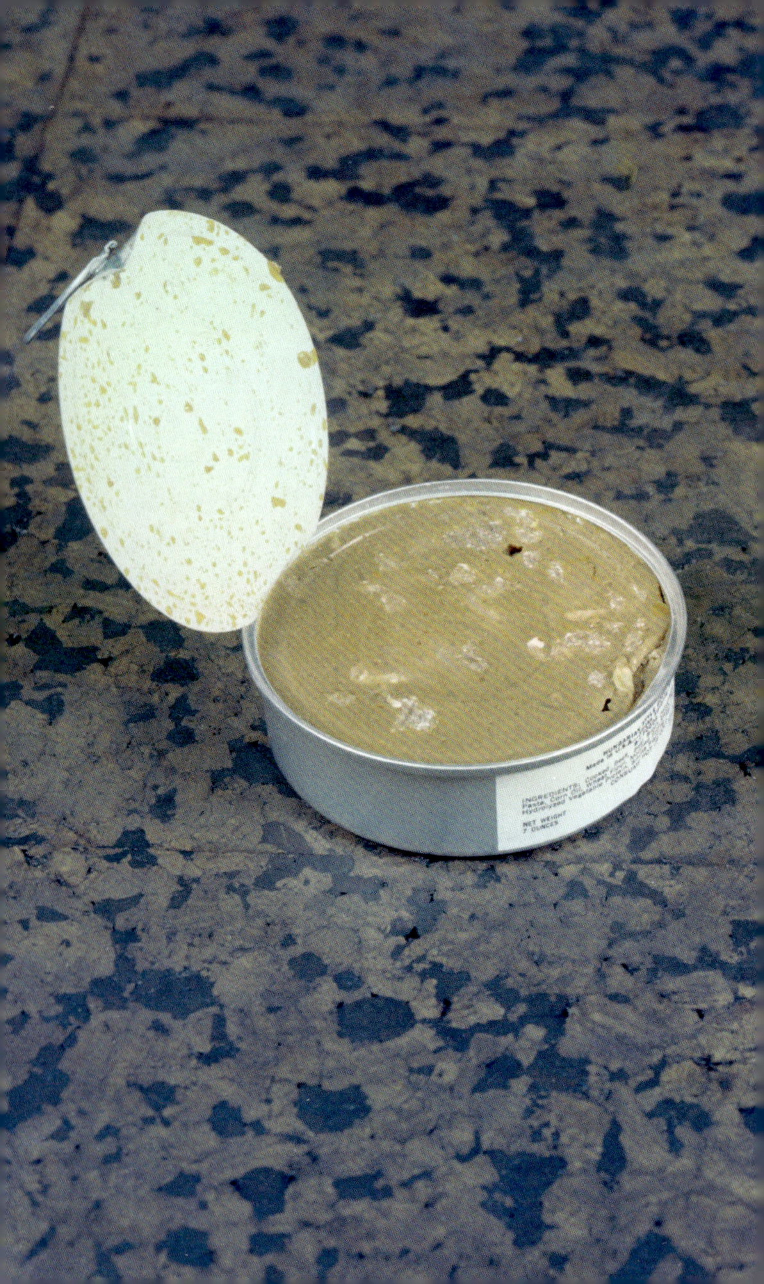
INGREDIENTS:
NET WEIGHT
7 OUNCES

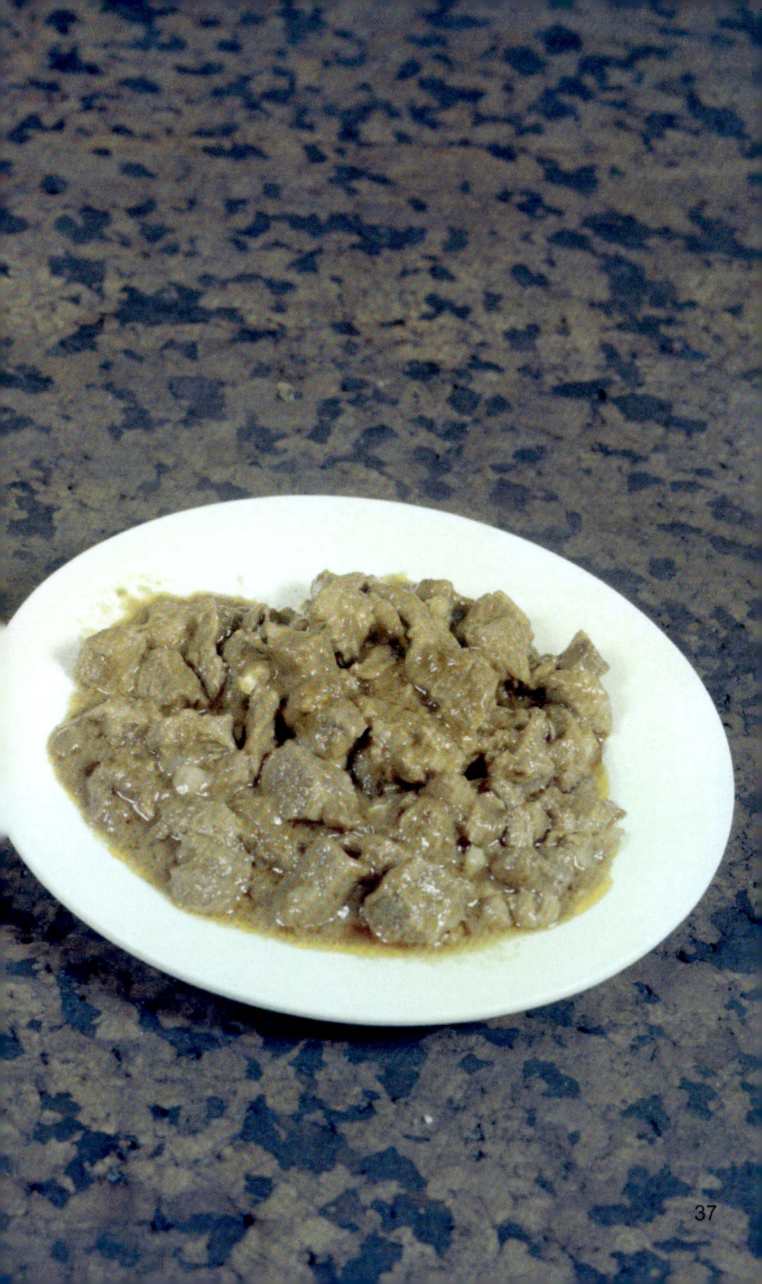

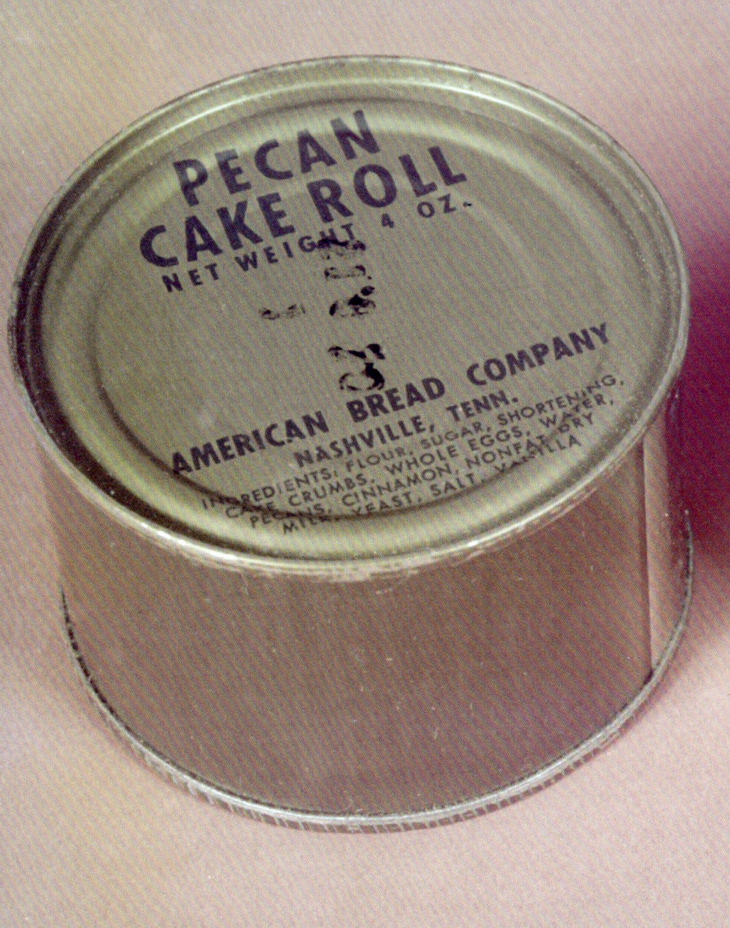
PECAN
CAKE ROLL
NET WEIGHT 4 OZ.
AMERICAN BREAD COMPANY
NASHVILLE, TENN.

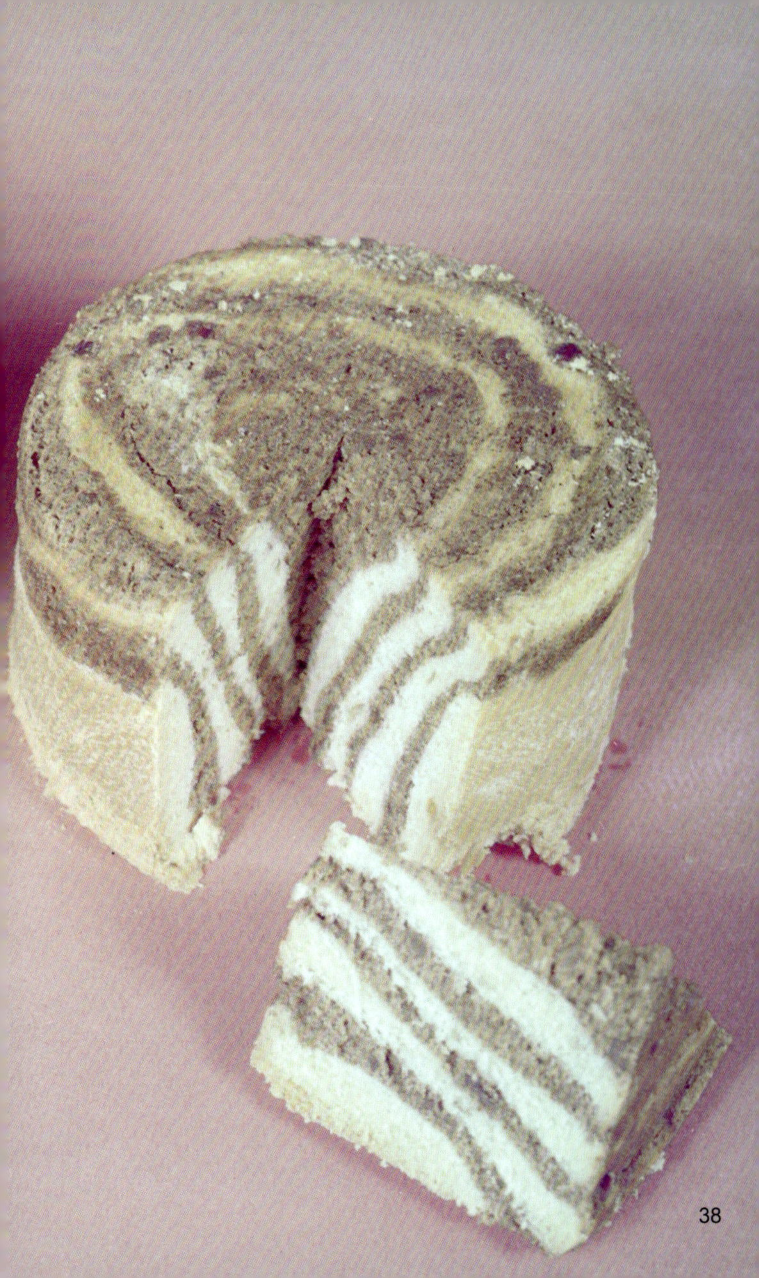

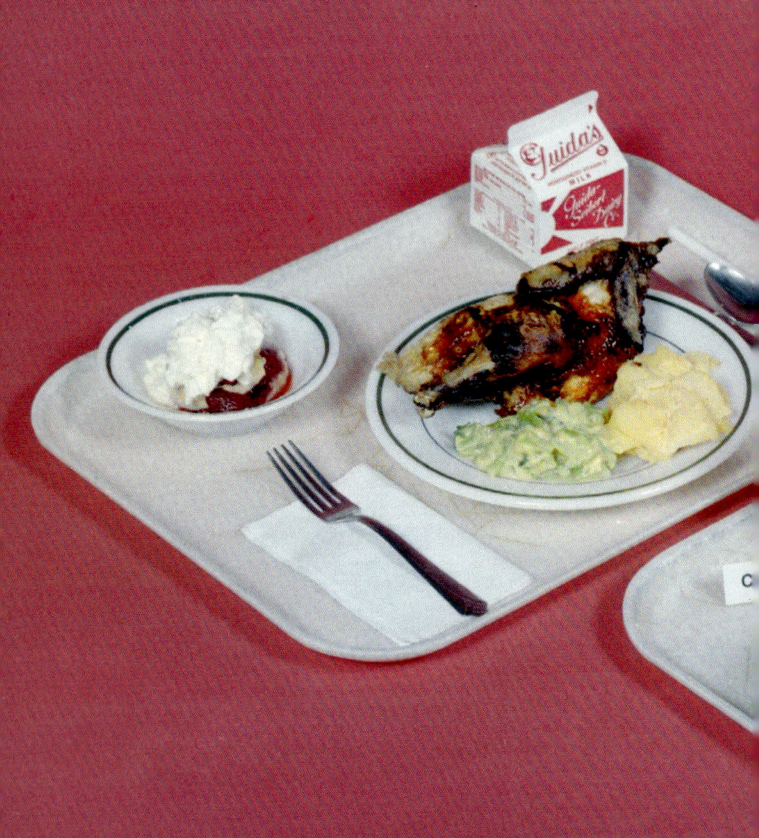
Guida's
MILK

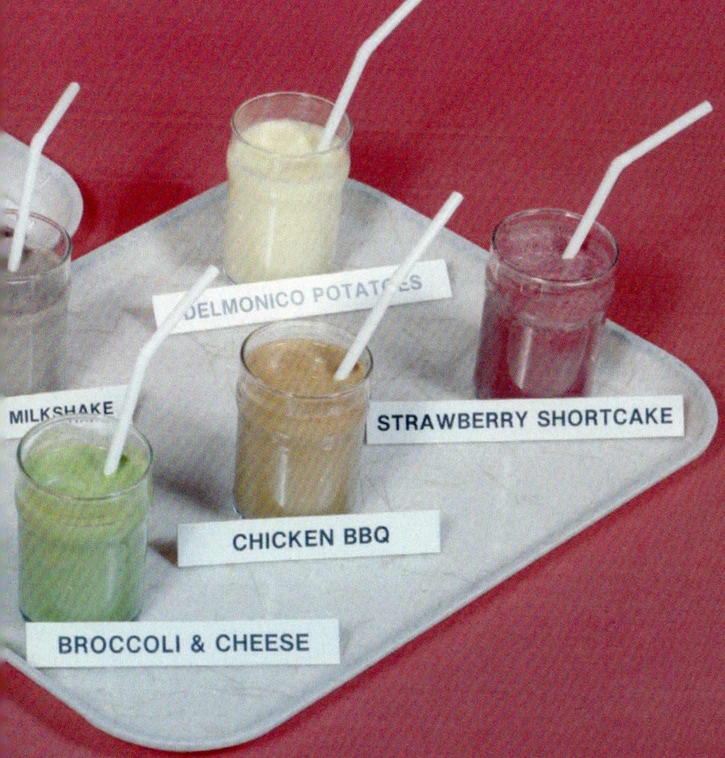
DELMONICO
MILKSHAKE
STRAWBERRY SHORTCAKE
CHICKEN BBQ
BROCCOLI & CHEESE

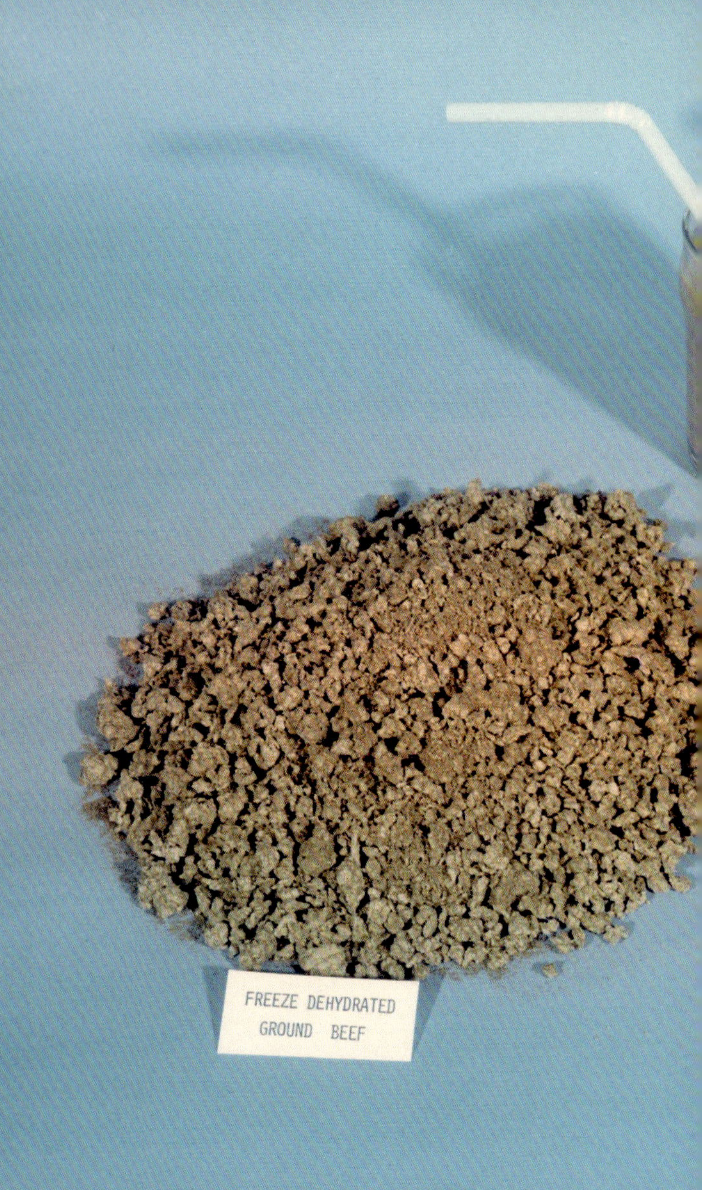
FREEZE DEHYDRATED
GROUND BEEF

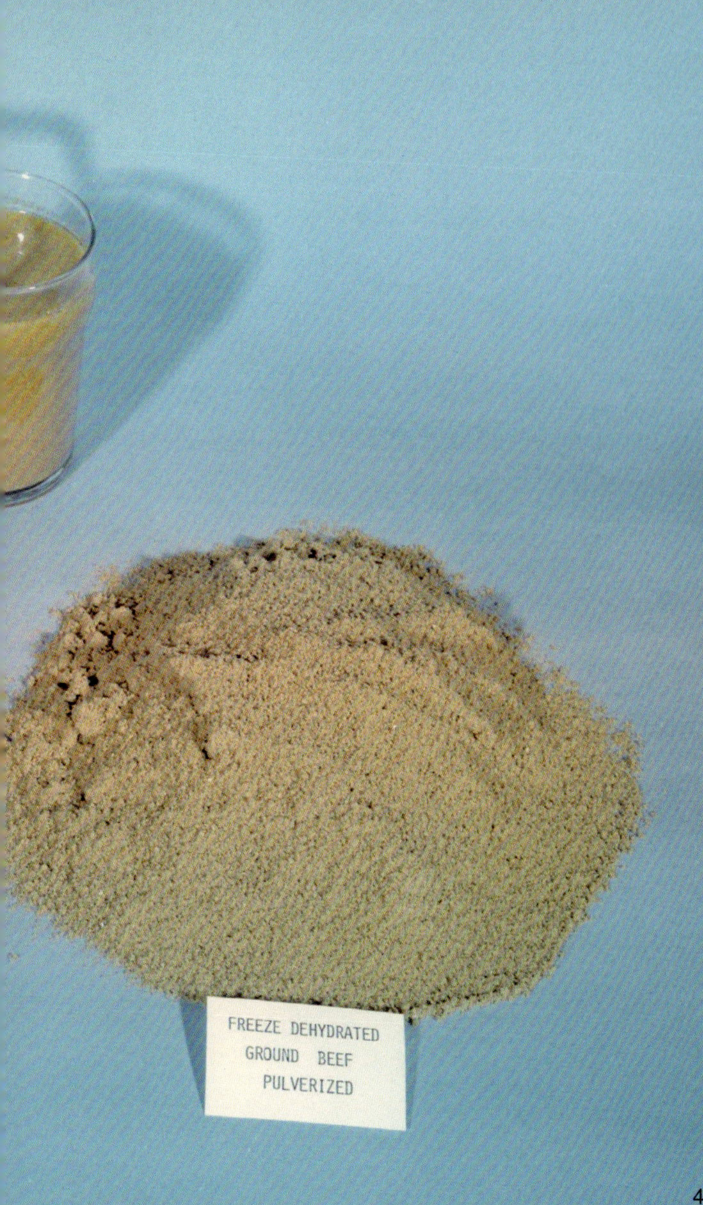
FREEZE DEHYDRATED
GROUND BEEF
PULVERIZED

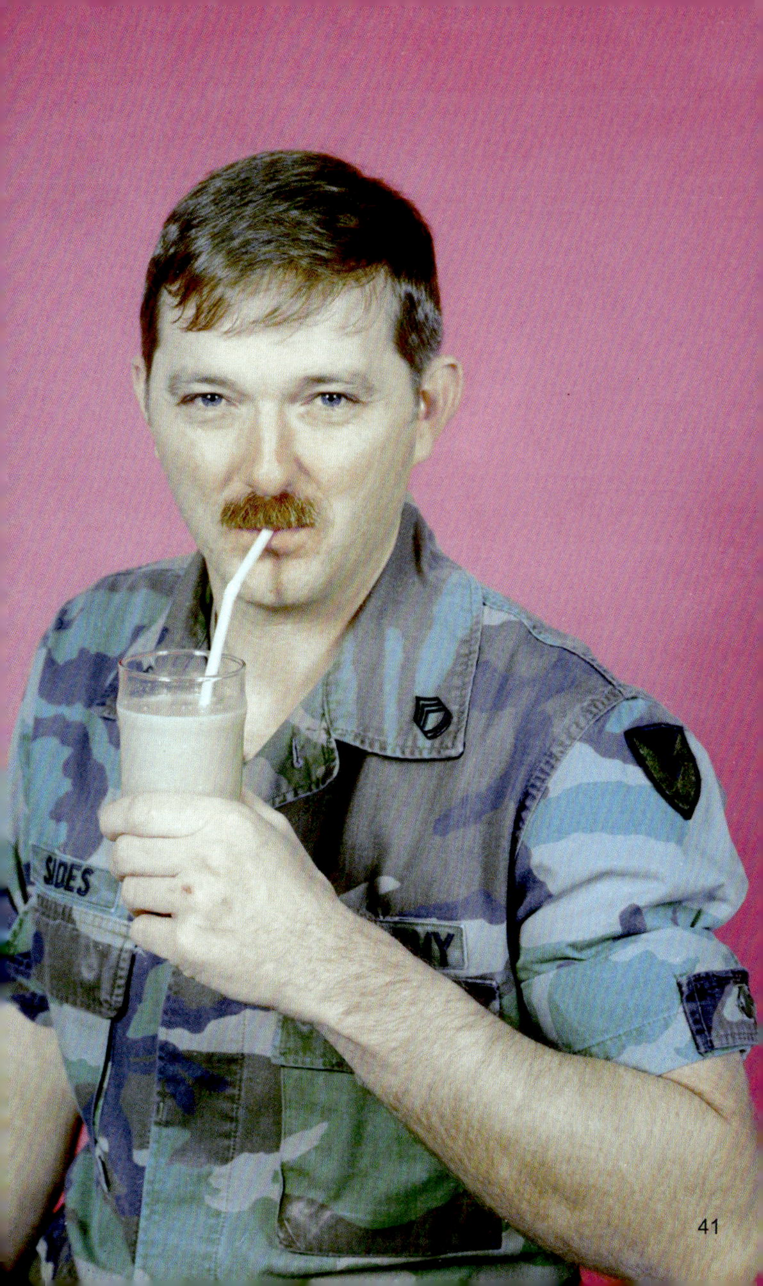
SIDES

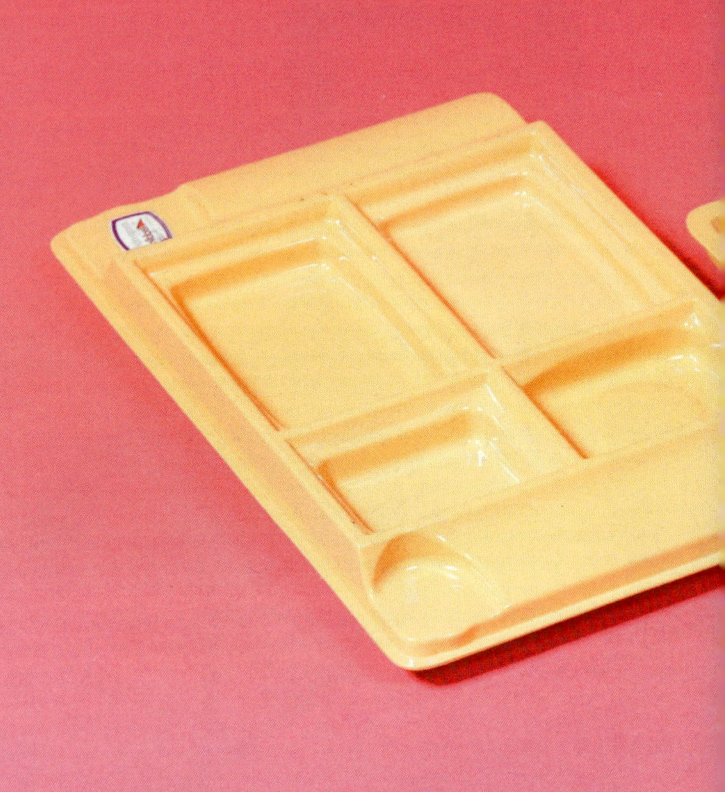

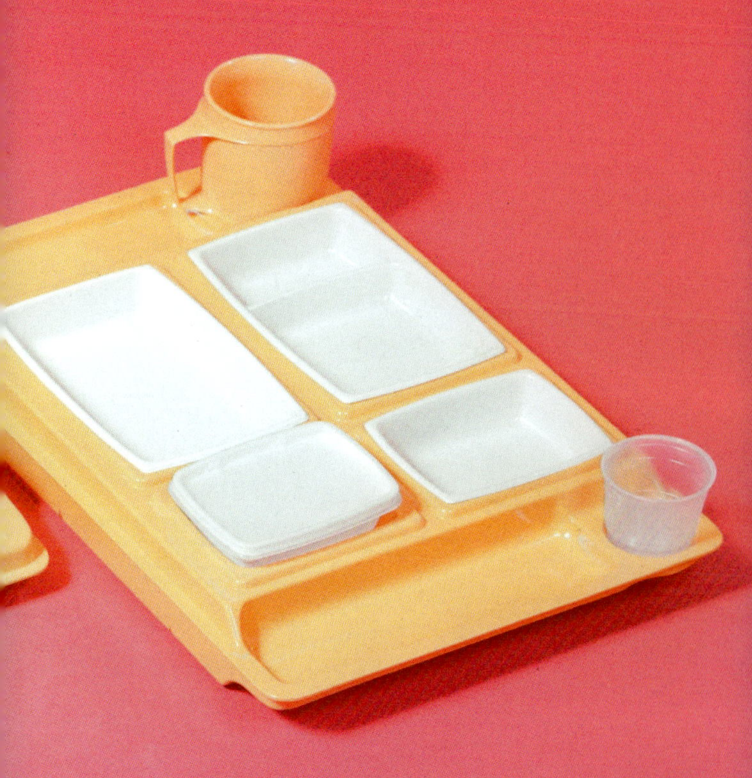

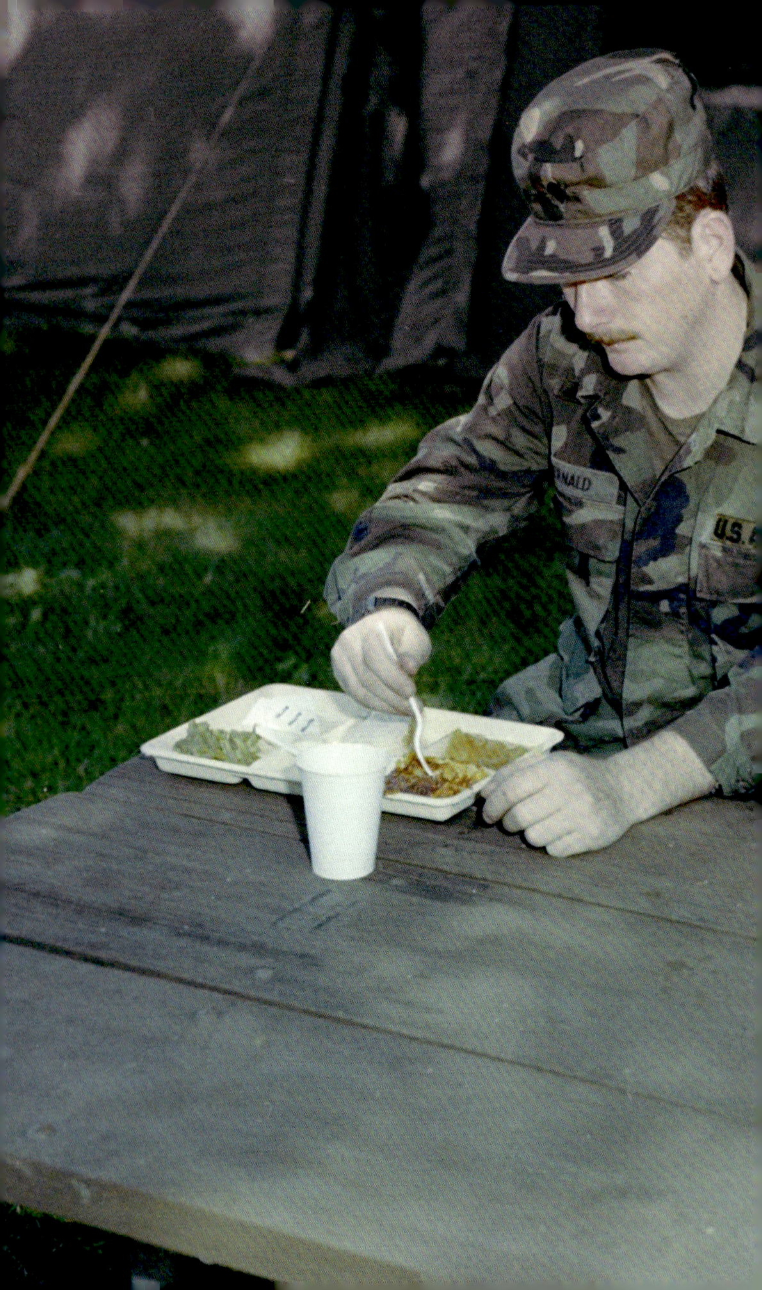

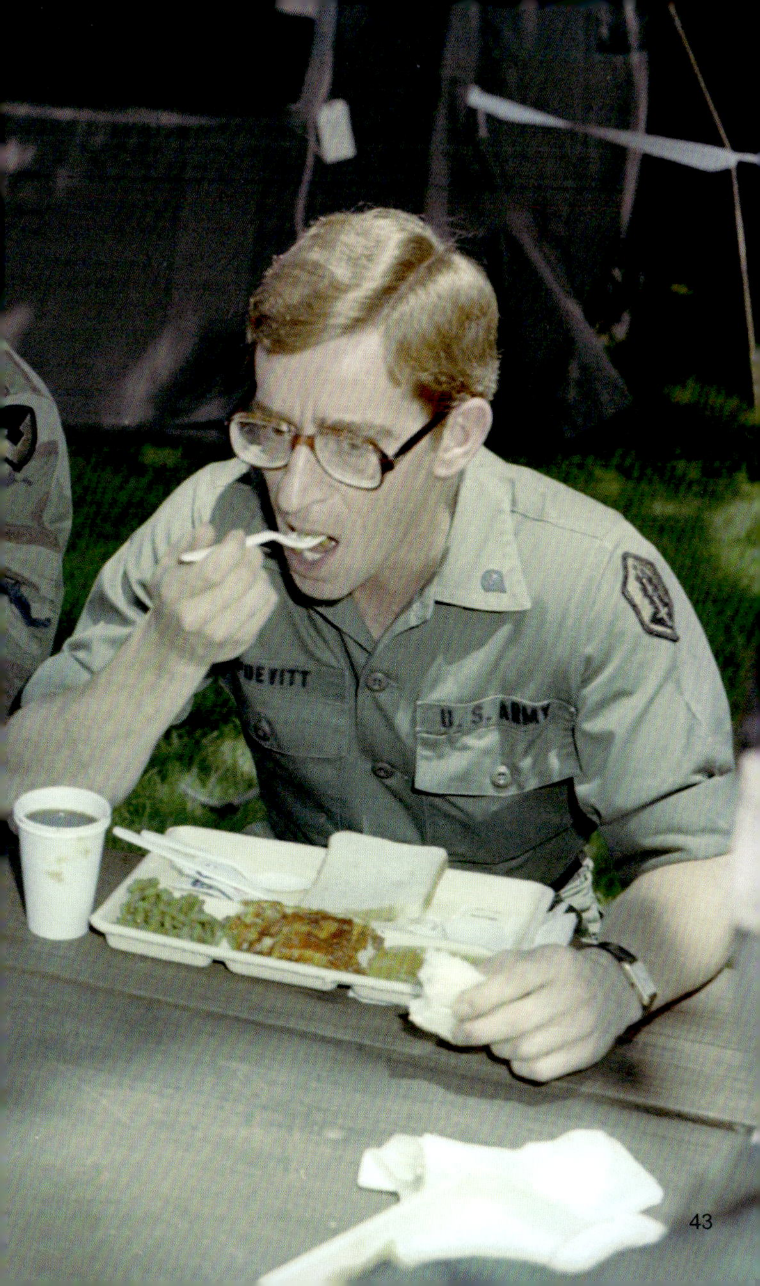
U. S. ARMY

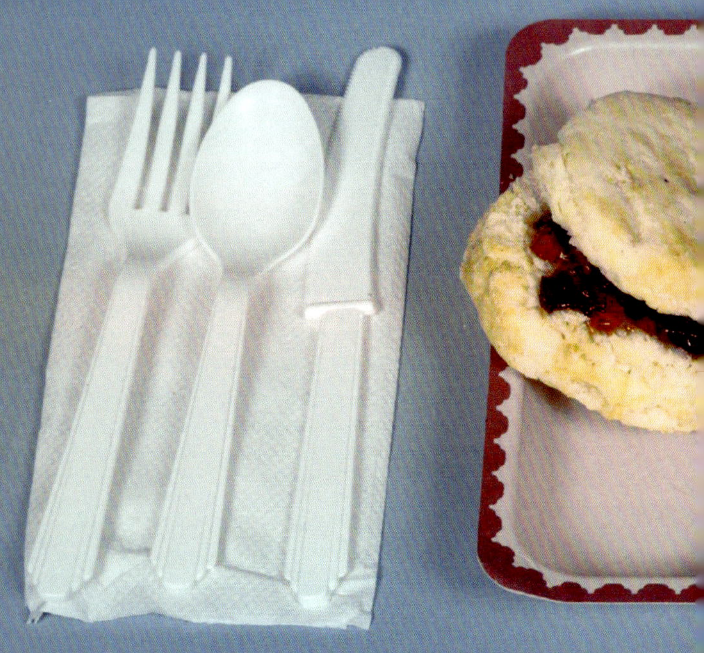

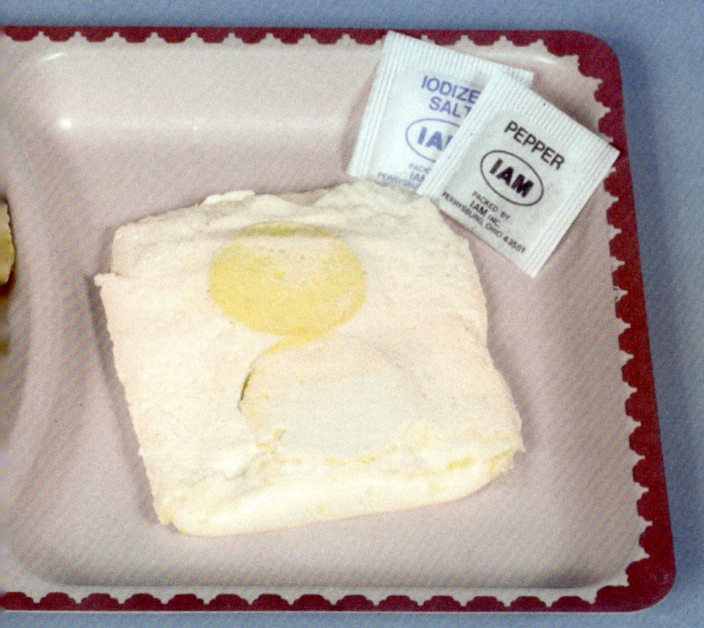

SERVING EGG

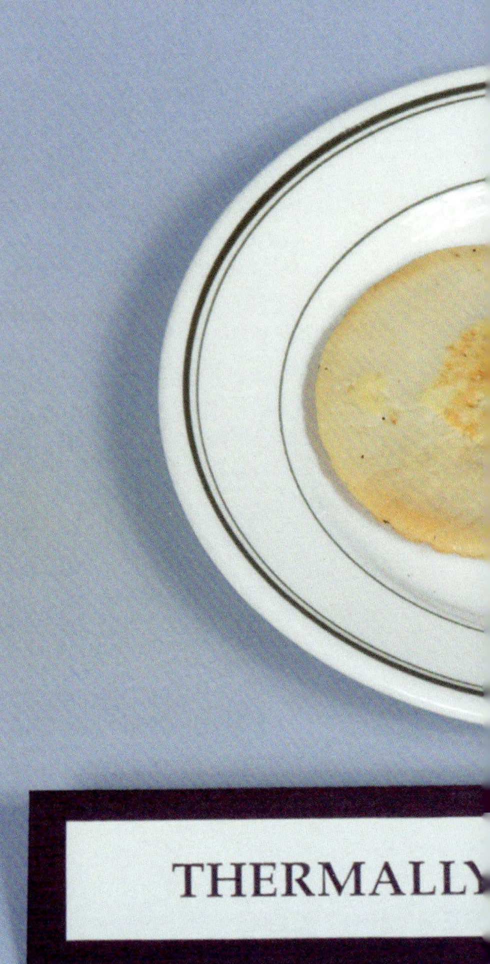
THERMALLY

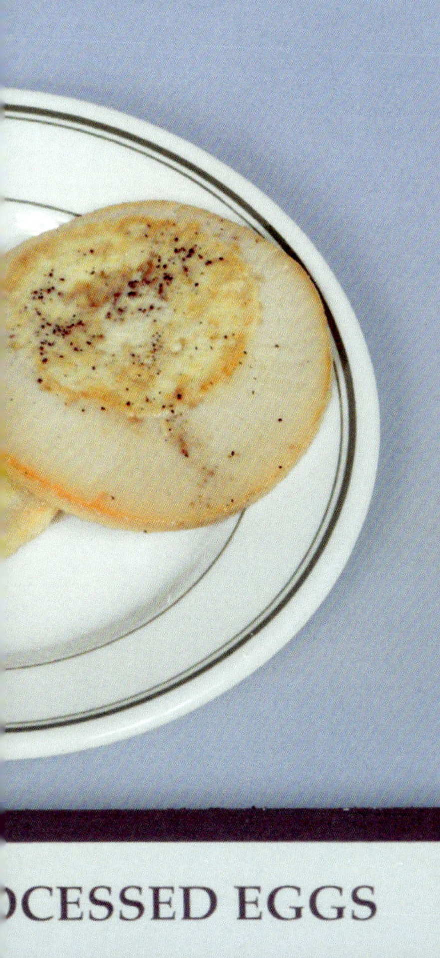
OCESSED EGGS

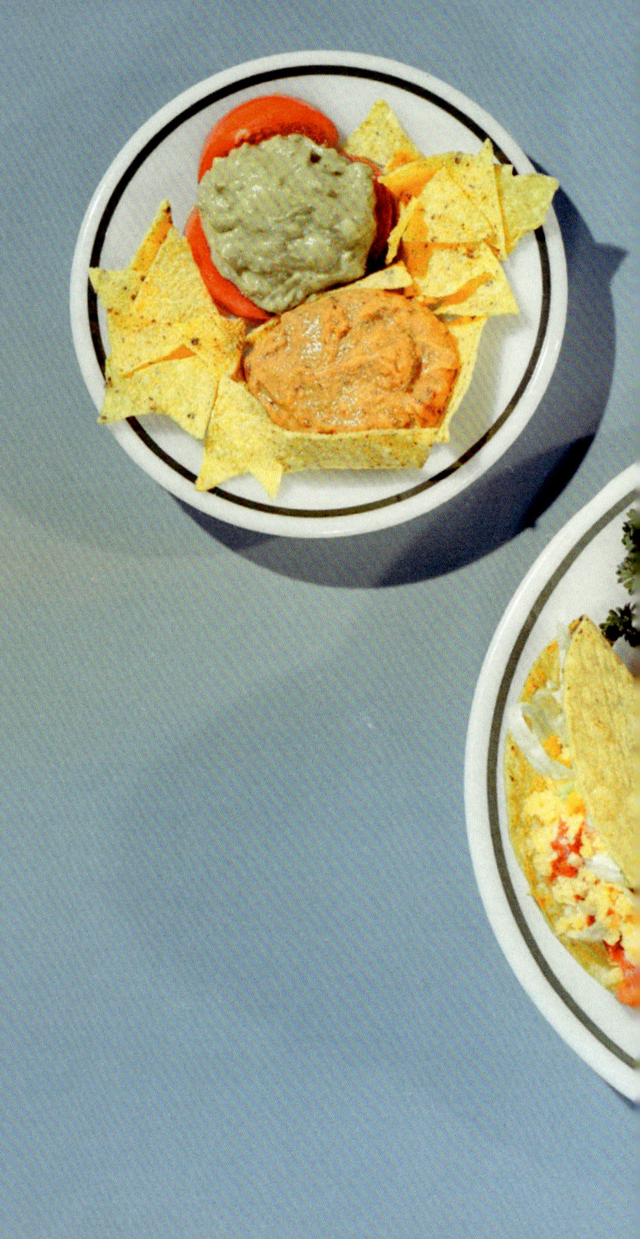

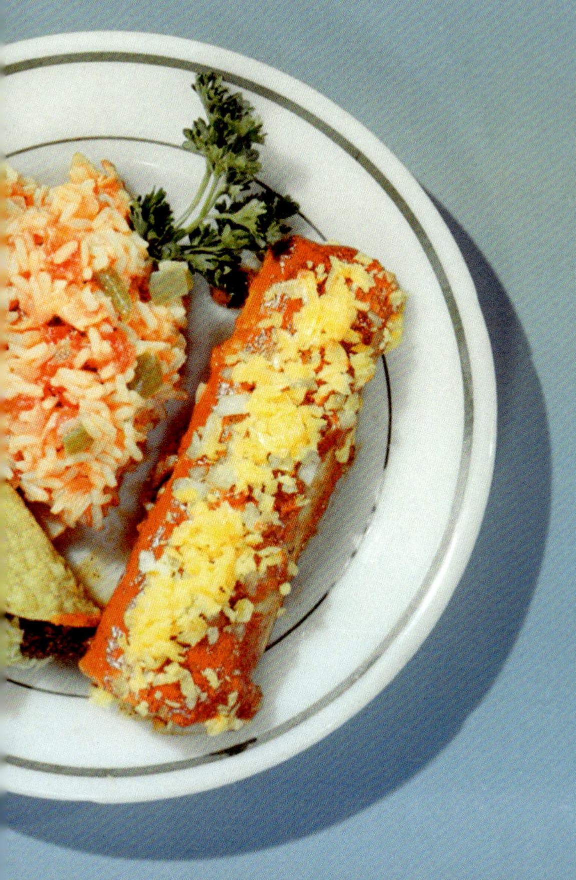

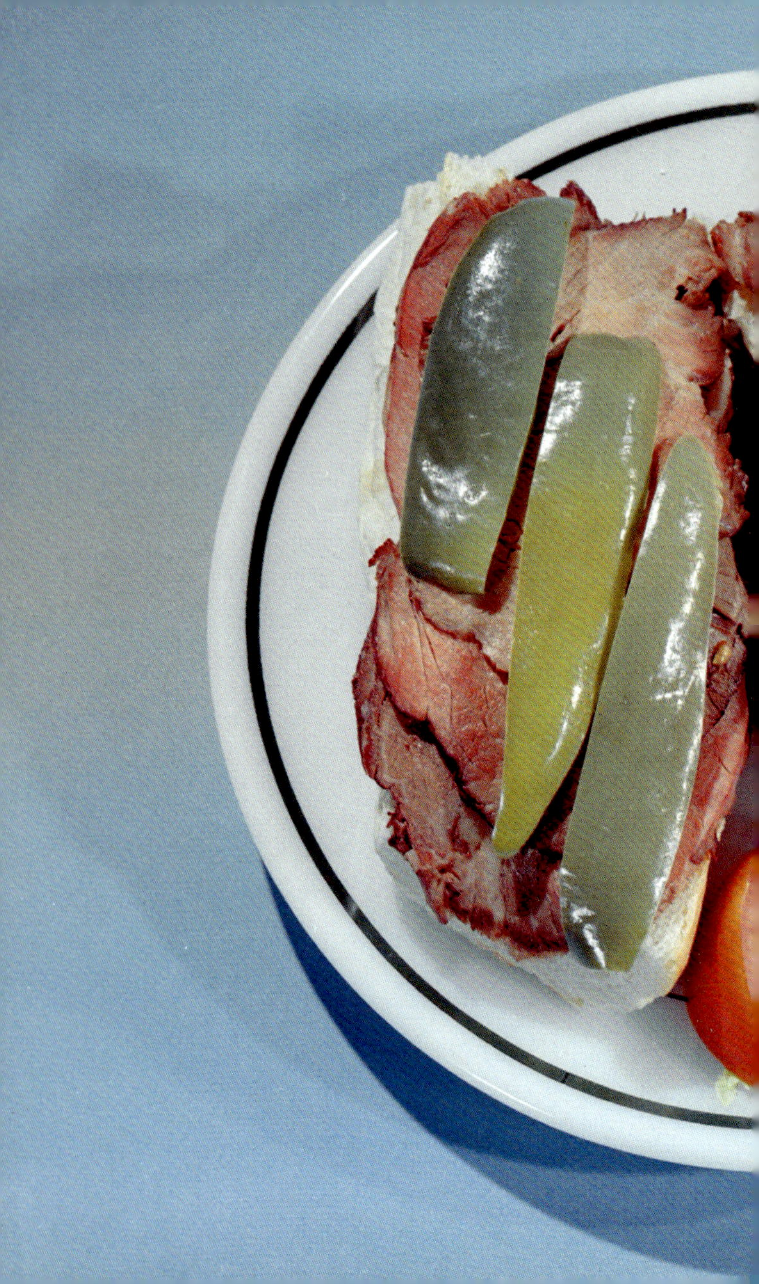

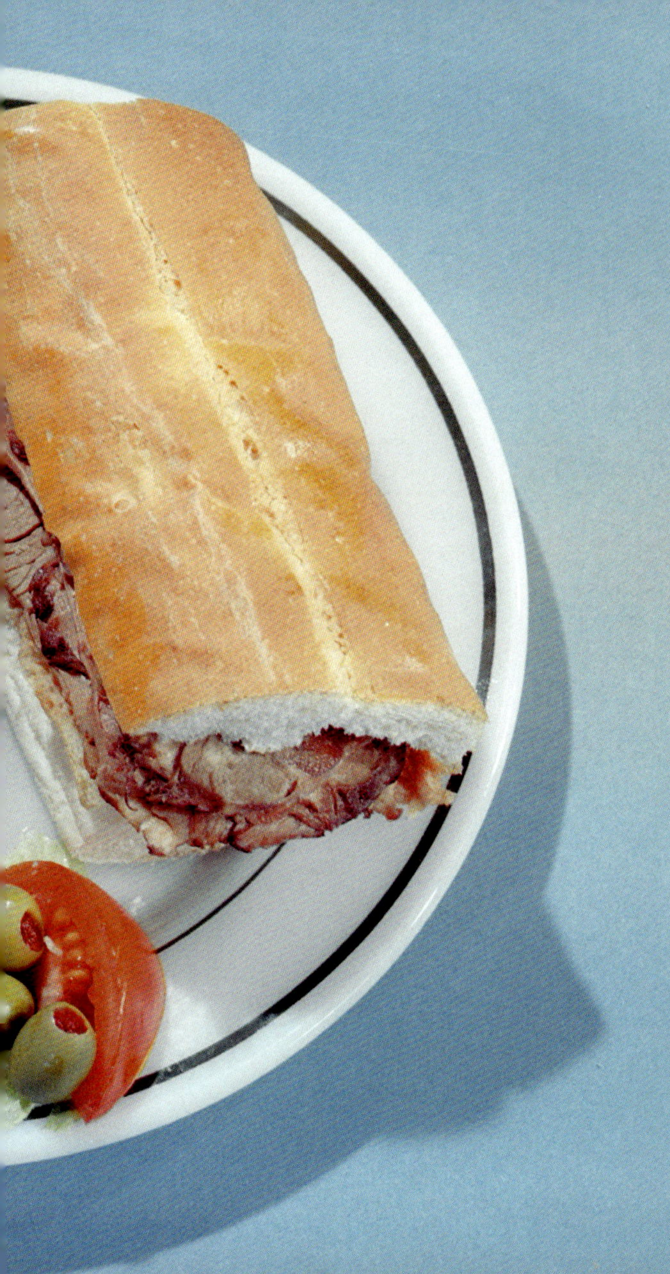

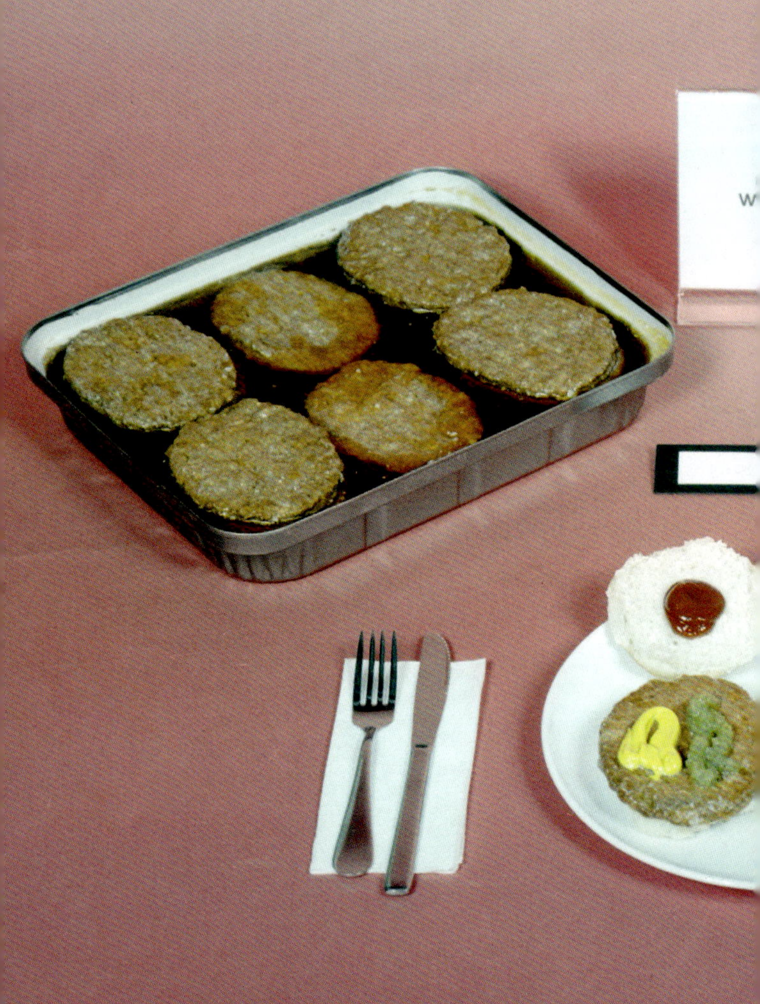

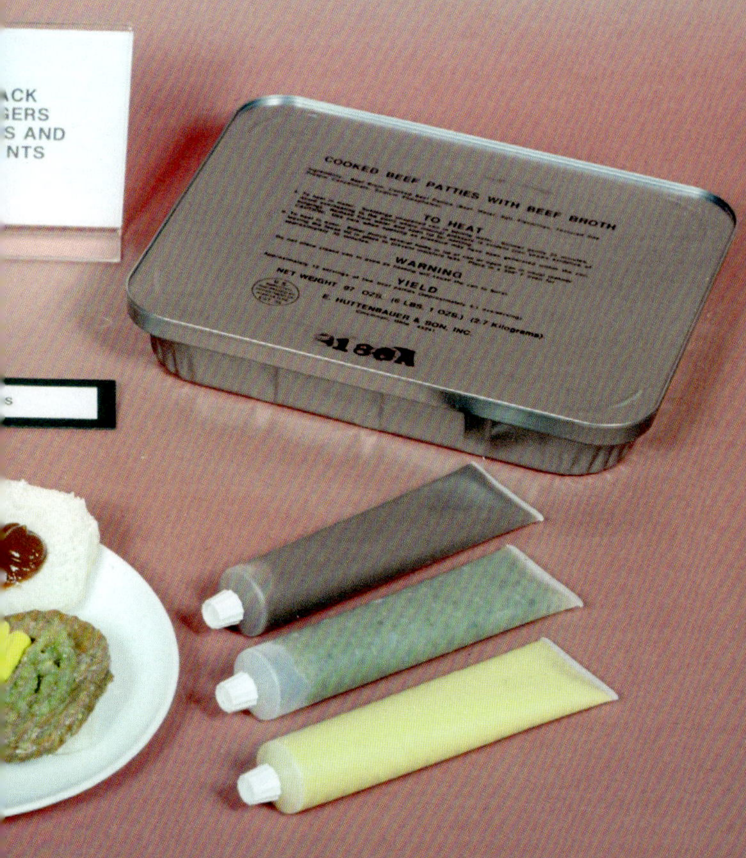
ACK
GERS
S AND
NTS
COOKED BEEF PATTIES WITH BEEF BROTH
TO HEAT
WARNING
YIELD
NET WEIGHT 97 OZS. (6 LBS. 1 OZS.) (2.7 Kilograms)
E. HUTTENBAUER & SON, INC.

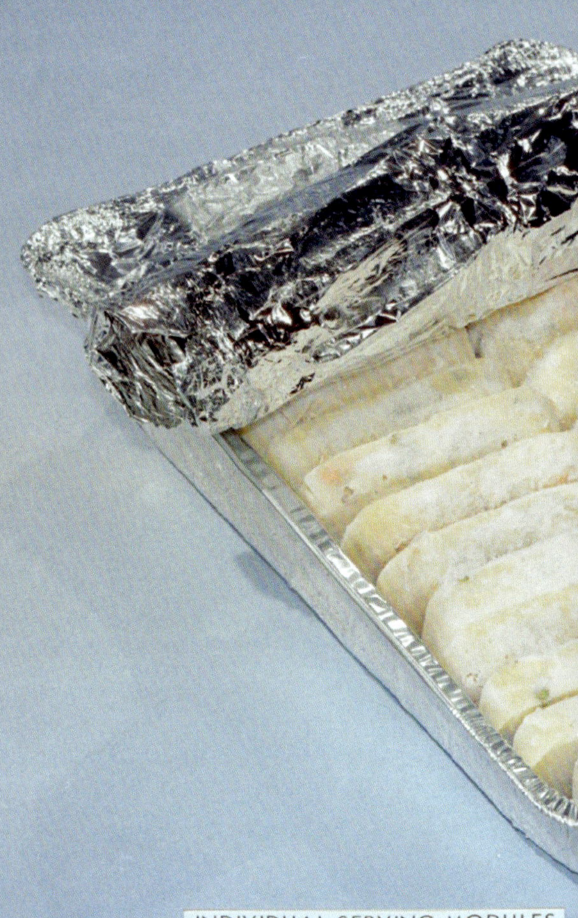

INDIVIDUAL SERVING MODULES

FROZEN CO

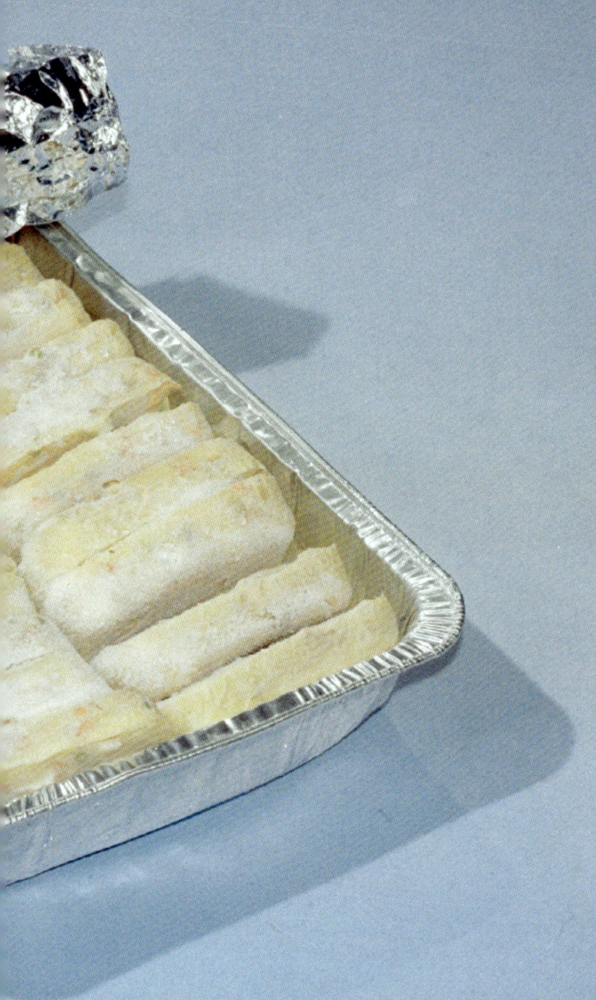

NIENCE FOODS

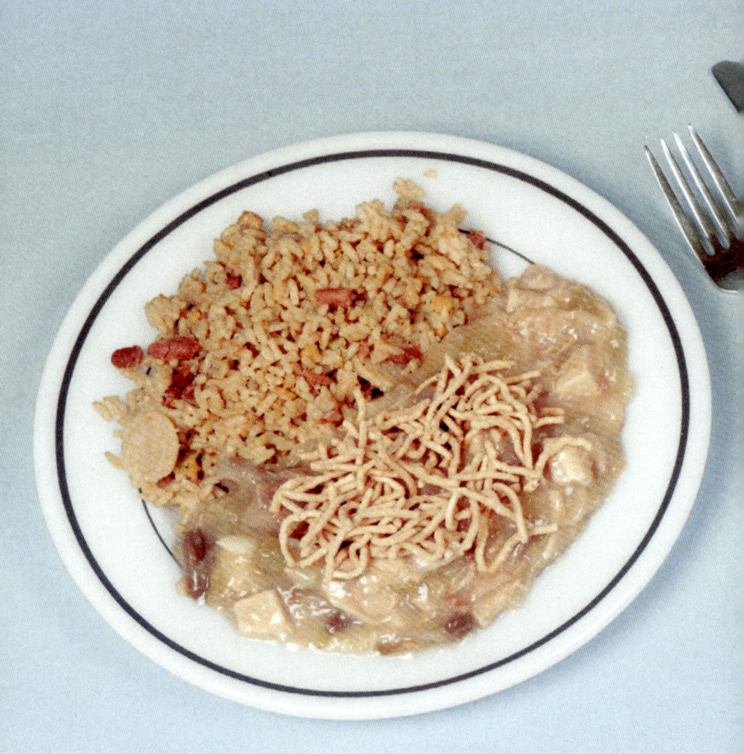

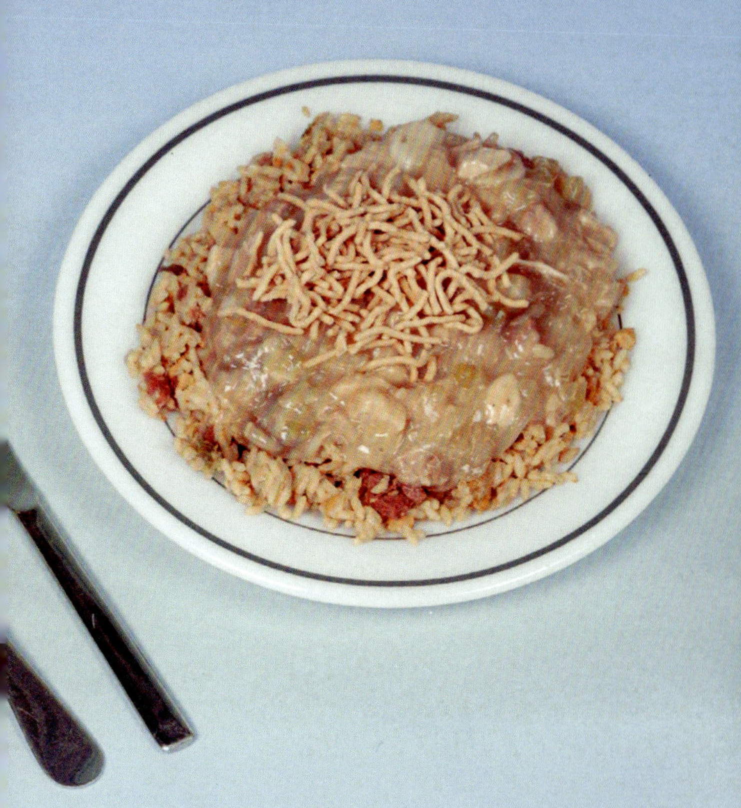

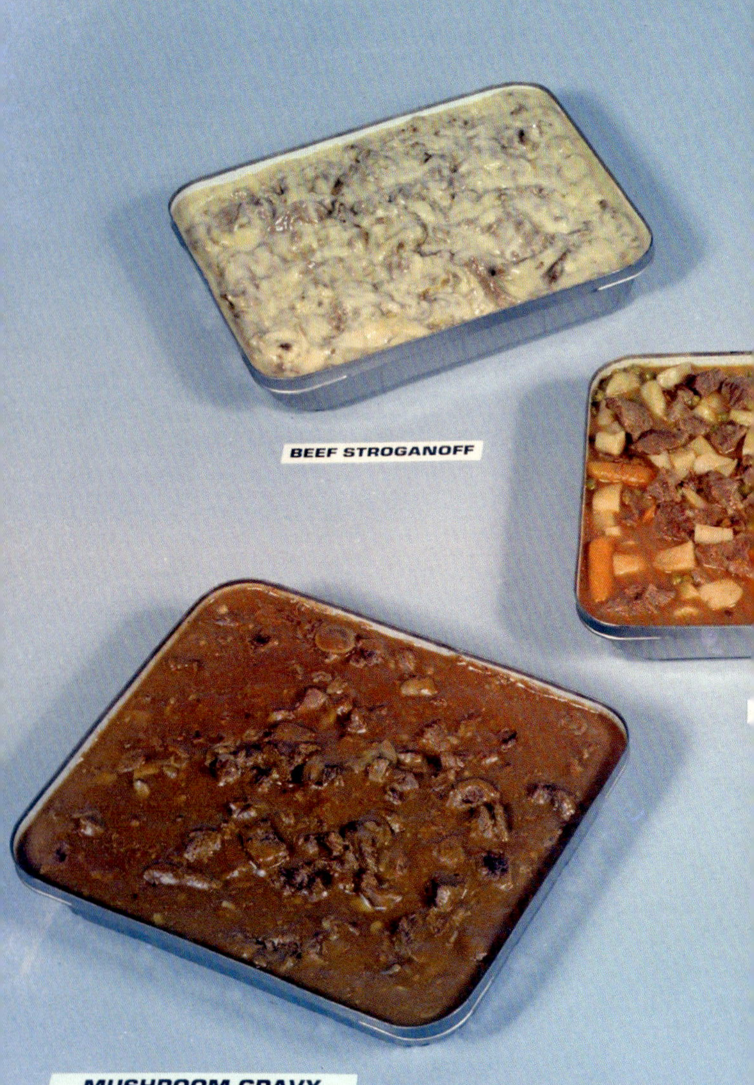
BEEF STROGANOFF
MUSHROOM GRAVY
with BRAISED BEEF TIPS

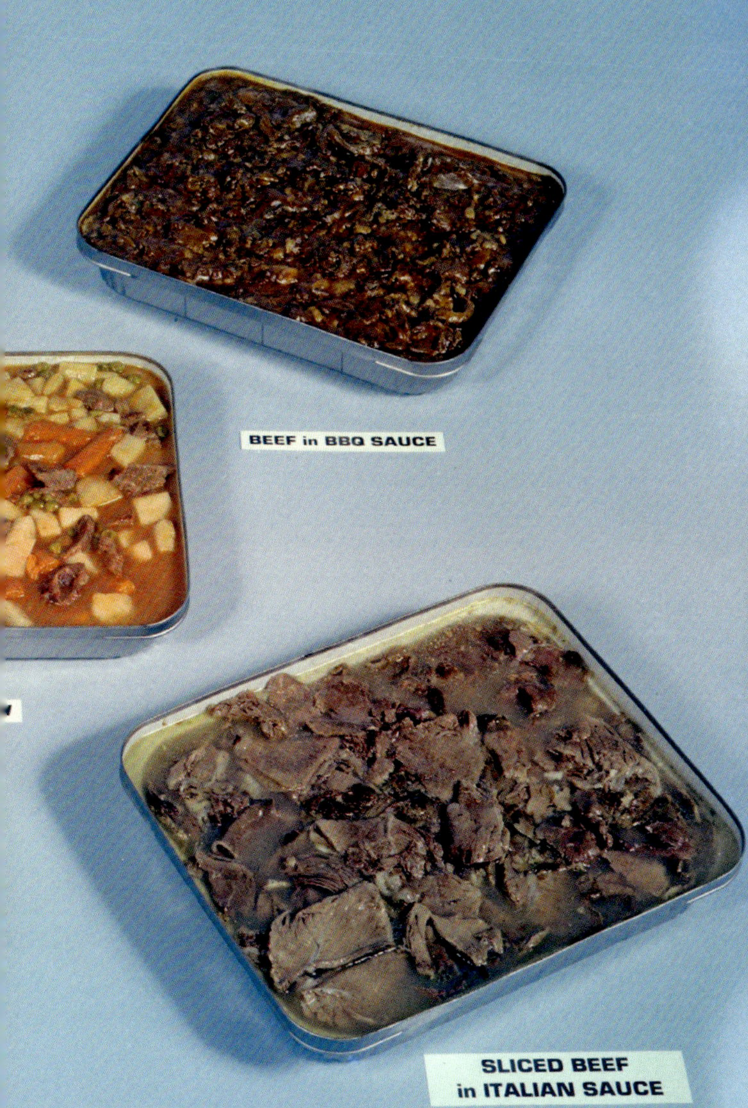
BEEF in BBQ SAUCE
SLICED BEEF
in ITALIAN SAUCE

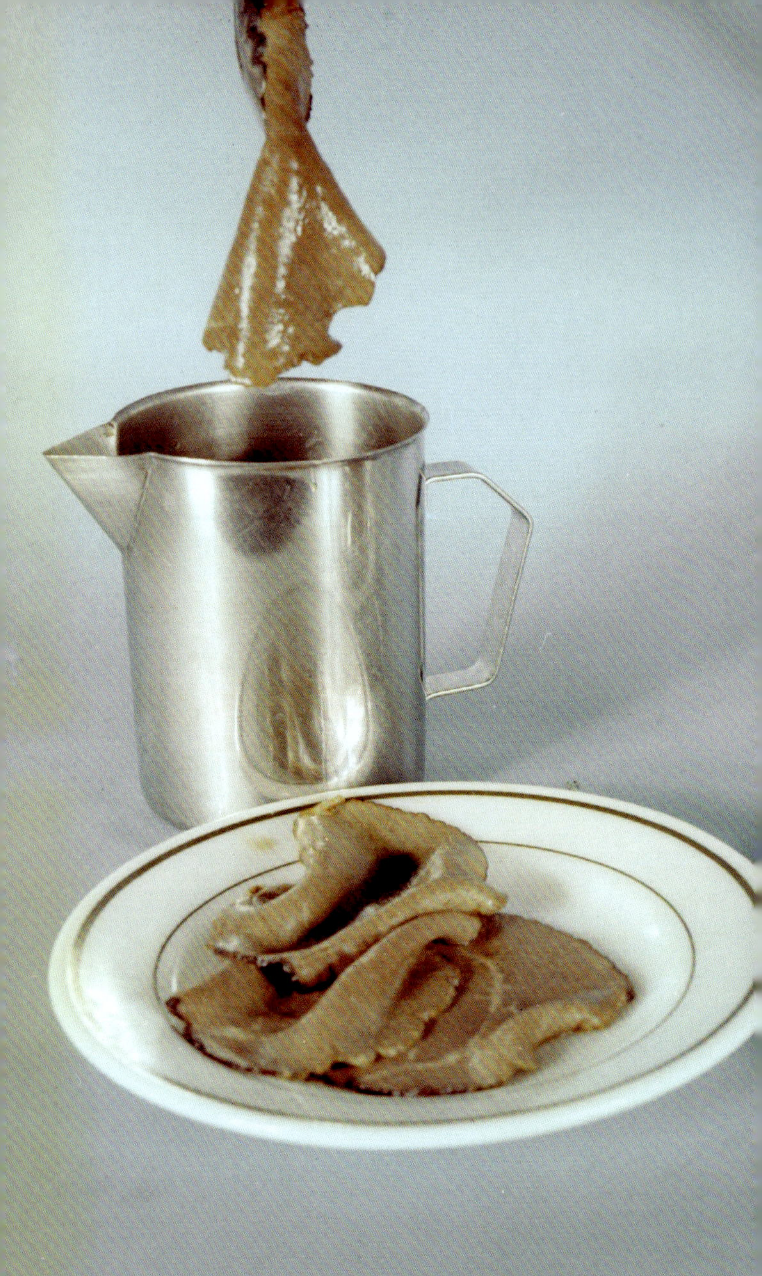

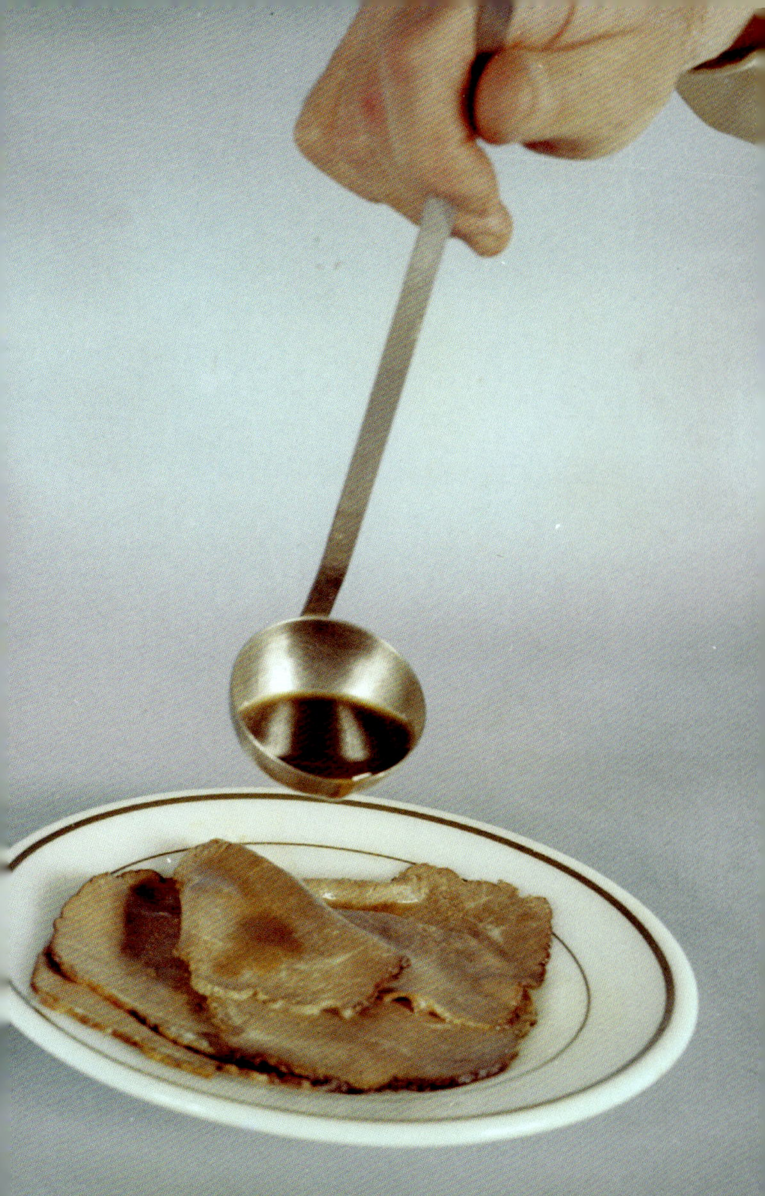

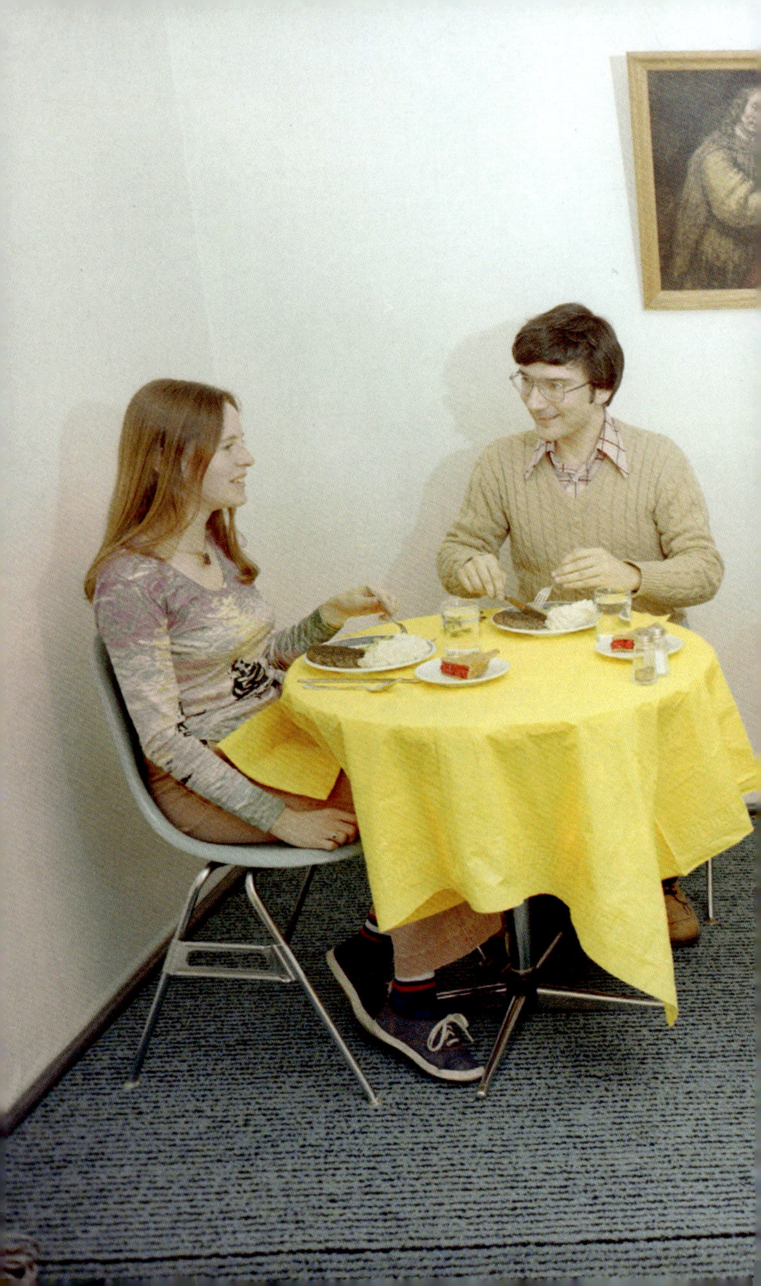

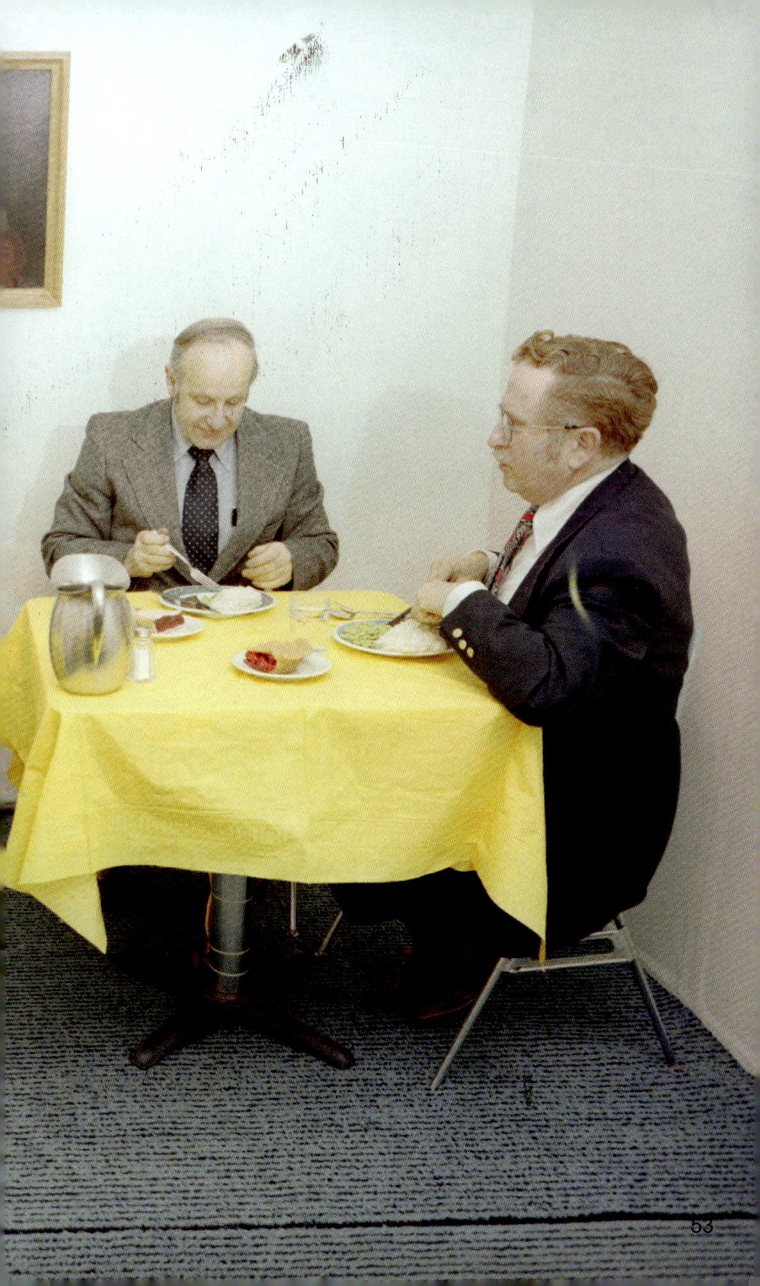

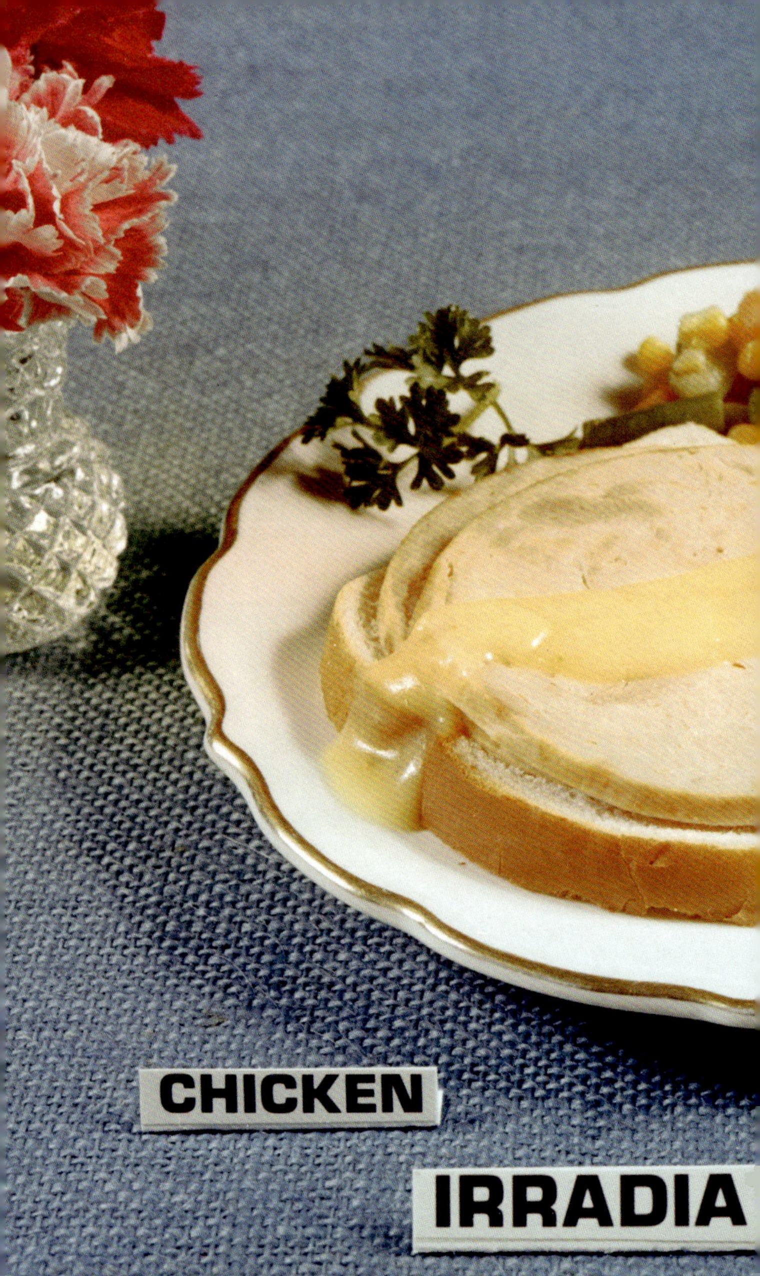
CHICKEN
IRRADIA

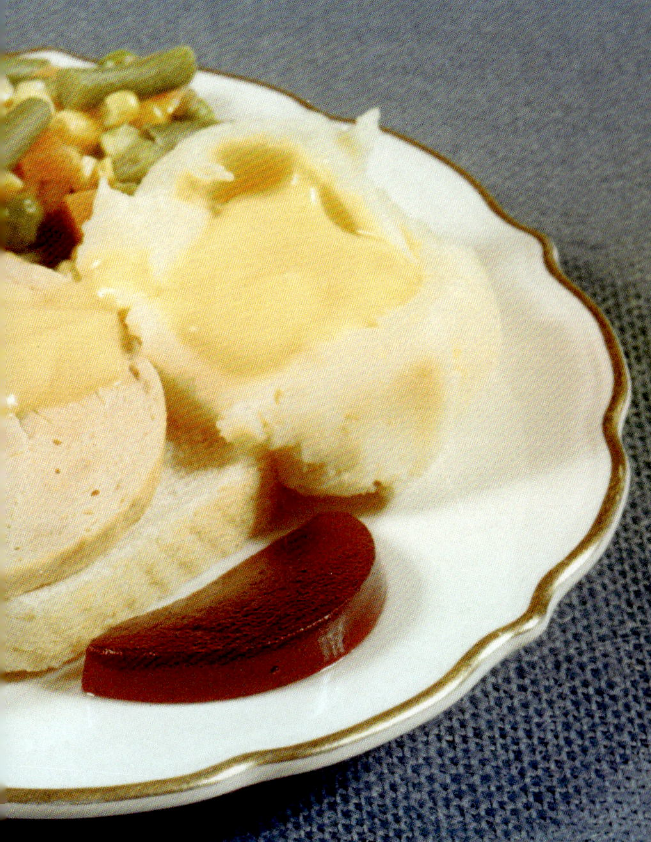

POTATO

FOODS

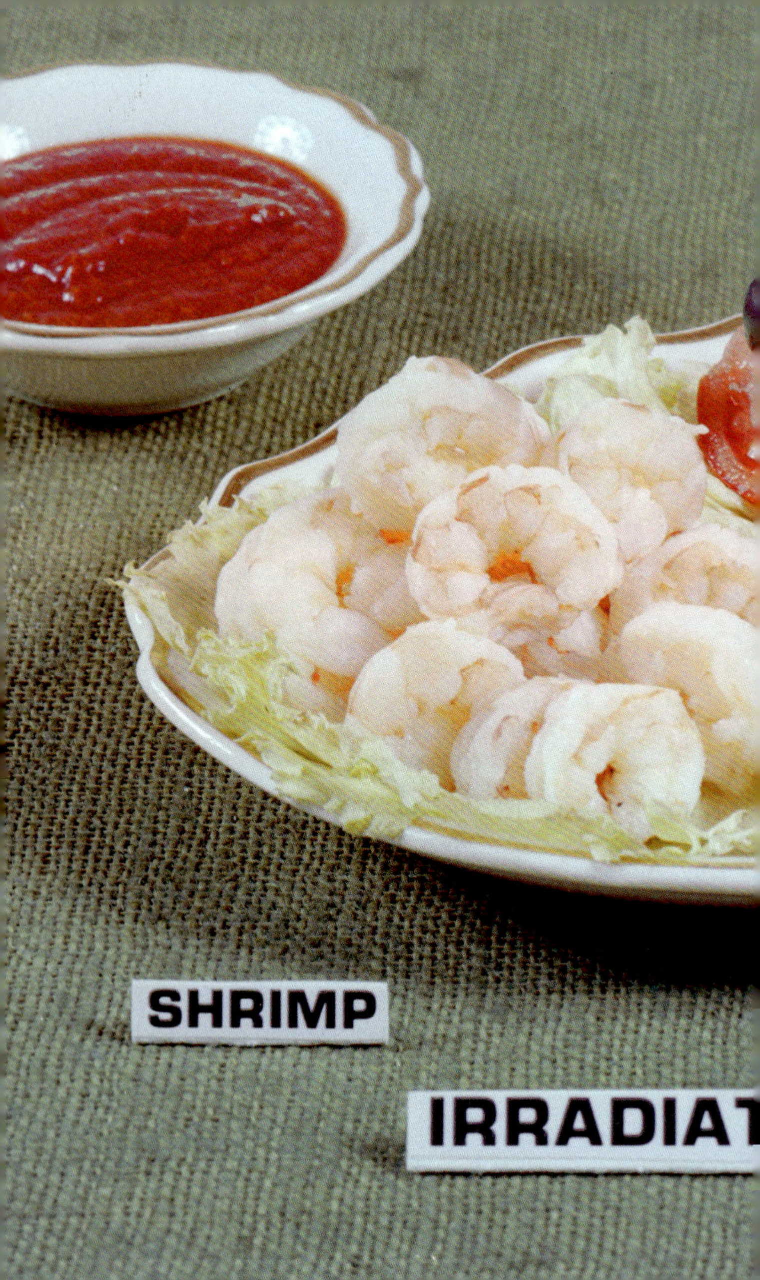
SHRIMP
IRRADIAT

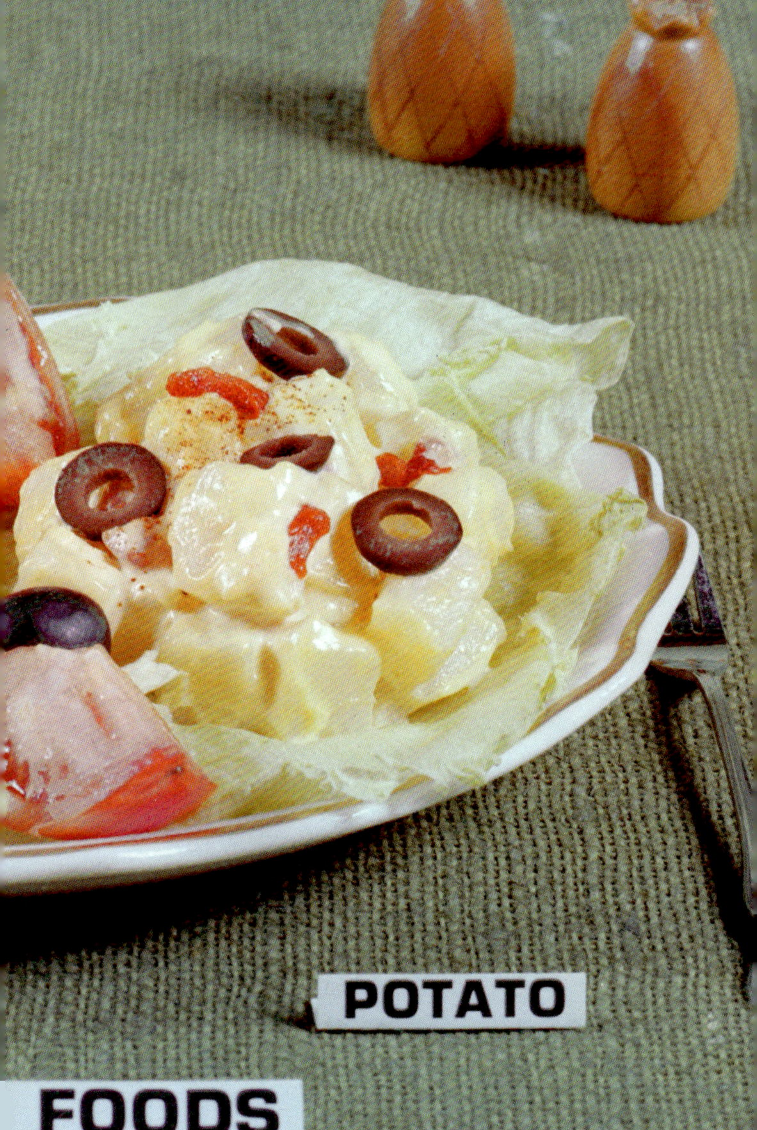
POTATO
FOODS

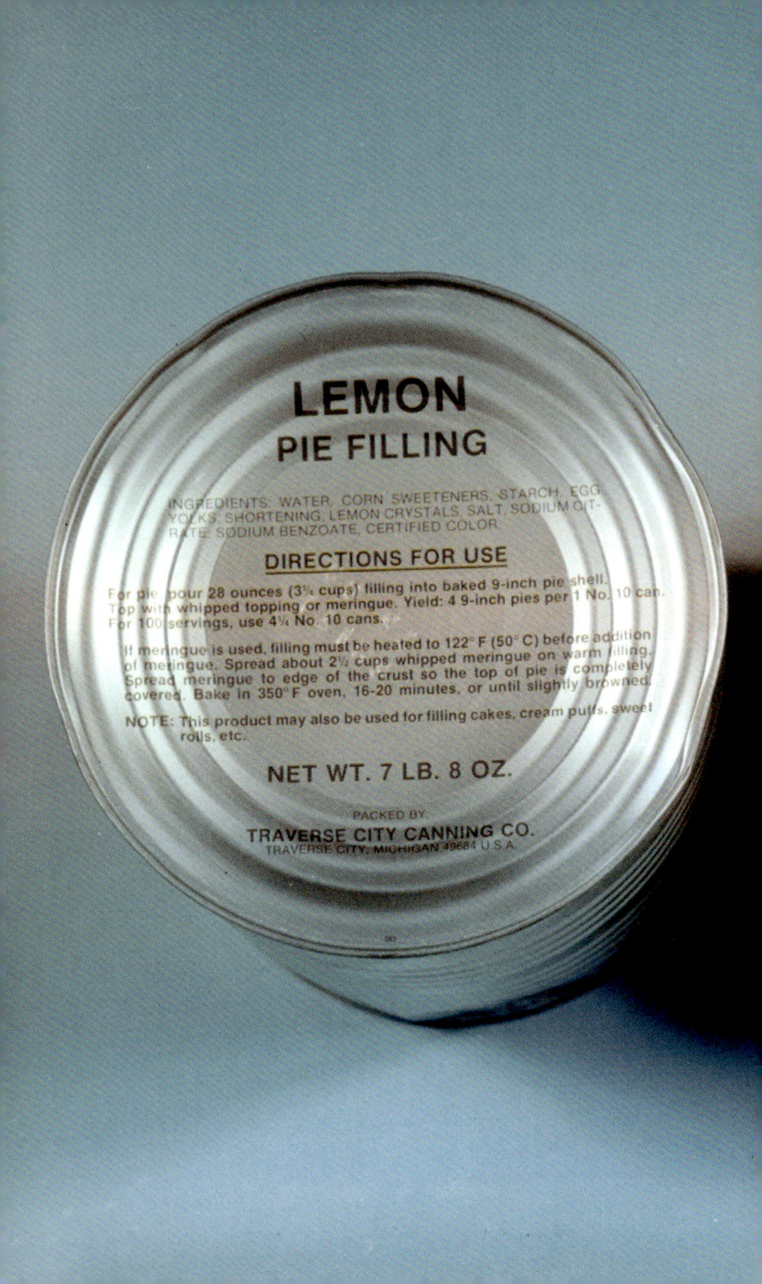

LEMON

PIE FILLING

INGREDIENTS: WATER, CORN SWEETENERS, STARCH, EGG YOLKS, SHORTENING, LEMON CRYSTALS, SALT, SODIUM CITRATE, SODIUM BENZOATE, CERTIFIED COLOR.

DIRECTIONS FOR USE

For pie, pour 28 ounces (3½ cups) filling into baked 9-inch pie shell. Top with whipped topping or meringue. Yield: 4 9-inch pies per 1 No. 10 can. For 100 servings, use 4¼ No. 10 cans.

If meringue is used, filling must be heated to 122° F (50° C) before addition of meringue. Spread about 2½ cups whipped meringue on warm filling. Spread meringue to edge of the crust so the top of pie is completely covered. Bake in 350° F oven, 16-20 minutes, or until slightly browned.

NOTE: This product may also be used for filling cakes, cream puffs, sweet rolls, etc.

NET WT. 7 LB. 8 OZ.

PACKED BY

TRAVERSE CITY CANNING CO.

TRAVERSE CITY, MICHIGAN 49684 U.S.A.

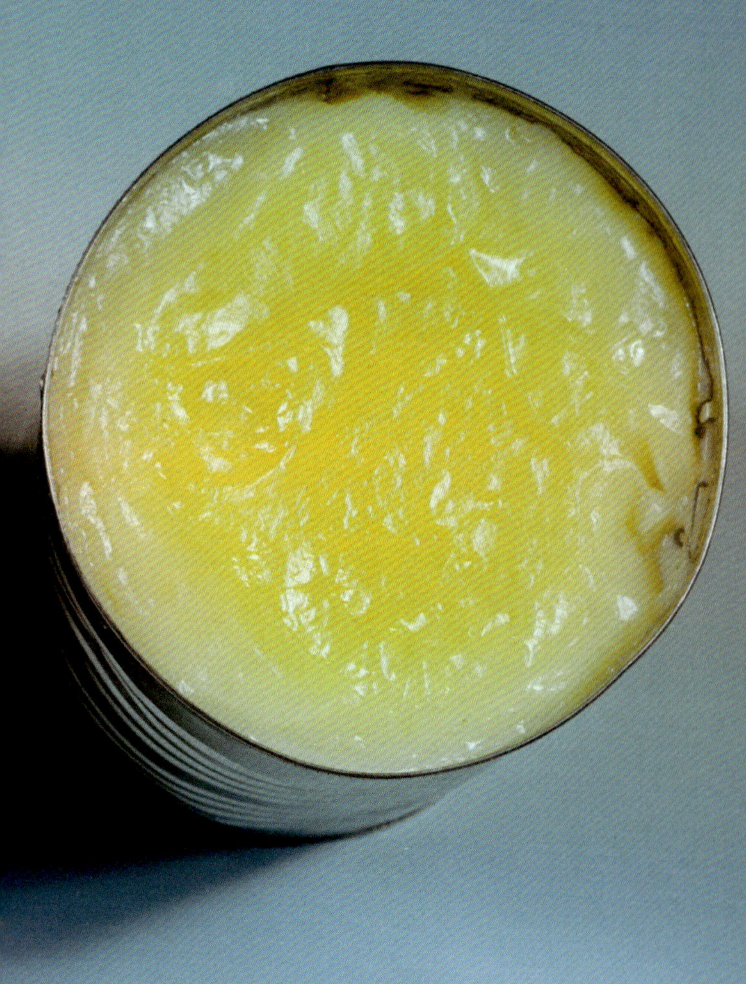

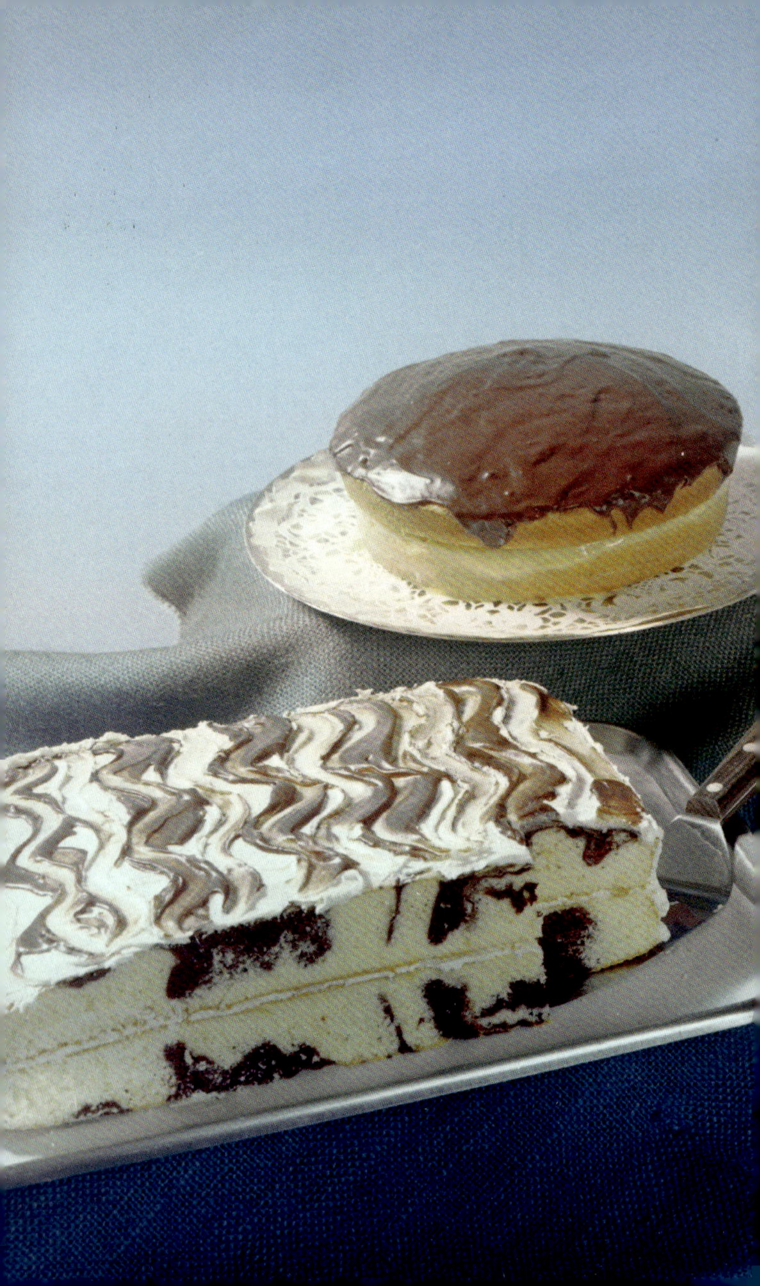

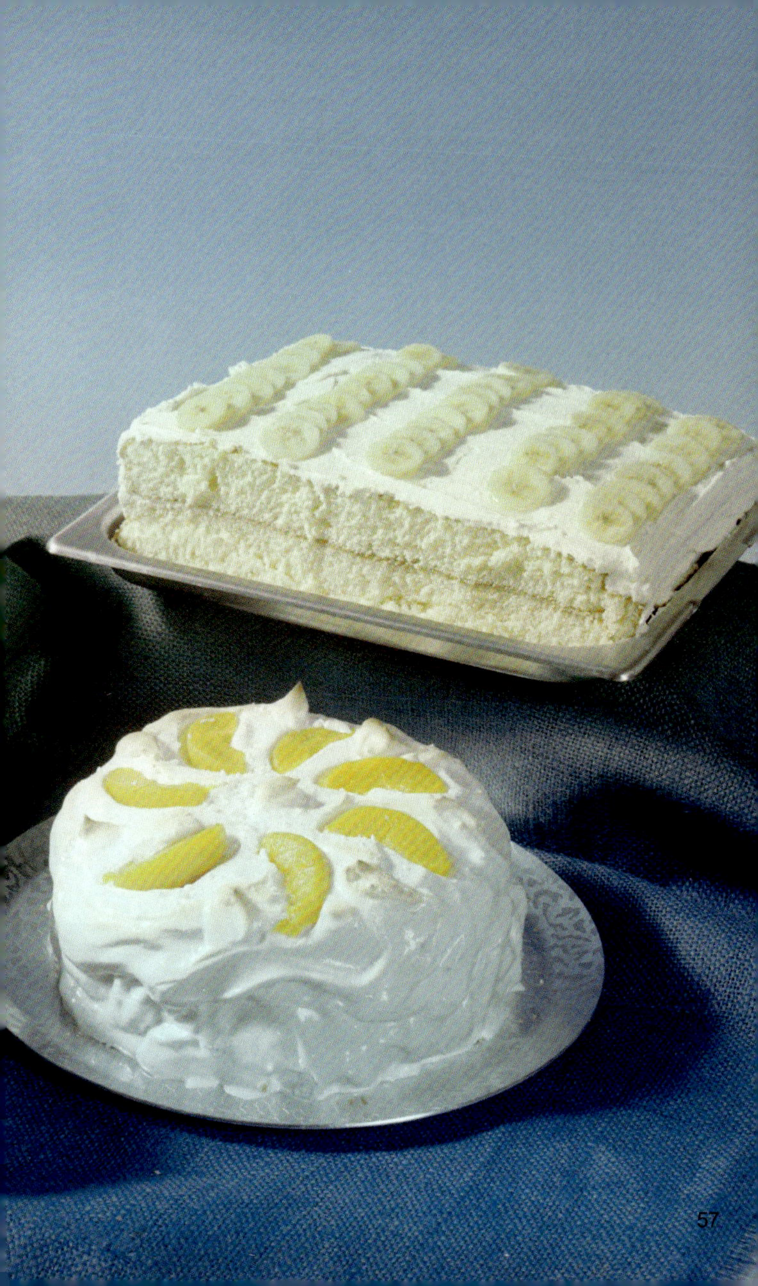

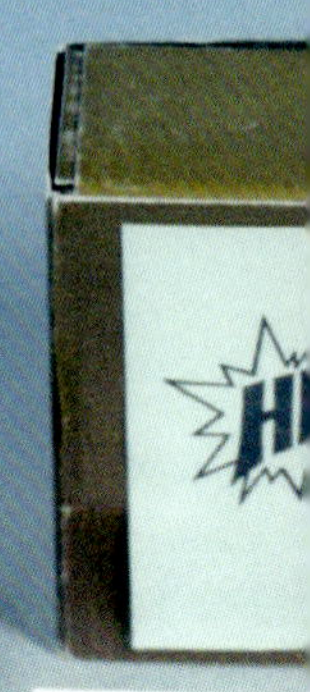
90
5.6
1

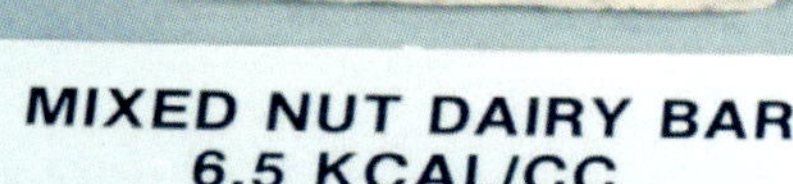
MIXED NUT DAIRY BAR
6.5 KCAL/CC

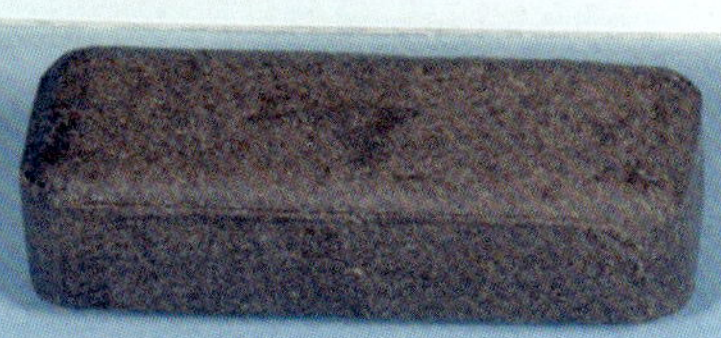
COCOA BAR
6.5 KCAL/CC

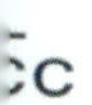

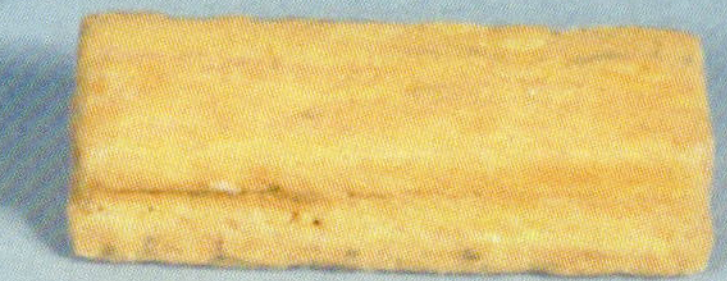
NACHO INFUSED CRUNCH
5.6 KCAL/CC

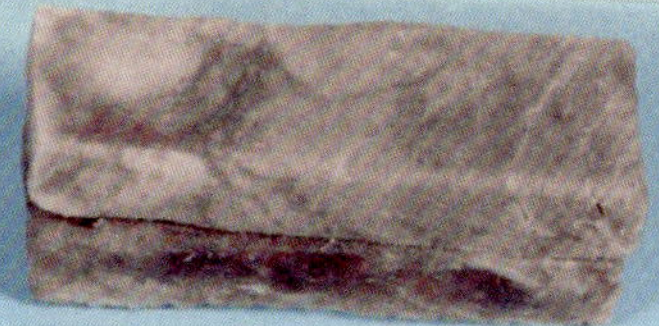
HAM MEAT STICK
6.4 KCAL/CC

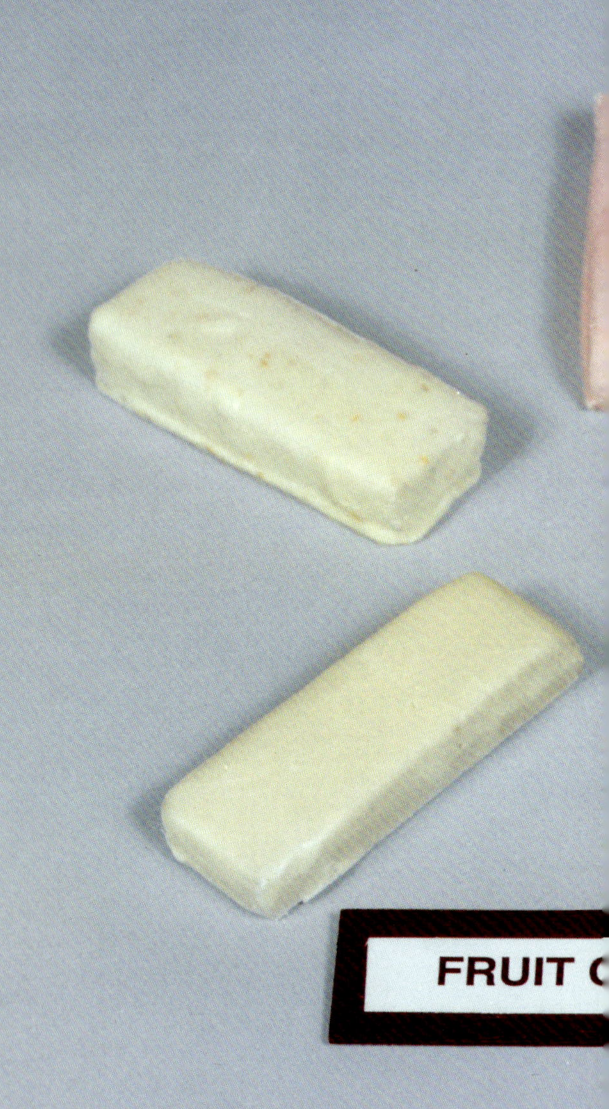
FRUIT C

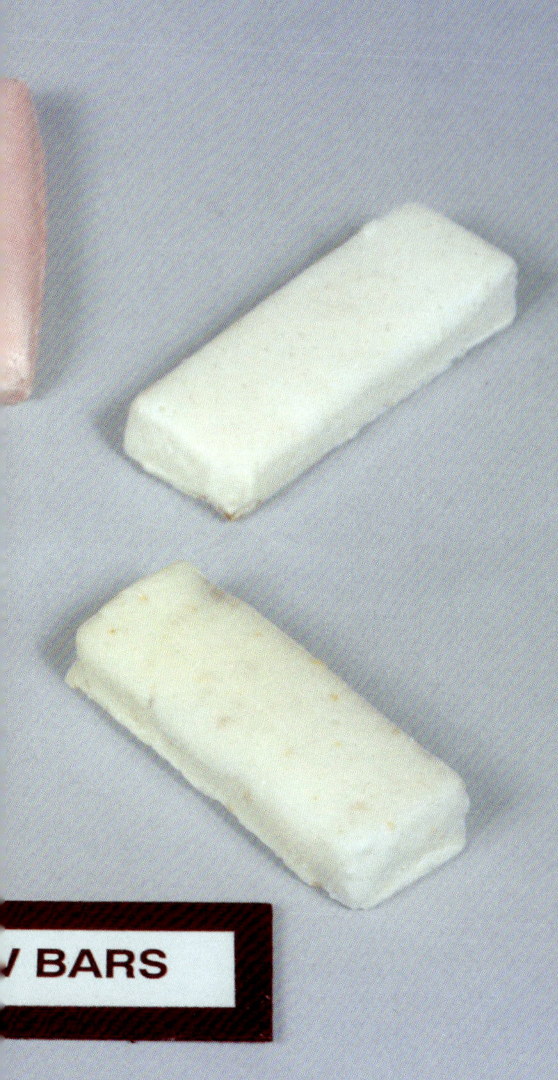
/ BARS

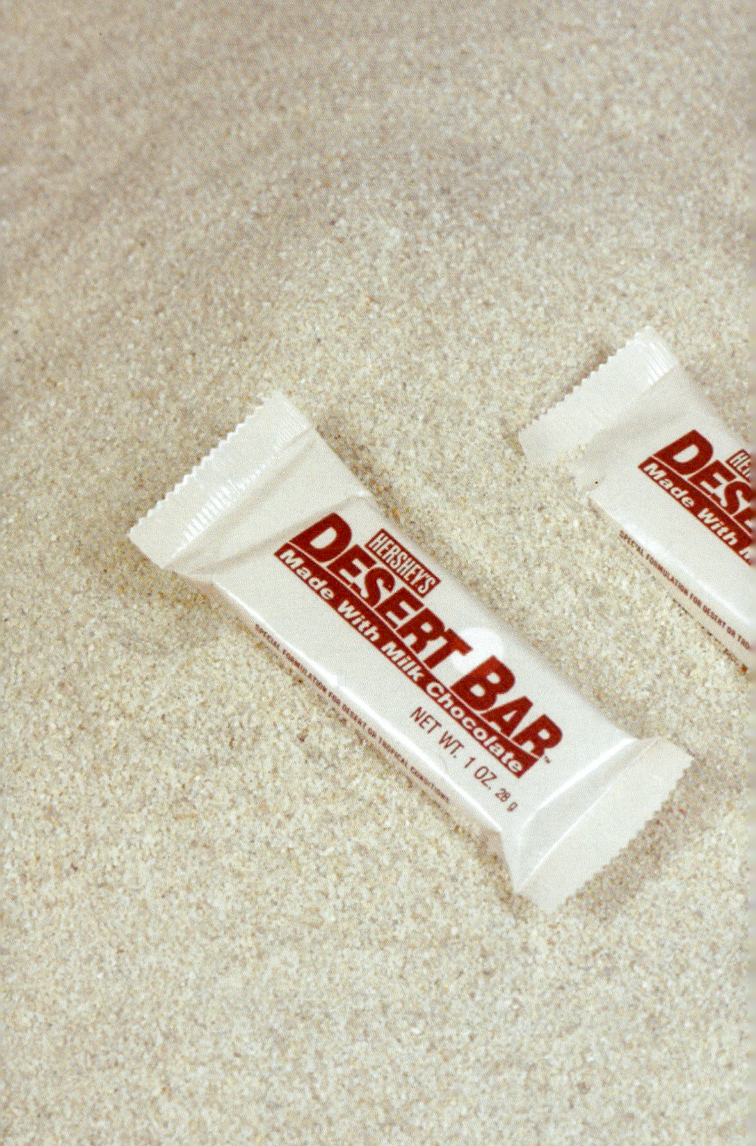
HERSHEY'S
DESERT BAR
Made With Milk Chocolate
NET WT. 1 OZ. 28 g
SPECIAL FORMULATION FOR DESERT OR TROPICAL CONDITIONS

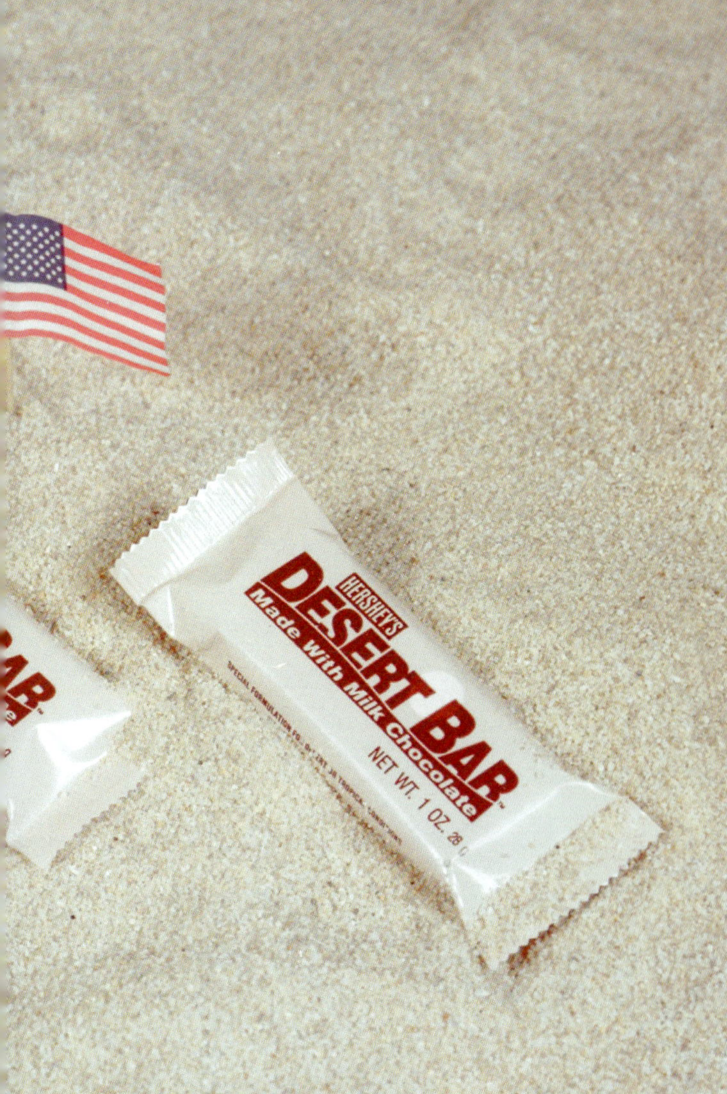
HERSHEY'S
DESERT BAR
Made With Milk Chocolate
NET WT. 1 OZ.

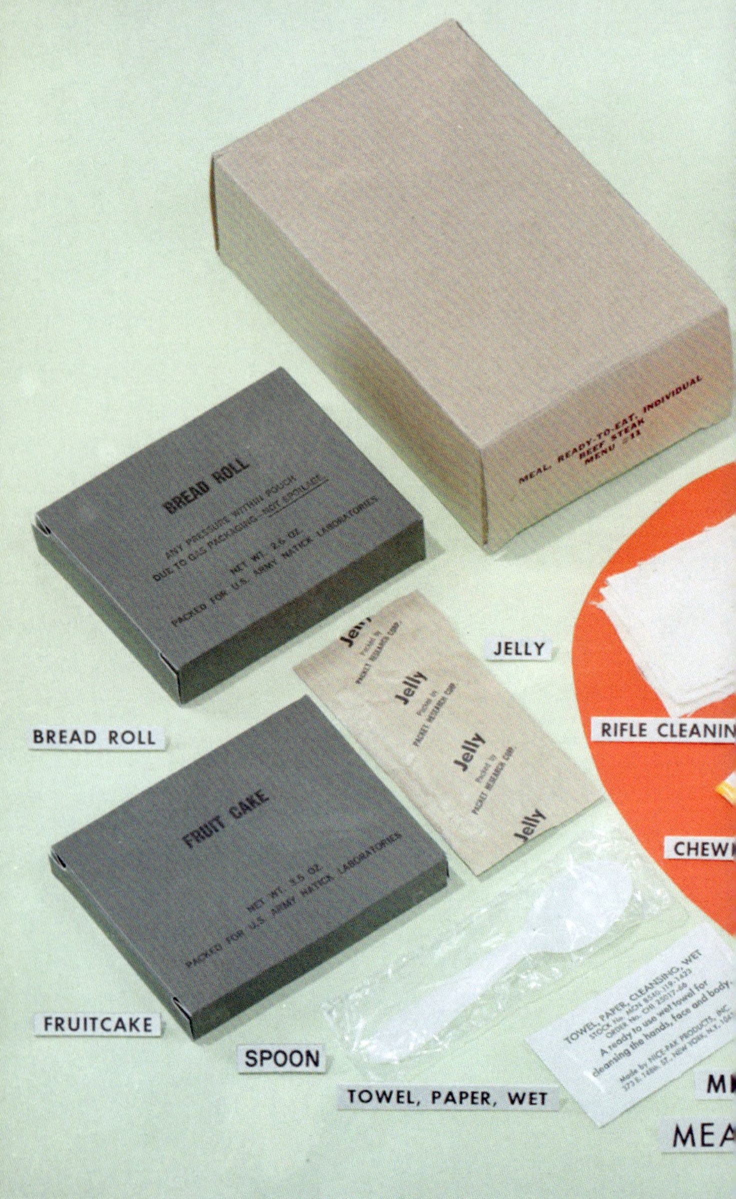
MEAL, READY-TO-EAT, INDIVIDUAL
BEEF STEAK
BREAD ROLL
ANY PRESSURE WITHIN POUCH
DUE TO GAS PACKAGING—NOT SPOILAGE
PACKED FOR U.S. ARMY NATICK LABORATORIES
JELLY
Jelly
Jelly
Jelly
Jelly
BREAD ROLL
FRUIT CAKE
PACKED FOR U.S. ARMY NATICK LABORATORIES
FRUITCAKE
SPOON
TOWEL, PAPER, WET
TOWEL, PAPER, CLEANSING, WET
A ready to use wet towel for cleansing the hands, face and body.

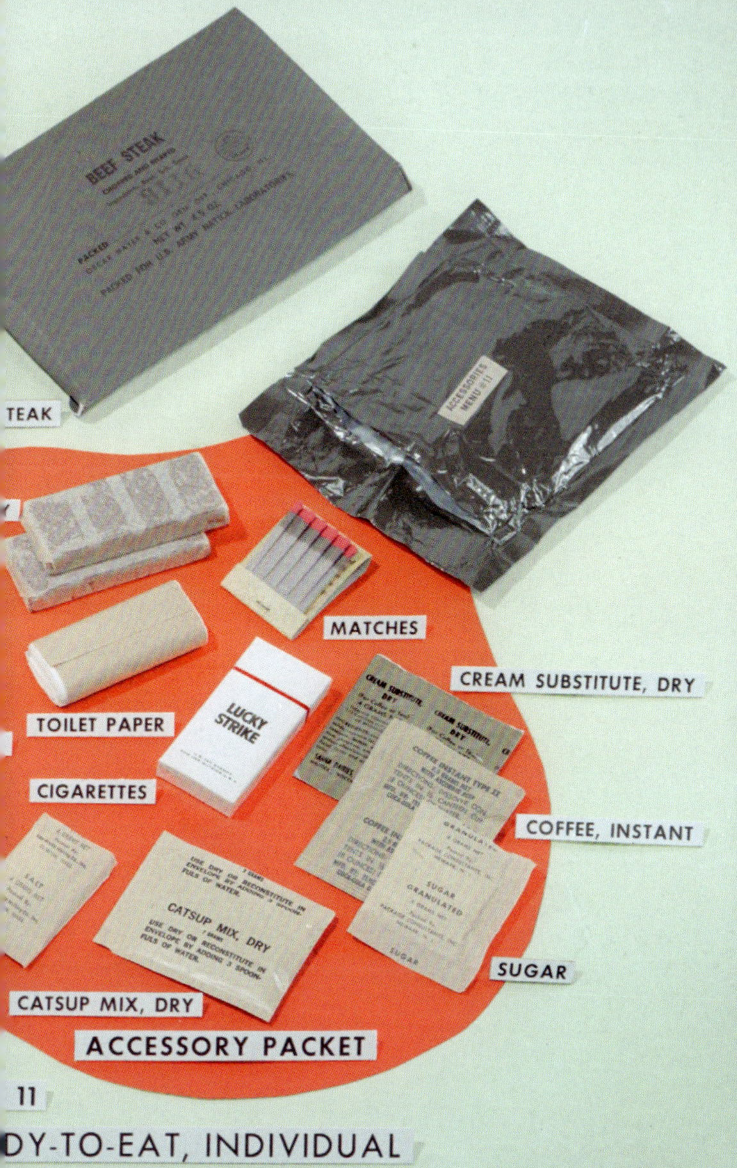
BEEF STEAK
TEAK
ACCESSORIES MENU #11
MATCHES
CREAM SUBSTITUTE, DRY
TOILET PAPER
LUCKY STRIKE
CIGARETTES
COFFEE, INSTANT
CATSUP MIX, DRY
SUGAR
CATSUP MIX, DRY
ACCESSORY PACKET
11
DY-TO-EAT, INDIVIDUAL

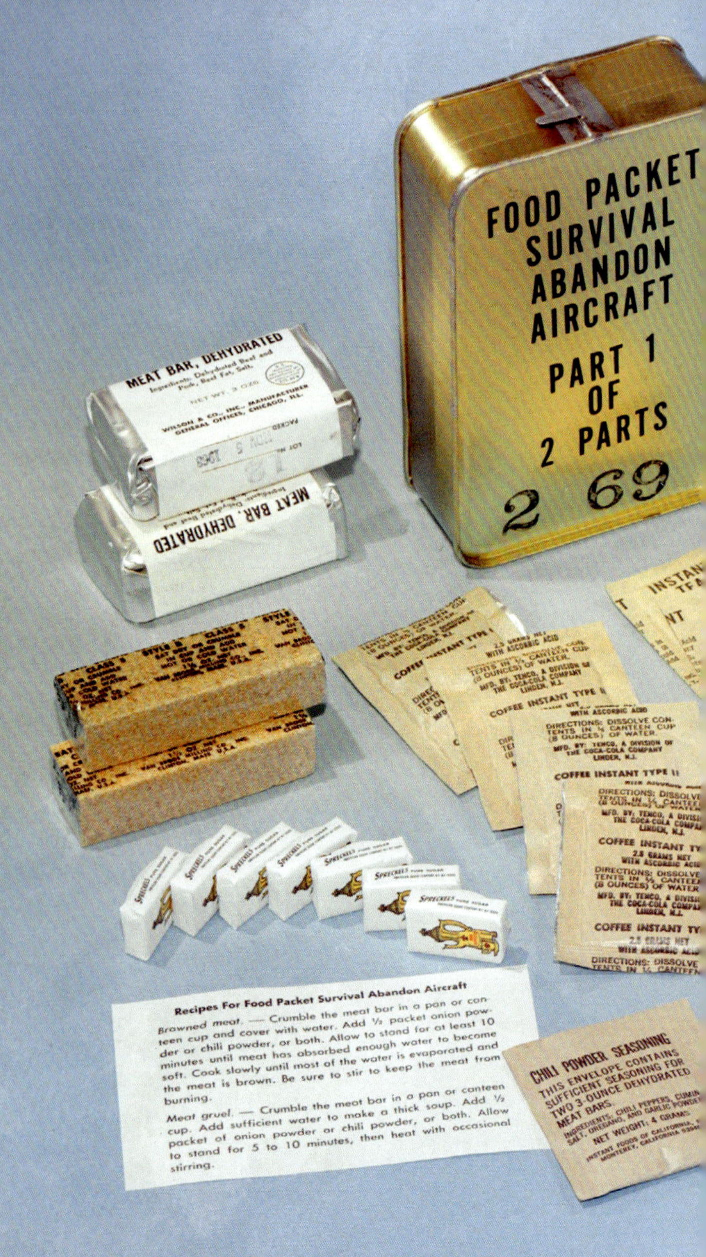
FOOD PACKET
SURVIVAL
ABANDON
AIRCRAFT
PART 1
OF
2 PARTS
2 69
MEAT BAR, DEHYDRATED
Ingredients: Dehydrated Beef and Pork, Beef Fat, Salt.
WILSON & CO., INC., MANUFACTURER
GENERAL OFFICES, CHICAGO, ILL.
MEAT BAR, DEHYDRATED
COFFEE INSTANT TYPE II
DIRECTIONS: DISSOLVE CONTENTS IN ½ CANTEEN CUP (8 OUNCES) OF WATER.
MFD. BY: TENCO, A DIVISION OF THE COCA-COLA COMPANY
LINDEN, N.J.
SPRECKELS PURE SUGAR
Recipes For Food Packet Survival Abandon Aircraft
Browned meat. — Crumble the meat bar in a pan or canteen cup and cover with water. Add ½ packet onion powder or chili powder, or both. Allow to stand for at least 10 minutes until meat has absorbed enough water to become soft. Cook slowly until most of the water is evaporated and the meat is brown. Be sure to stir to keep the meat from burning.
Meat gruel. — Crumble the meat bar in a pan or canteen cup. Add sufficient water to make a thick soup. Add ½ packet of onion powder or chili powder, or both. Allow to stand for 5 to 10 minutes, then heat with occasional stirring.
CHILI POWDER SEASONING
THIS ENVELOPE CONTAINS SUFFICIENT SEASONING FOR TWO 3-OUNCE DEHYDRATED MEAT BARS.
NET WEIGHT: 4 GRAMS

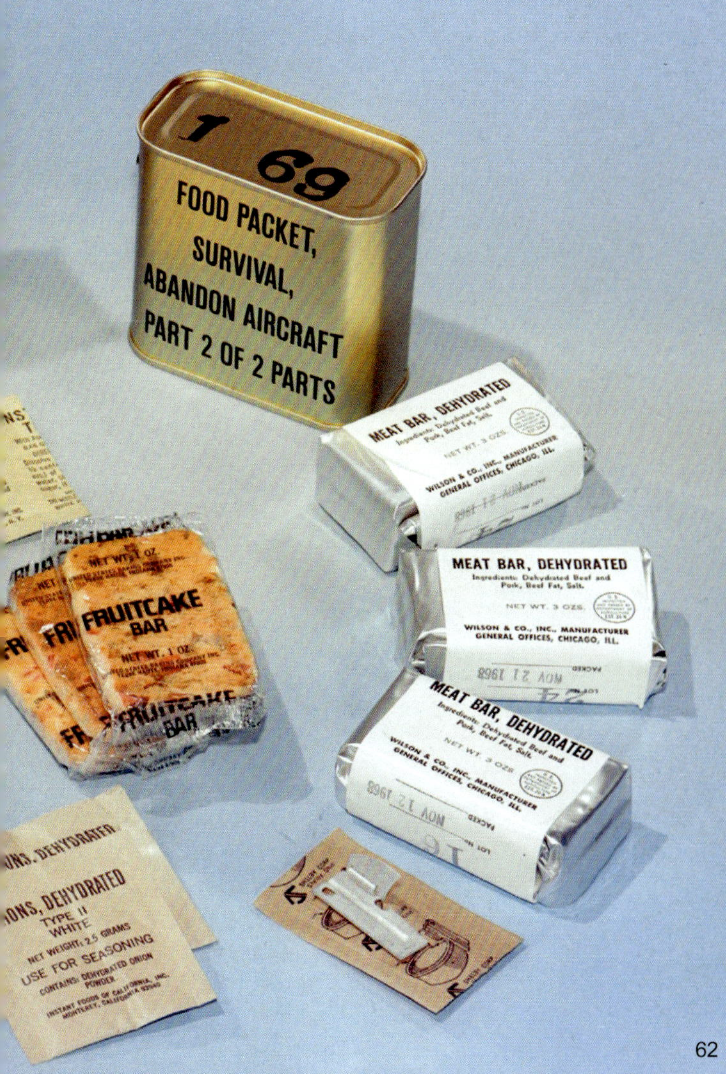
FOOD PACKET,
SURVIVAL,
ABANDON AIRCRAFT
PART 2 OF 2 PARTS
MEAT BAR, DEHYDRATED
Ingredients: Dehydrated Beef and Pork, Beef Fat, Salt.
NET WT. 3 OZS.
WILSON & CO., INC., MANUFACTURER
GENERAL OFFICES, CHICAGO, ILL.
PACKED NOV 21 1968
FRUITCAKE BAR
NET WT. 1 OZ.
TYPE II
WHITE
NET WEIGHT: 2.5 GRAMS
USE FOR SEASONING
CONTAINS: DEHYDRATED ONION POWDER
INSTANT FOODS OF CALIFORNIA, INC.
MONTEREY, CALIFORNIA 93940

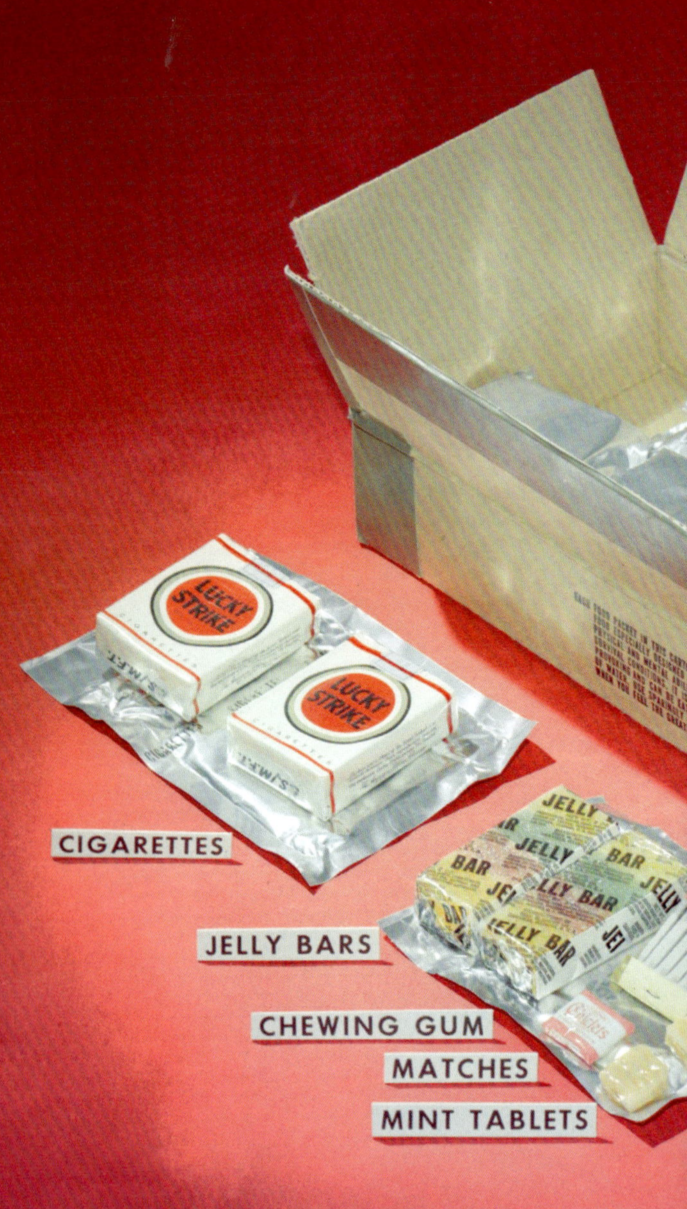
LUCKY STRIKE
LUCKY STRIKE
CIGARETTES
JELLY BARS
CHEWING GUM
MATCHES
MINT TABLETS

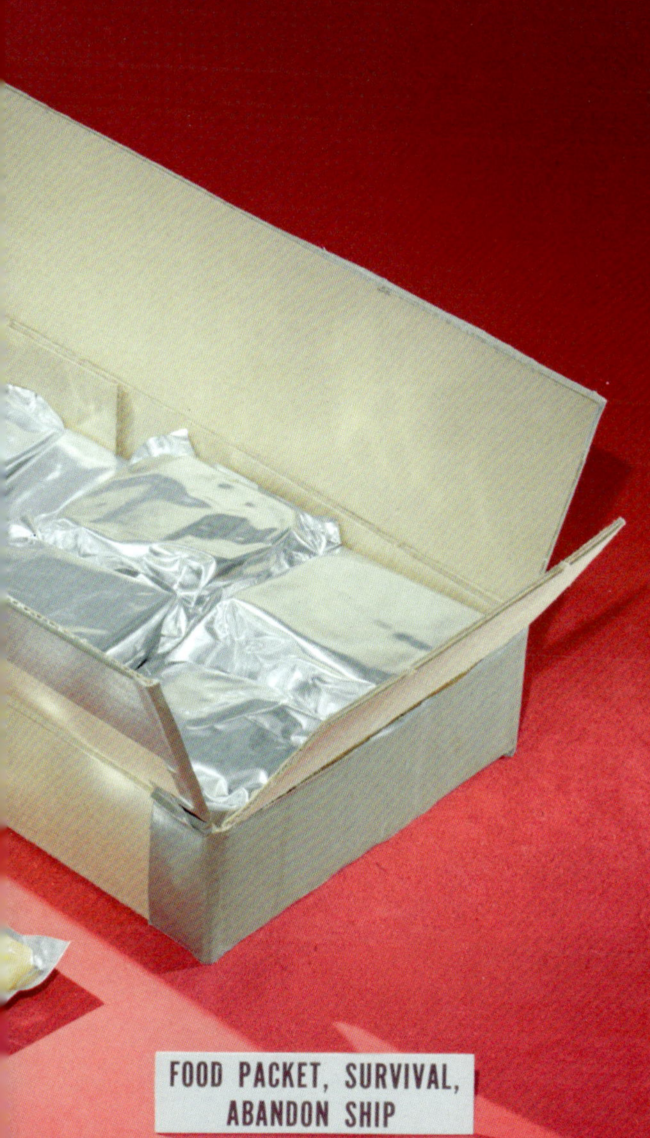
FOOD PACKET, SURVIVAL,
ABANDON SHIP

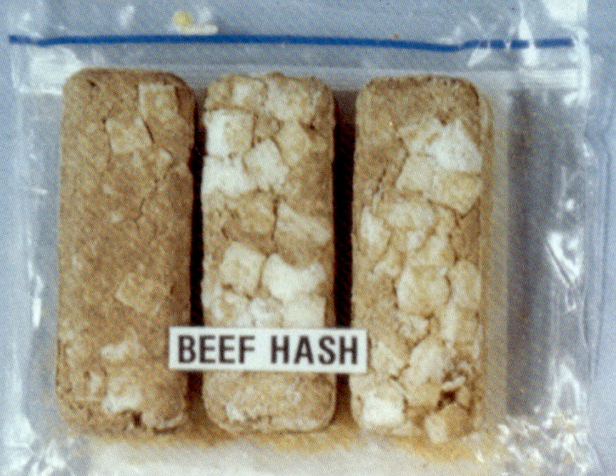
BEEF HASH

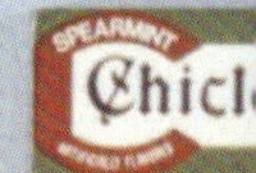
SPEARMINT

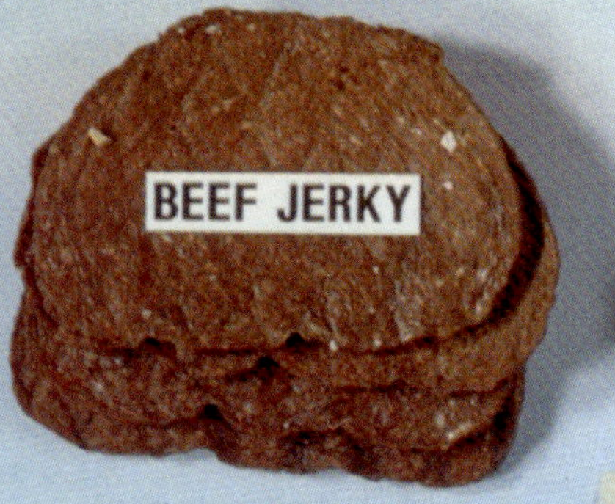
BEEF JERKY

CHEWING
GRANOLA
COFFEE INSTANT TYPE I
STYLE I COMPOSITION (2)
COFFEE
OATMEAL COOKIE
EMERGENC

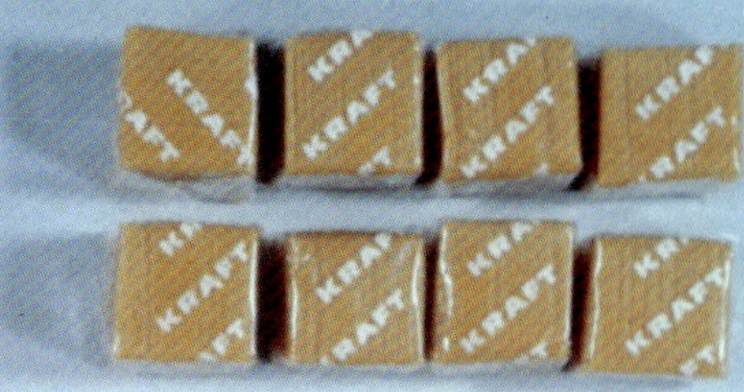

CARAMELS

TOILET PAPER

ORANGE BEVERAGE

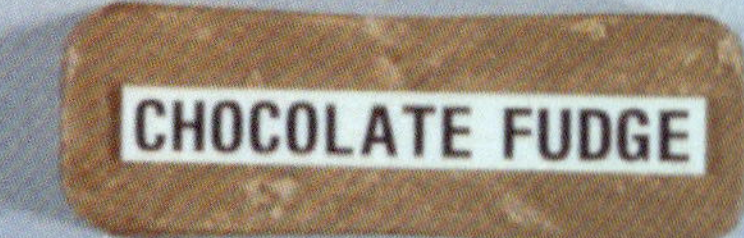

CREAM

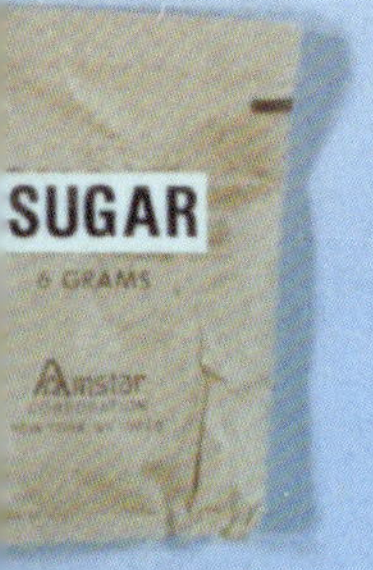

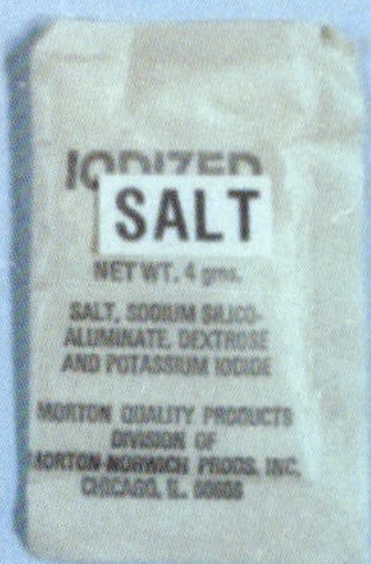

#6
SAULT PACKET

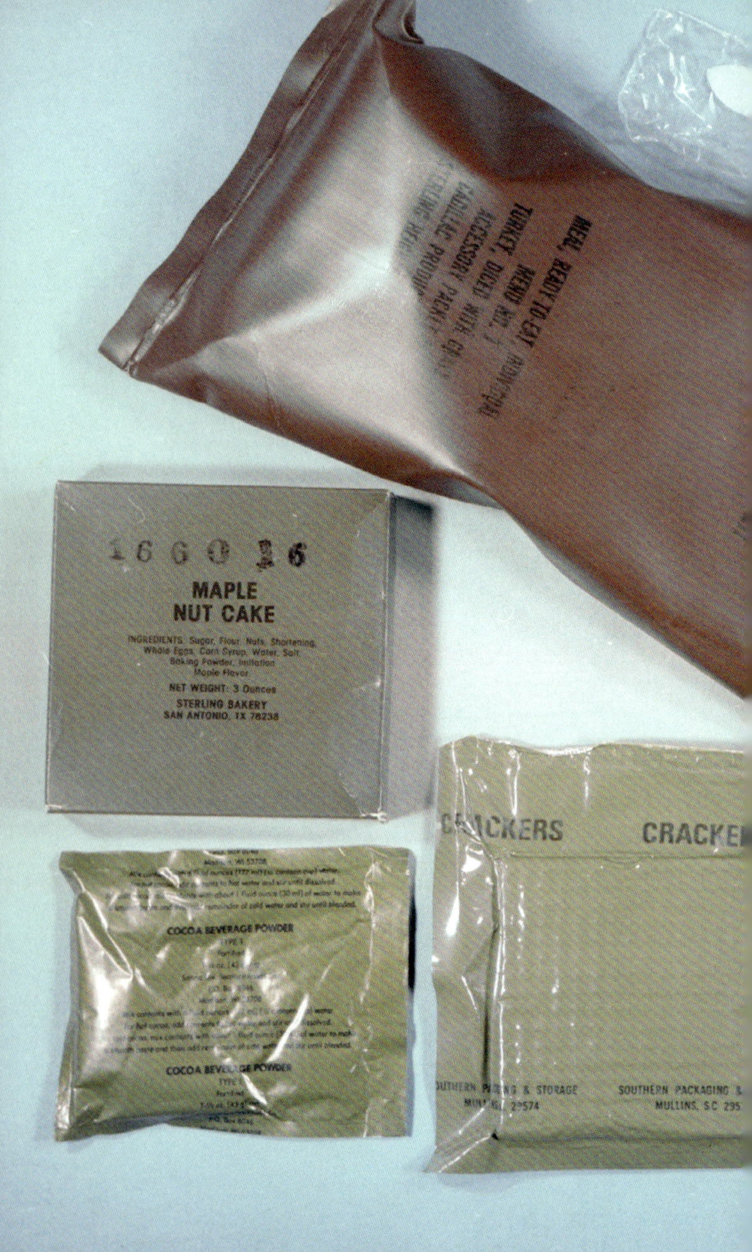
MEAL, READY-TO-EAT, INDIVIDUAL
MAPLE
NUT CAKE
INGREDIENTS: Sugar, Flour, Nuts, Shortening, Whole Eggs, Corn Syrup, Water, Salt Baking Powder, Imitation Maple Flavor
NET WEIGHT: 3 Ounces
STERLING BAKERY
SAN ANTONIO, TX 78238
COCOA BEVERAGE POWDER
CRACKERS

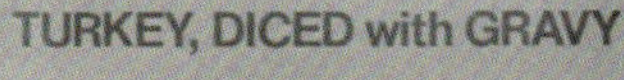
TURKEY, DICED with GRAVY
INGREDIENTS: Turkey, water, soup and gravy base (containing salt, hydrolyzed vegetable protein, monosodium glutamate, sugar, food starch modified, dried chicken meat, chicken fat, hydrogenated shortening, onion powder, garlic, turmeric and spice), cornstarch modified, flour, vegetable oil, salt, and onion salt.
1405 0 A
DISTRIBUTED BY
GREEN GIANT CO.
LE SUEUR, MN 56058
NET WT. 5 OZ.

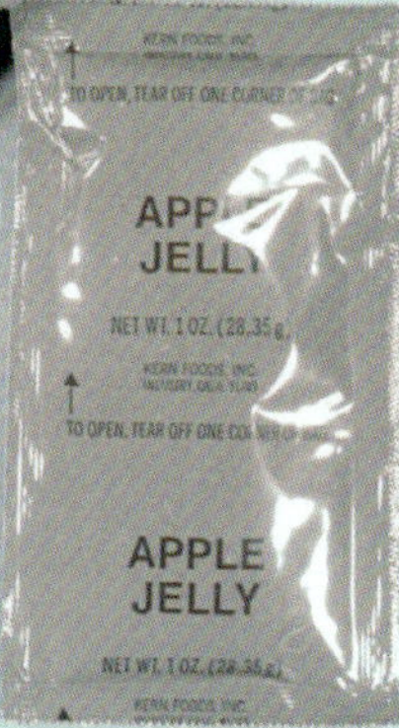
TO OPEN, TEAR OFF ONE CORNER OF BAG
APPLE
JELLY
NET WT. 1 OZ. (28.35 g)
TO OPEN, TEAR OFF ONE CORNER OF BAG
APPLE
JELLY

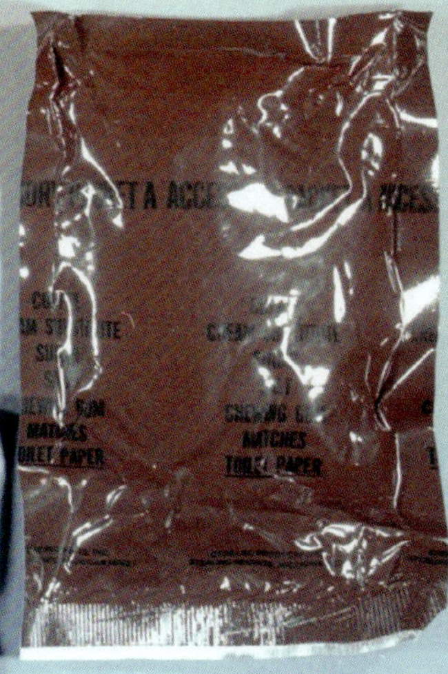

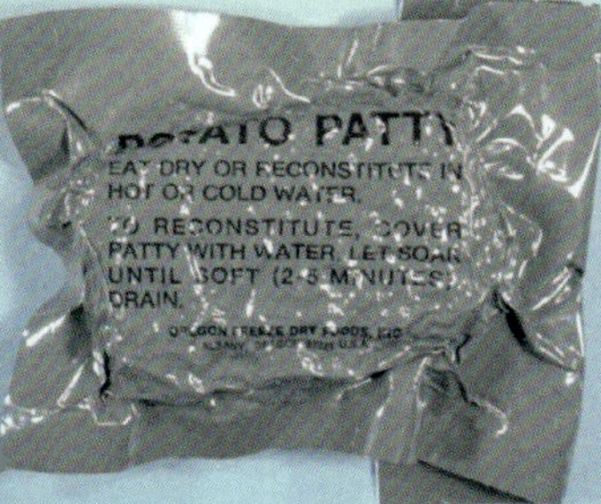
POTATO PATTY
EAT DRY OR RECONSTITUTE IN HOT OR COLD WATER.
TO RECONSTITUTE, COVER PATTY WITH WATER. LET SOAK UNTIL SOFT (2-5 MINUTES). DRAIN.

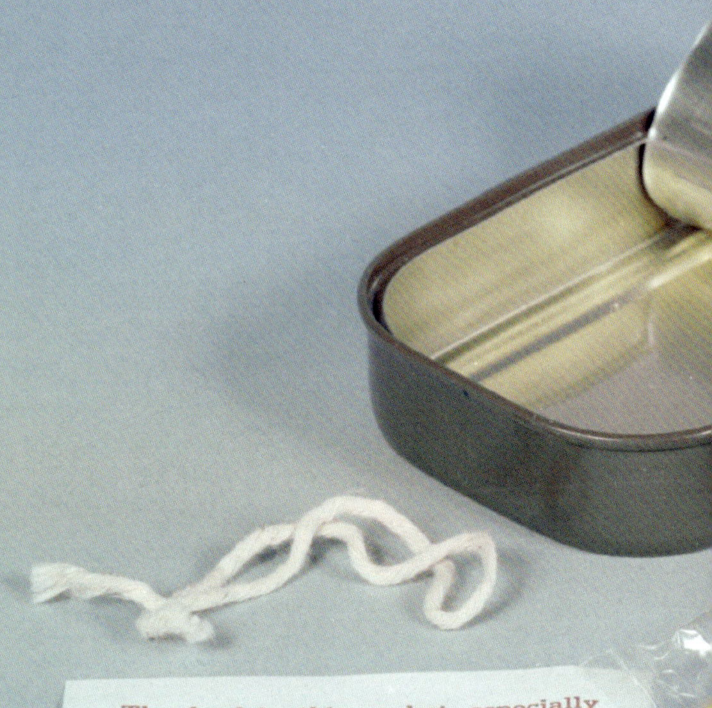
The food in this packet, especially developed for survival use, will be beneficial even when water supply is limited. When entirely consumed by one man in one day, the packet will maintain survival efficiency. Items must not be allowed to get wet. Keep unused components in plastic bag. Use Twine to tie mouth securely.

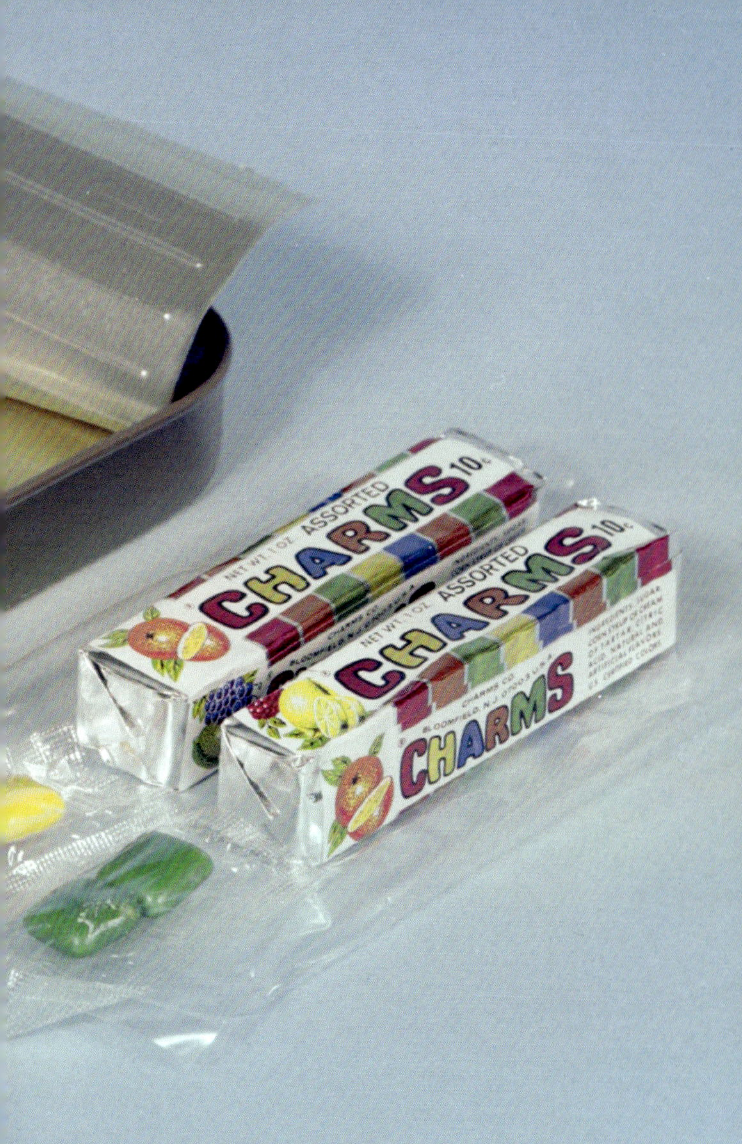
CHARMS 10¢
ASSORTED
CHARMS 10¢
ASSORTED
CHARMS

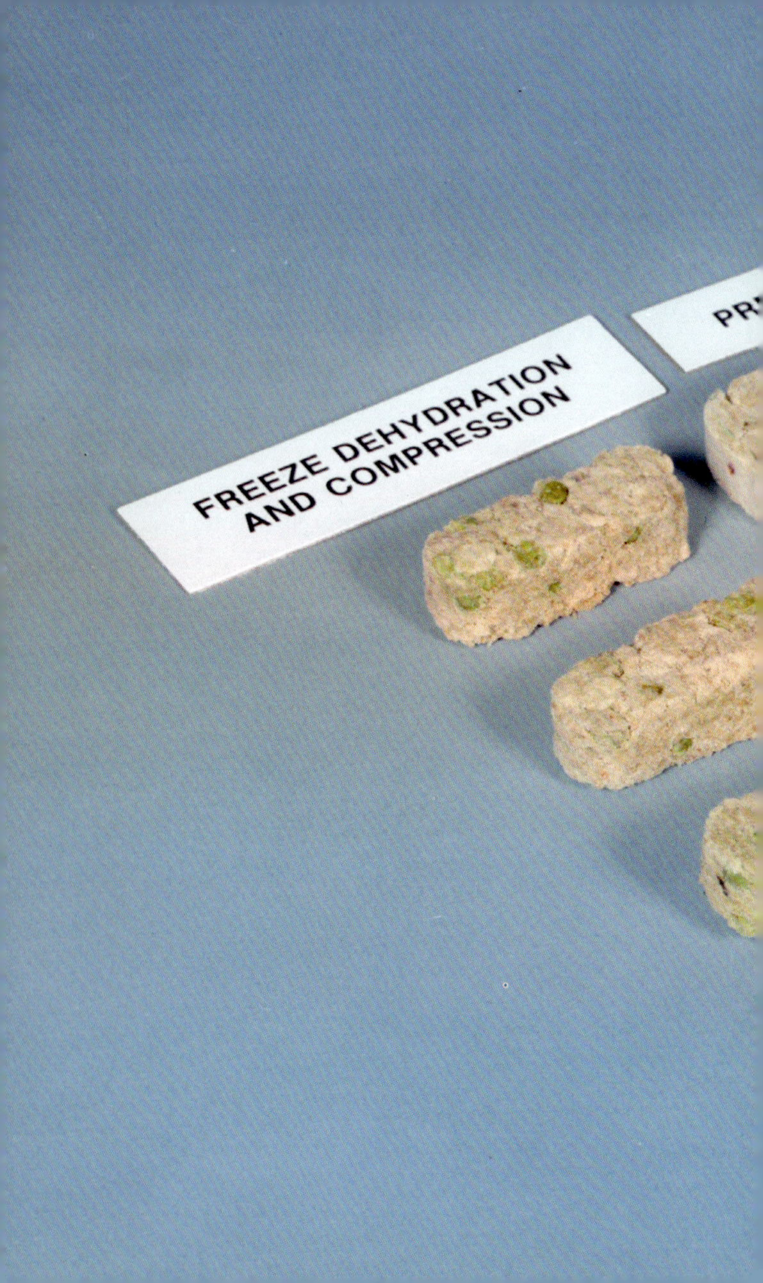

FREEZE DEHYDRATION
AND COMPRESSION

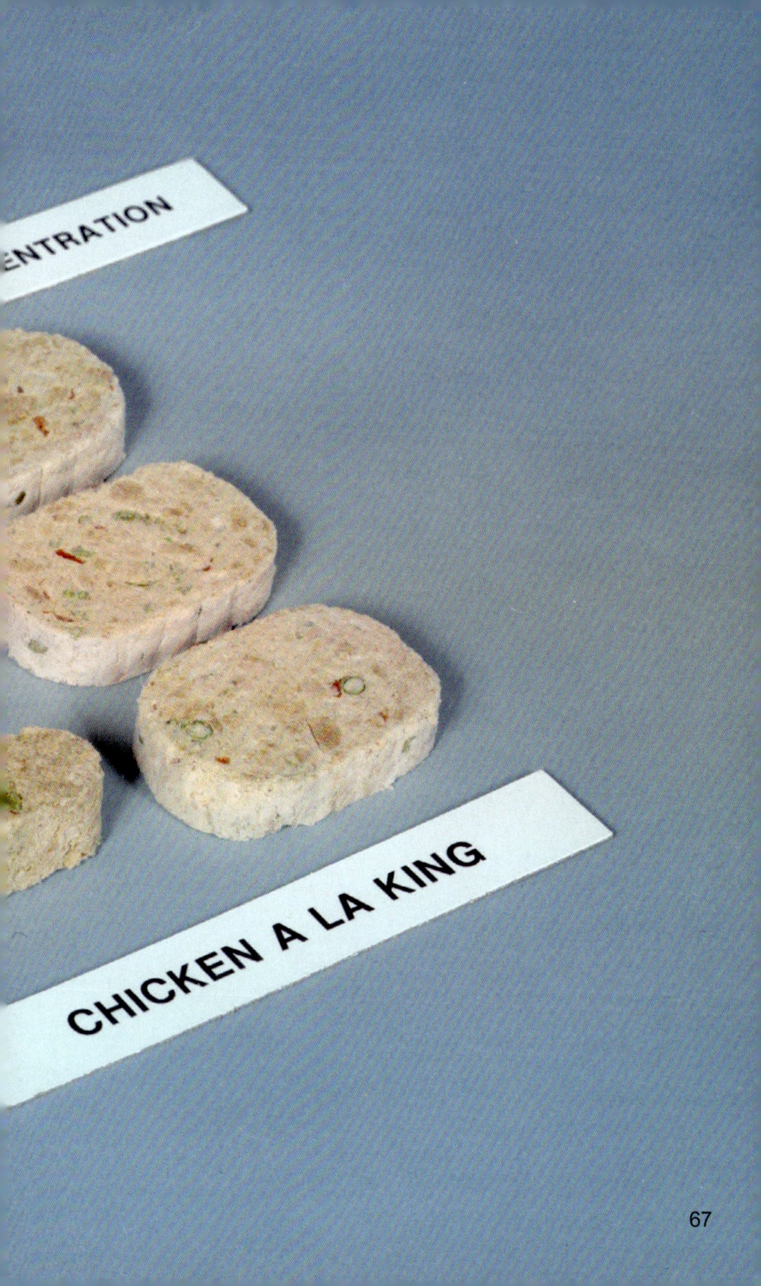

CHICKEN A LA KING

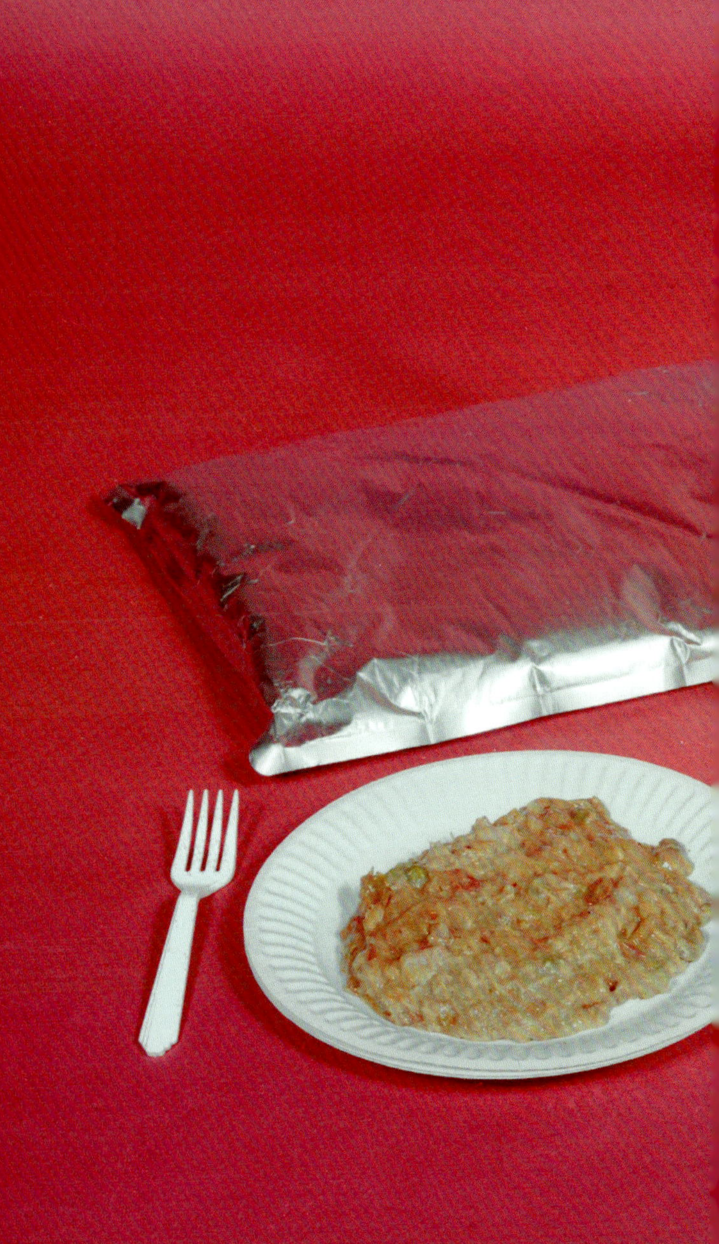

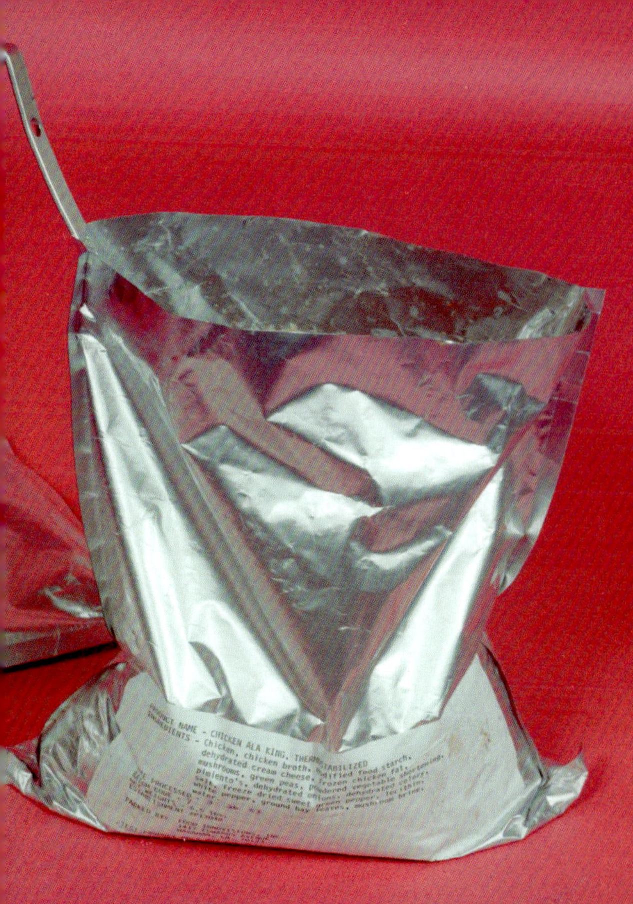

CHICKEN A LA KING
INSTITUTIONAL POUCH

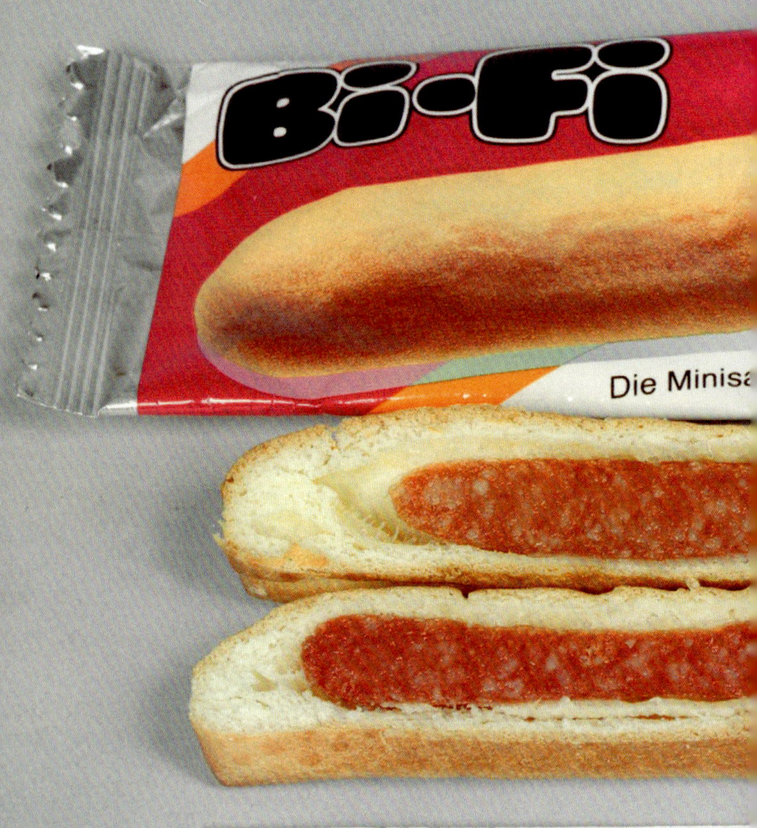

FOREIGN T
SHELF STAB

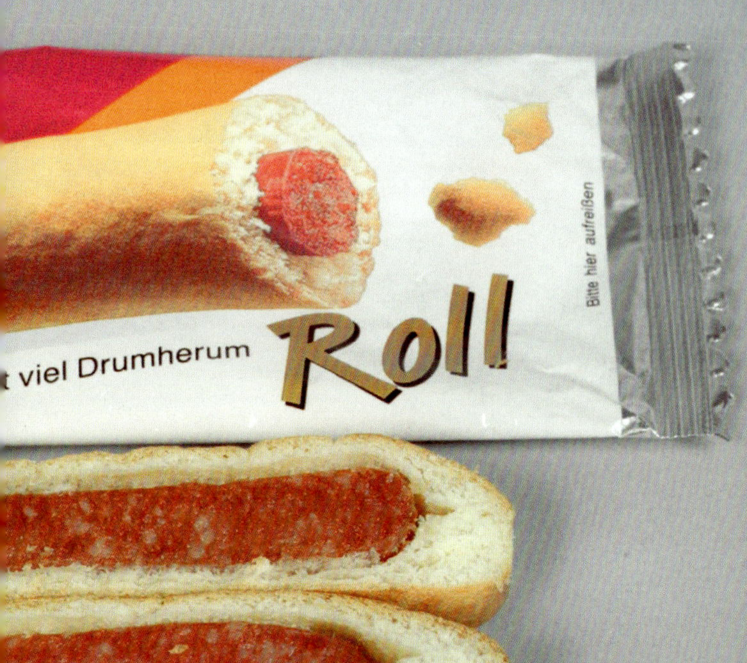

HNOLOGY
SANDWICH

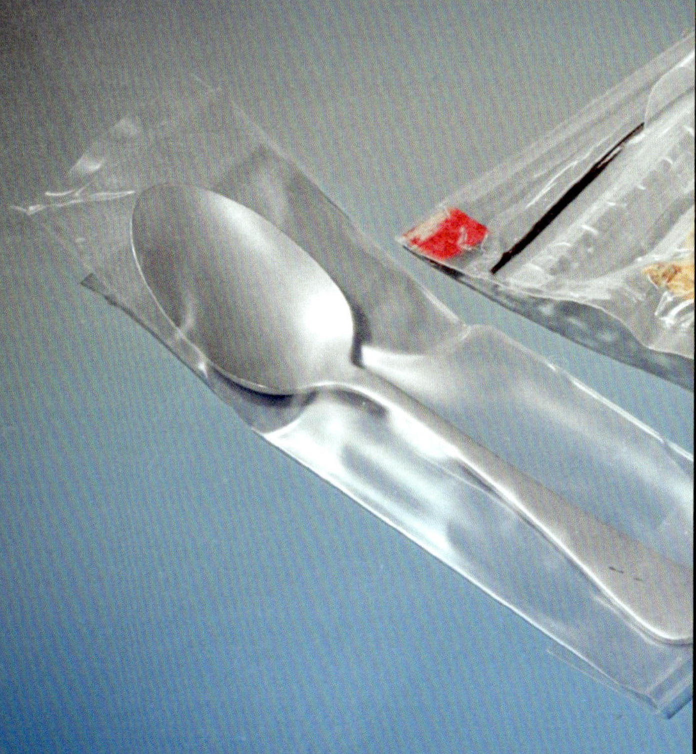
SPOON & BOWL FEEDE
(SPAGHETTI WITH MEAT SAU

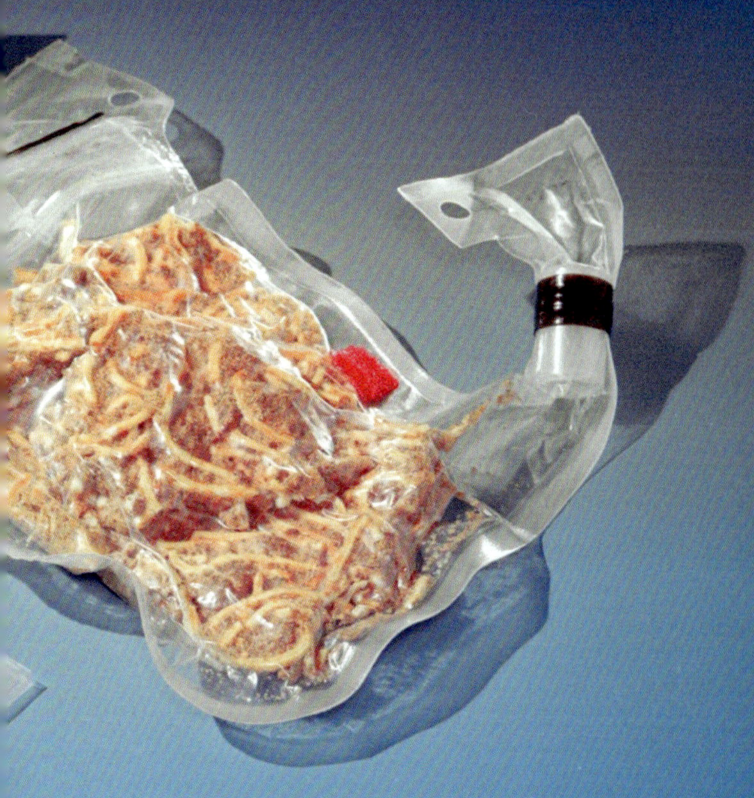

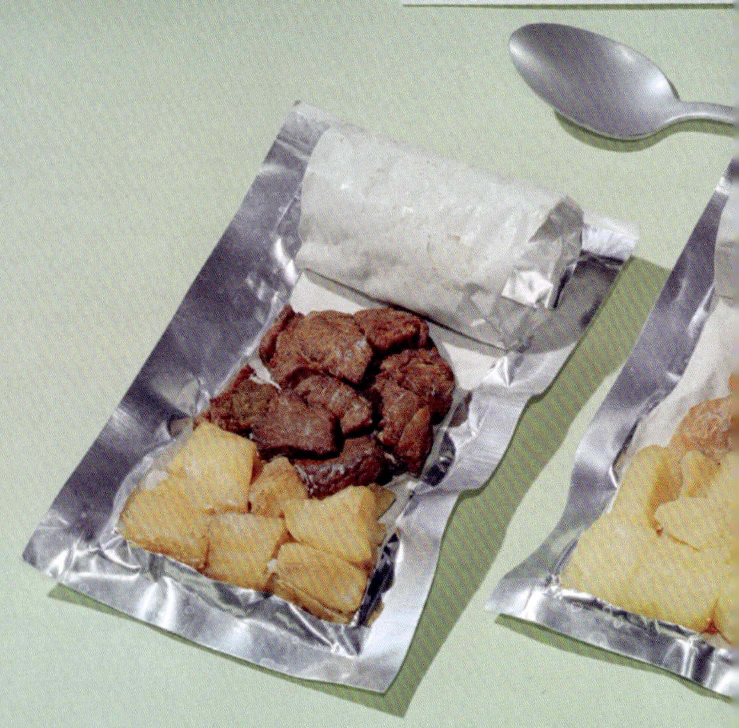
THERMOSTABILIZE
BEEF & POTATOES
HAM & PO

T MEAT PRODUCTS

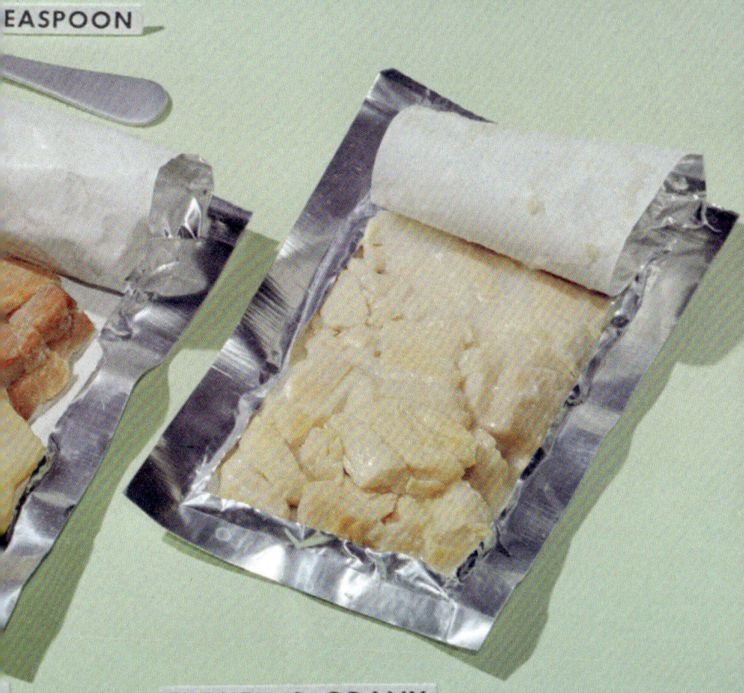

TURKEY & GRAVY

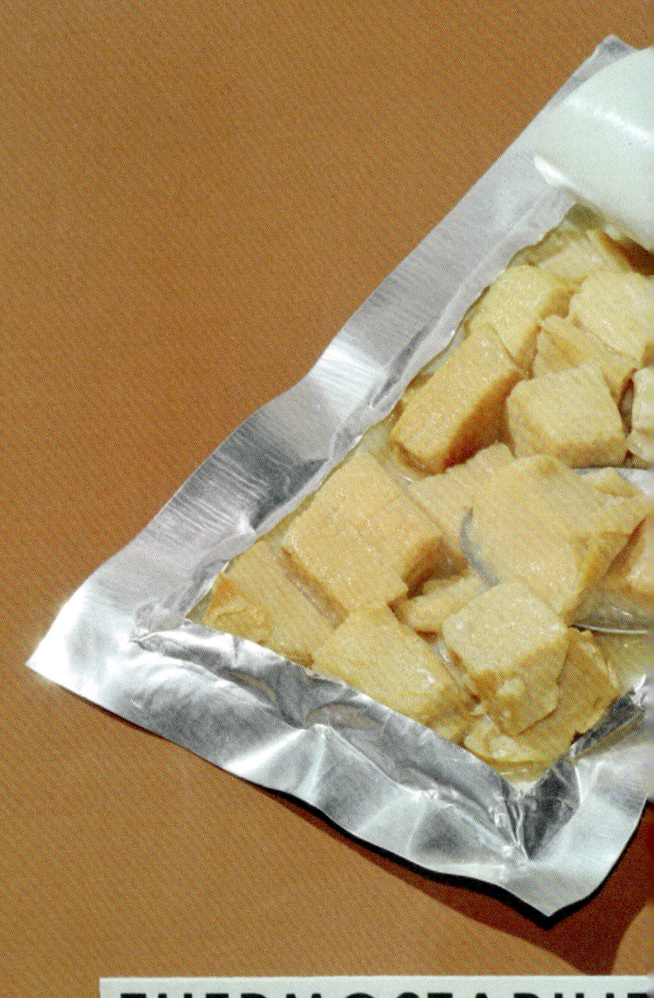

THERMOSTABILIZ

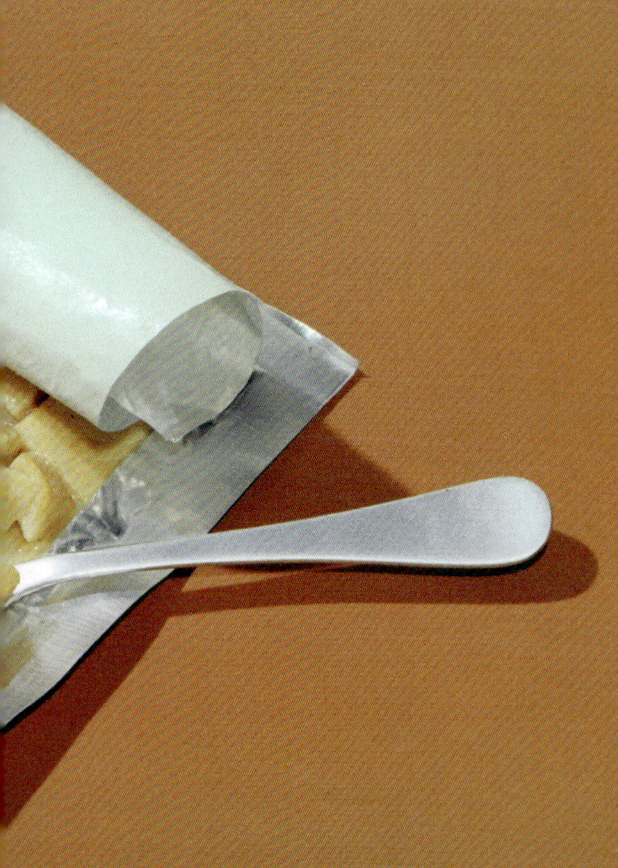
TURKEY & GRAVY
WET MEAT PRODUCT

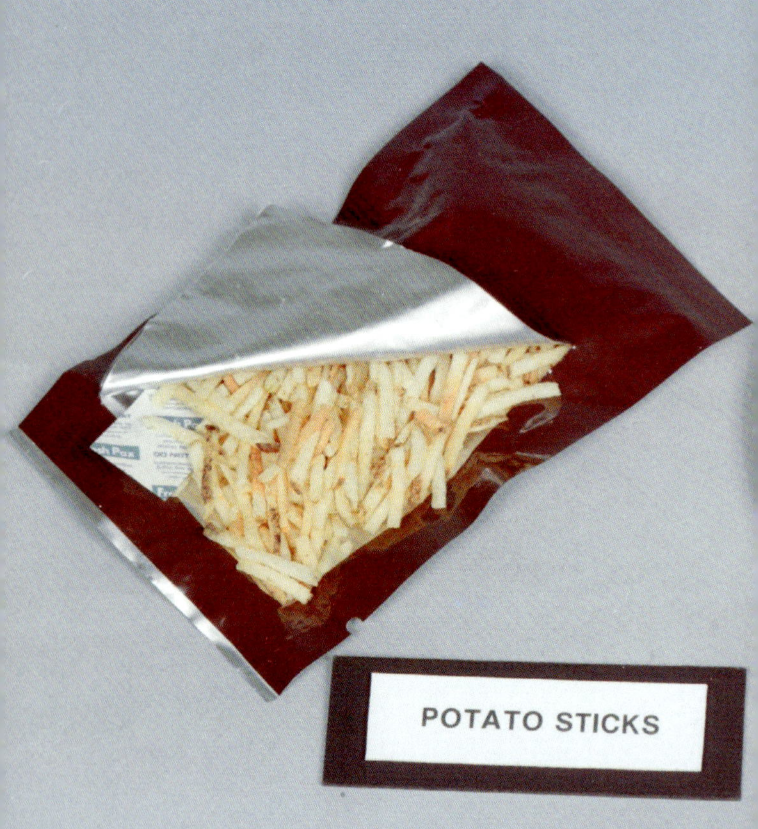
POTATO STICKS

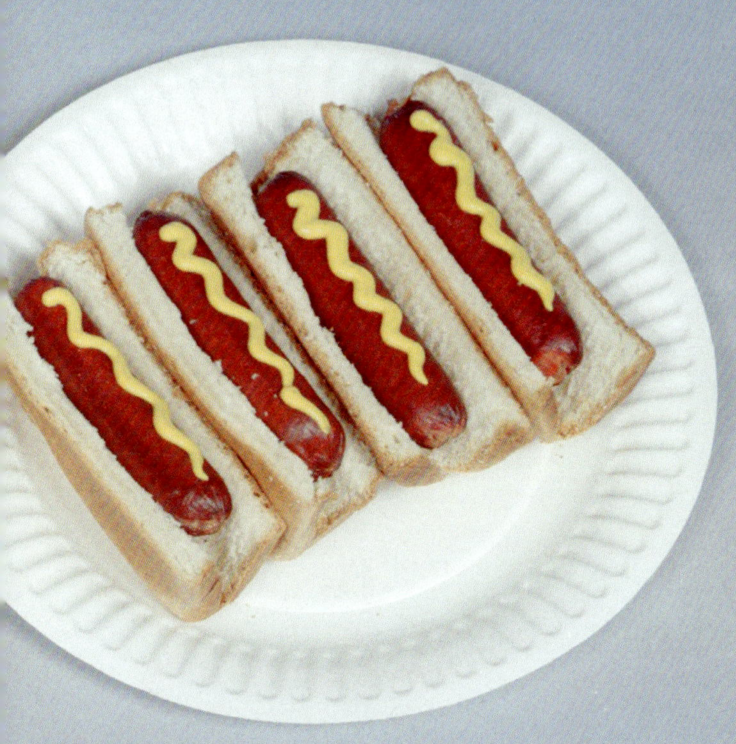

SMOKEY FRANKFURTERS

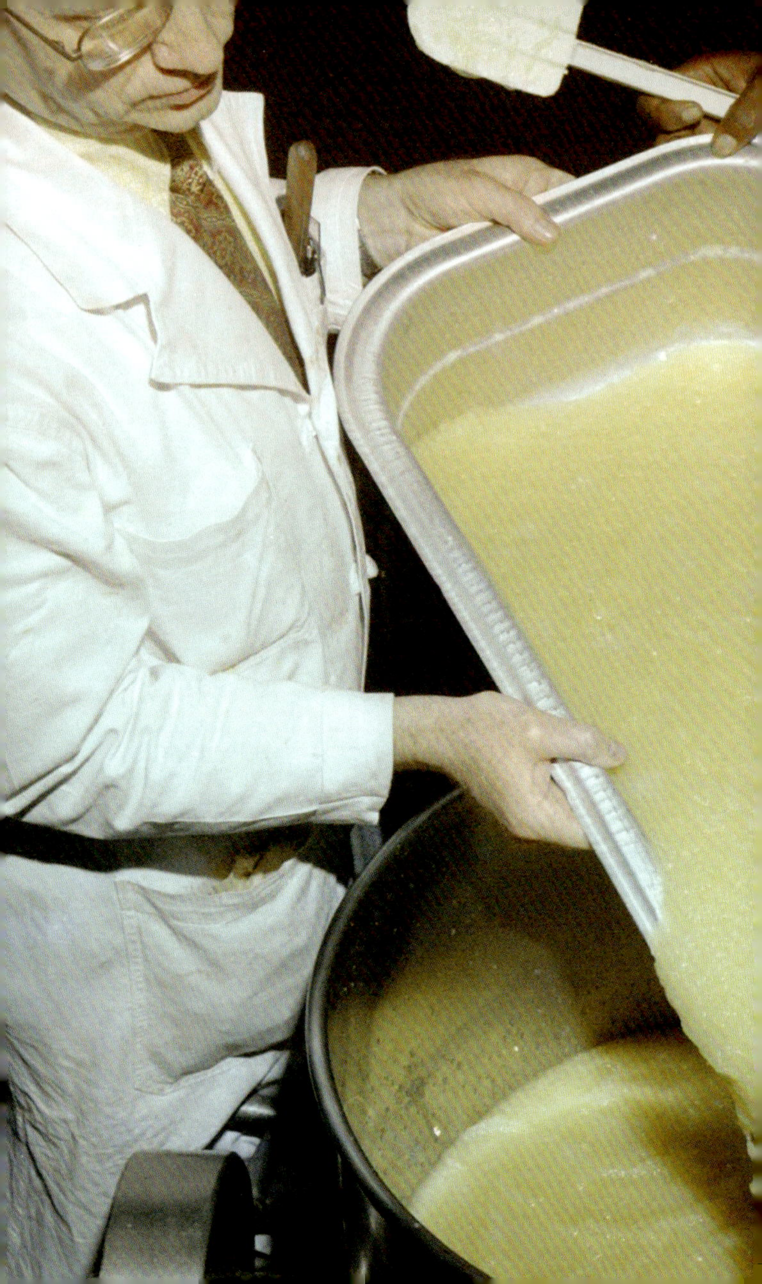

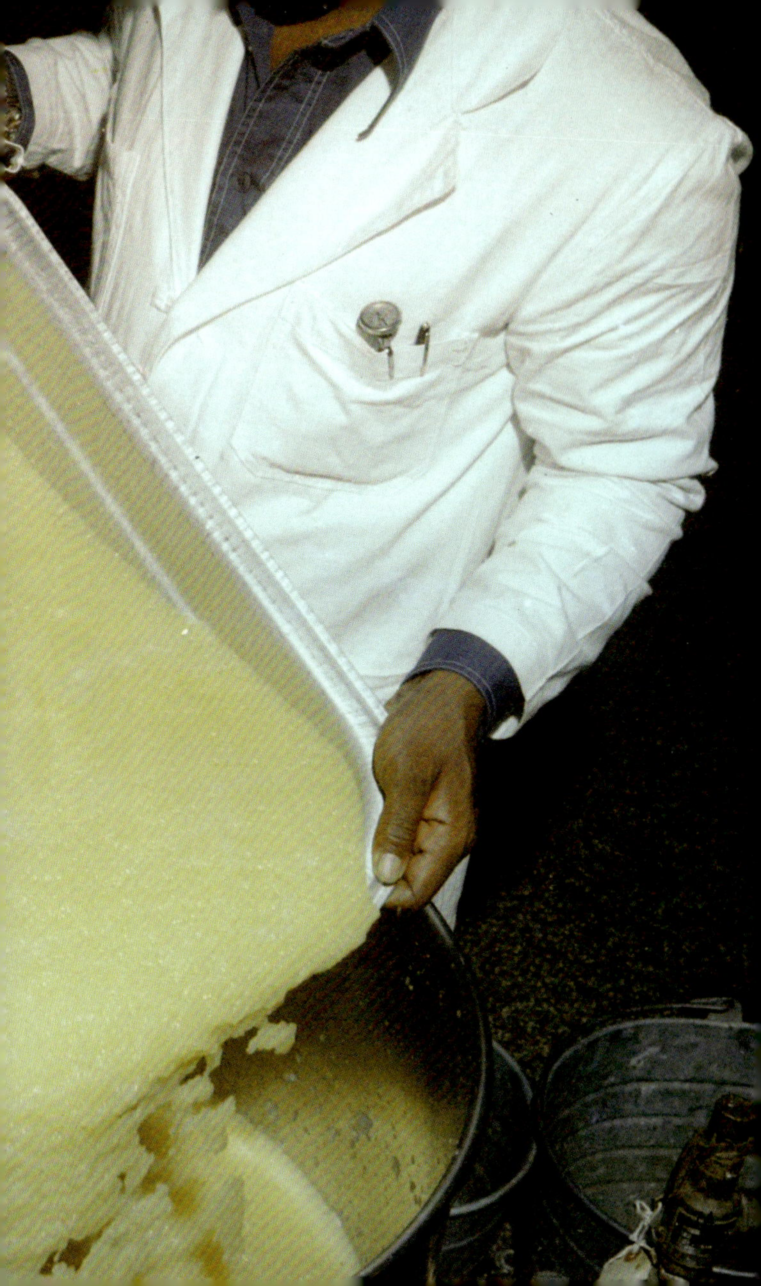

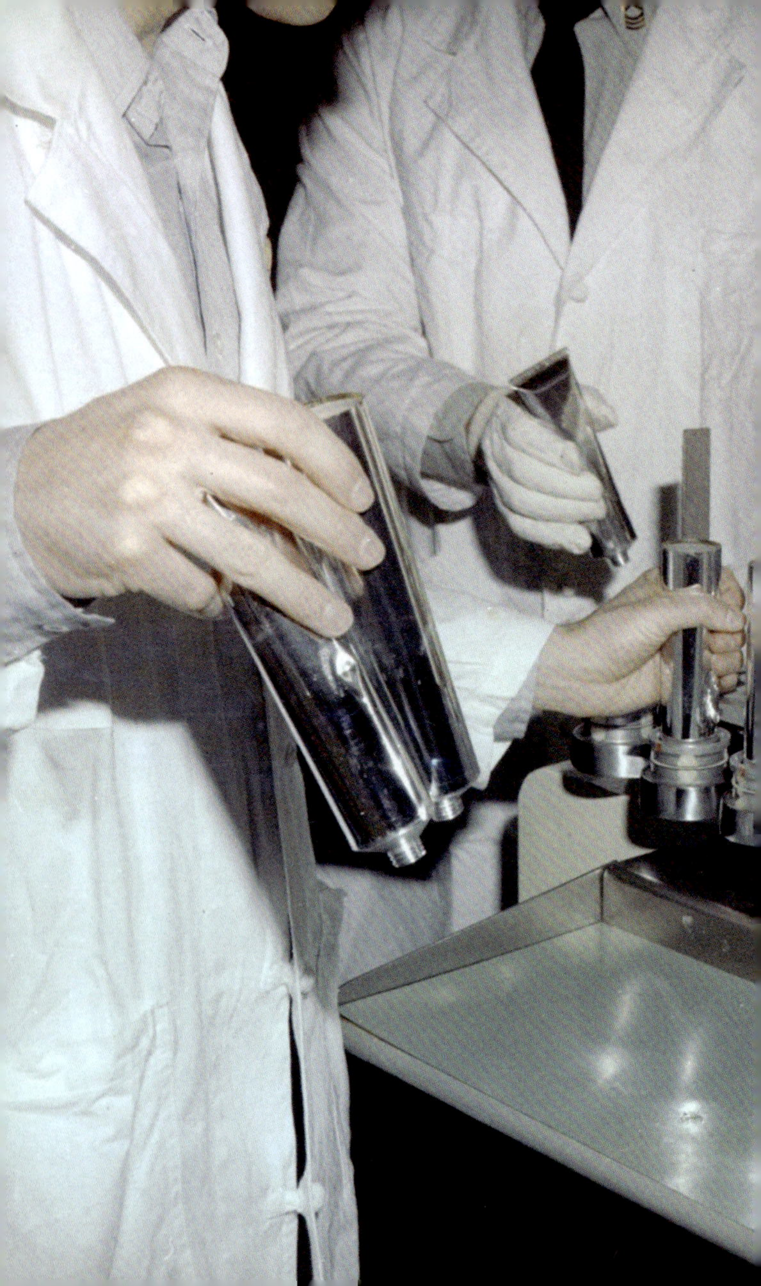

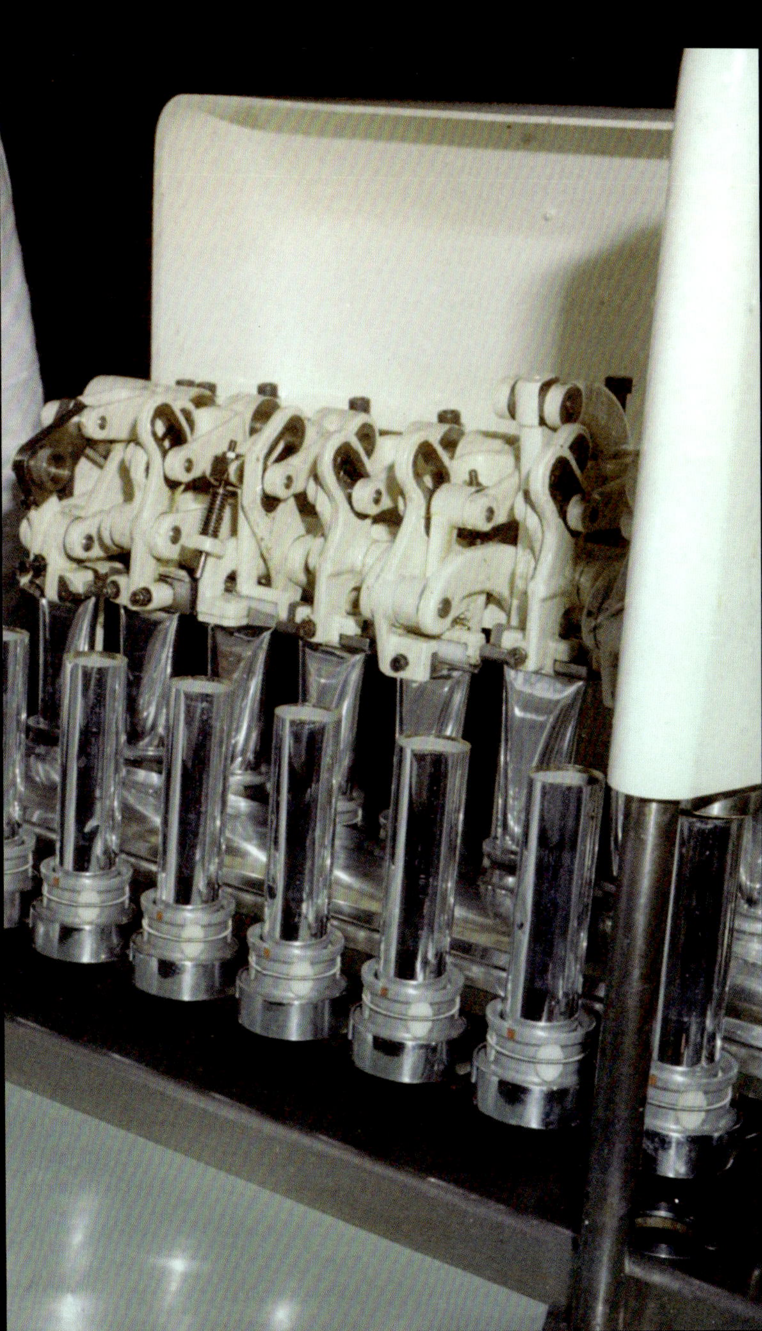

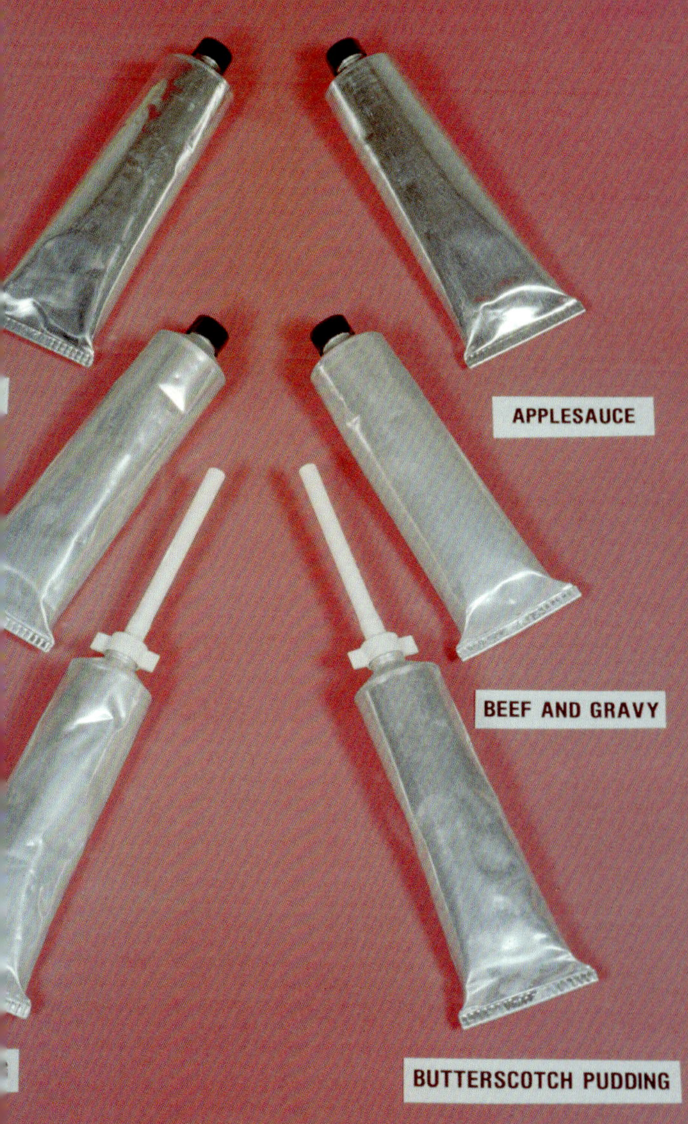
APPLESAUCE
BEEF AND GRAVY
BUTTERSCOTCH PUDDING

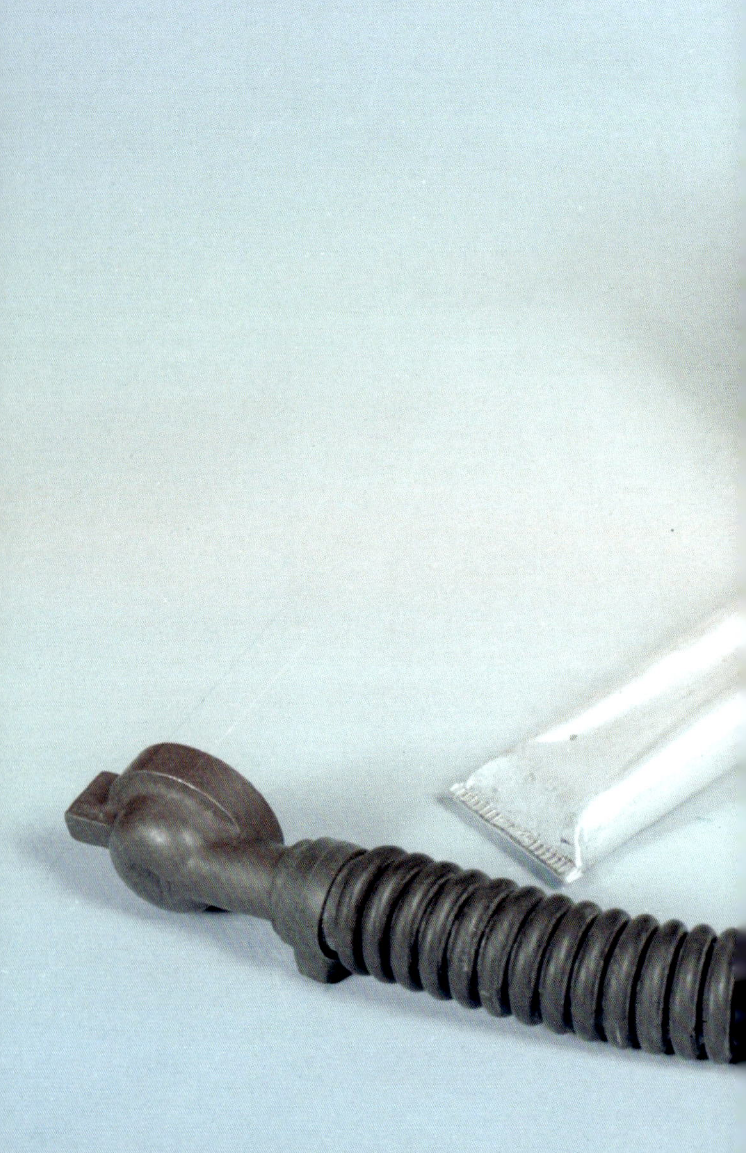

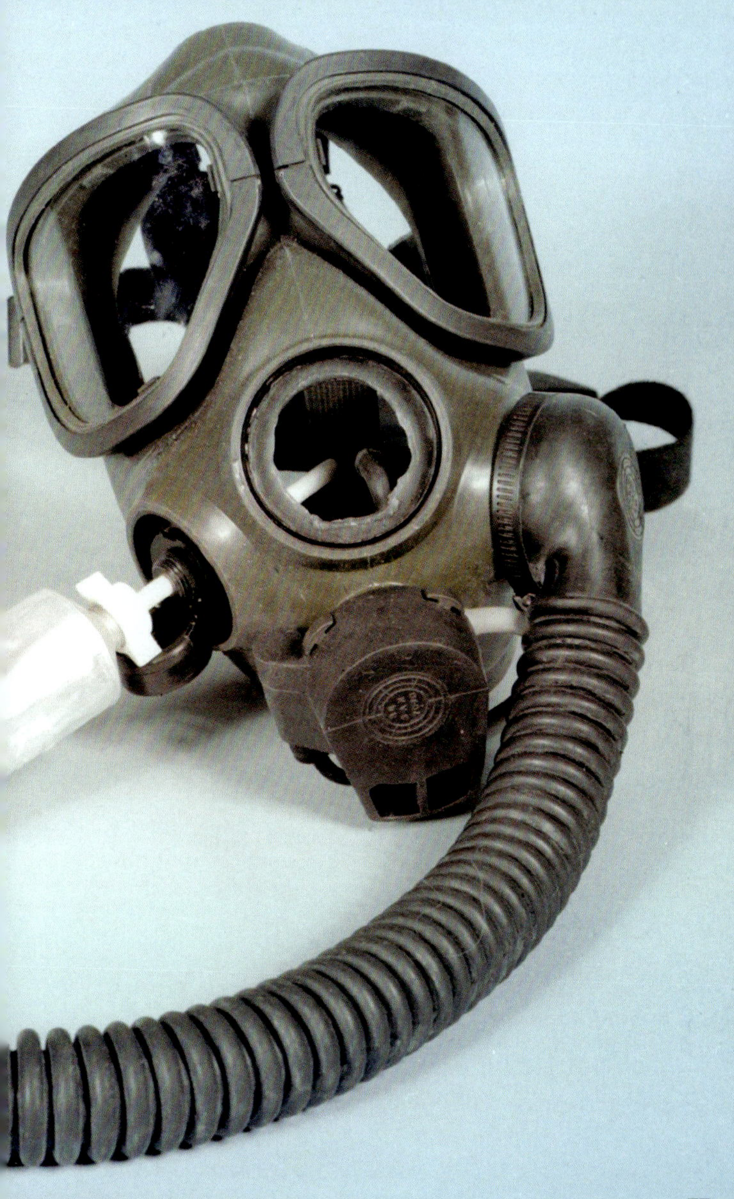

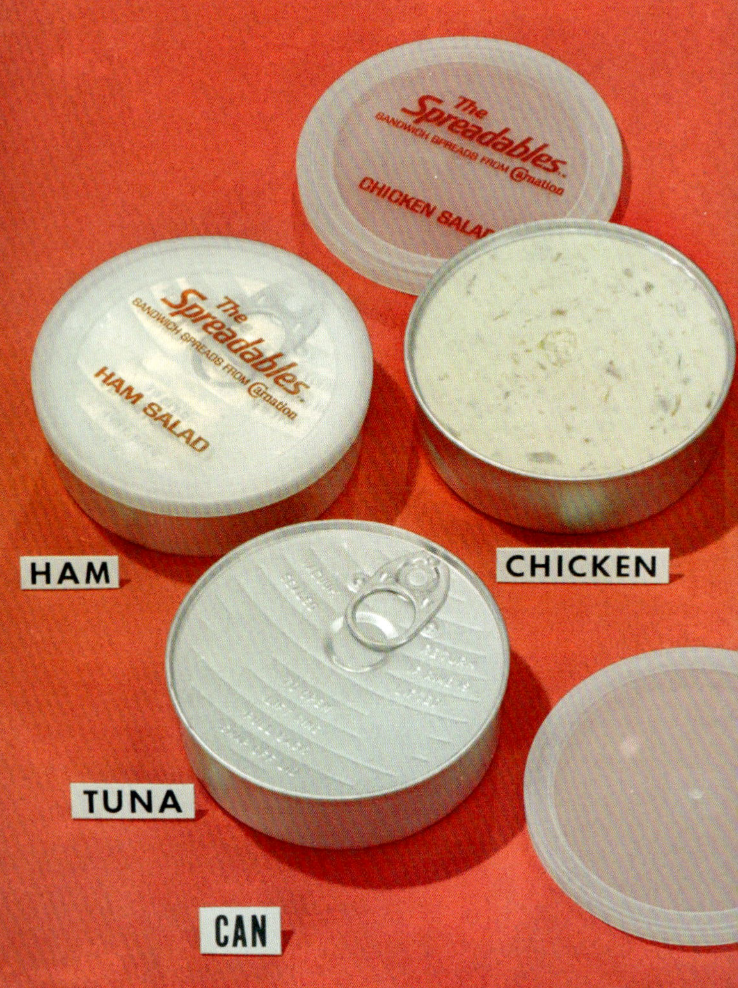

THERMOSTABILIZED SALA

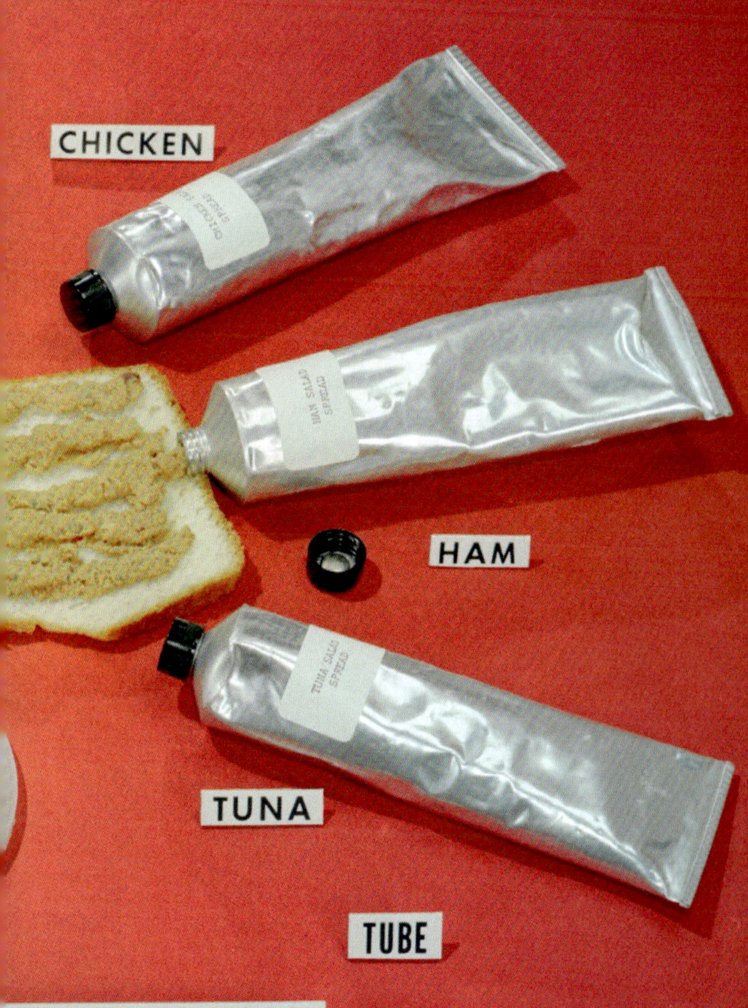

NDWICH FILLINGS)

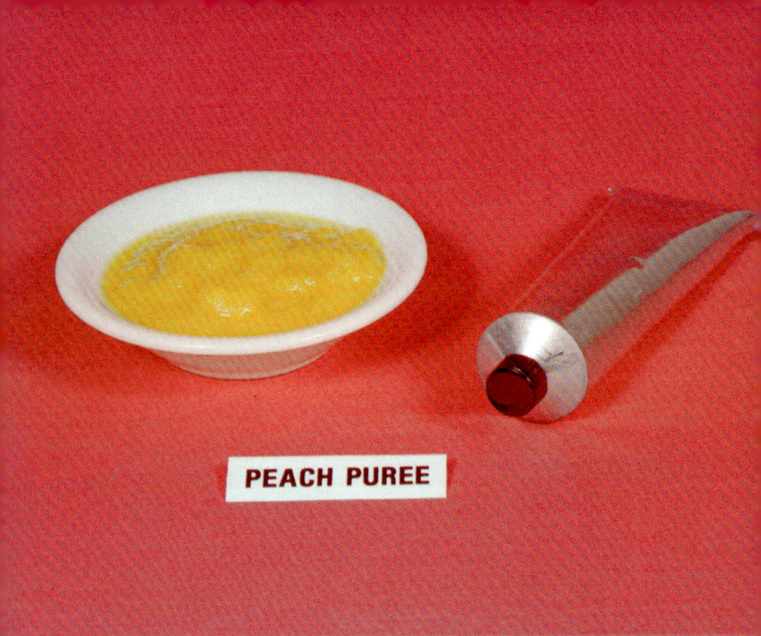

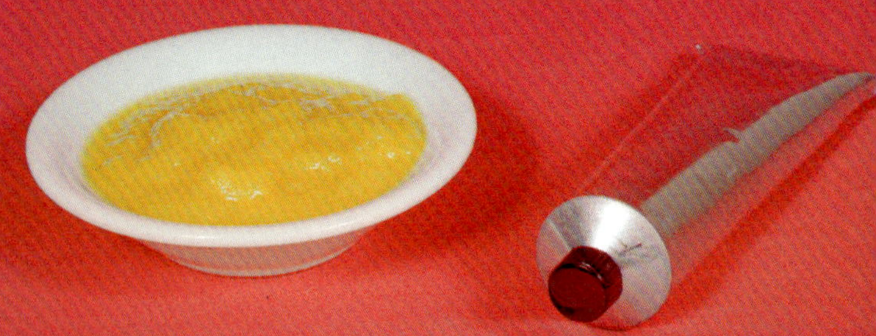

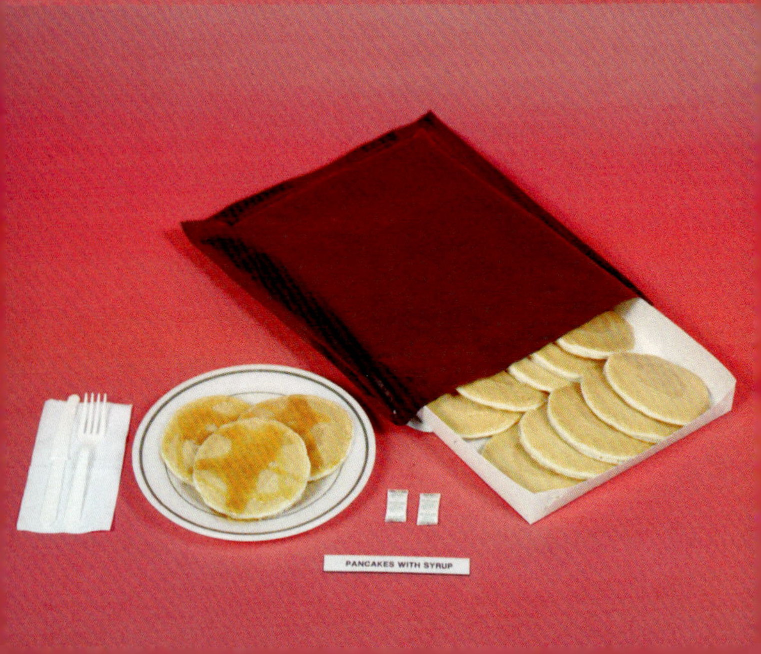

PANCAKES WITH SYRUP

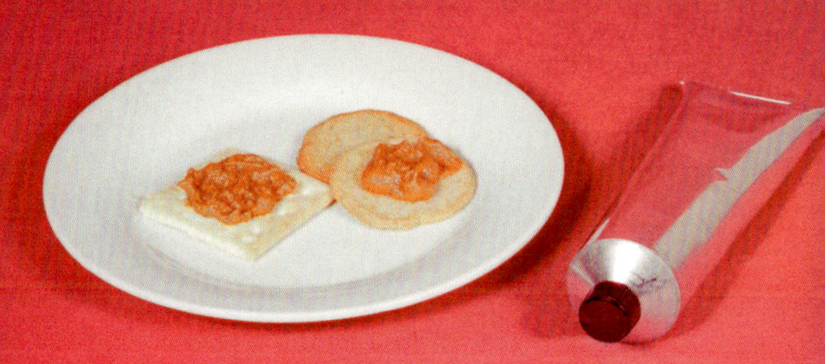

SLOPPY JOE

80

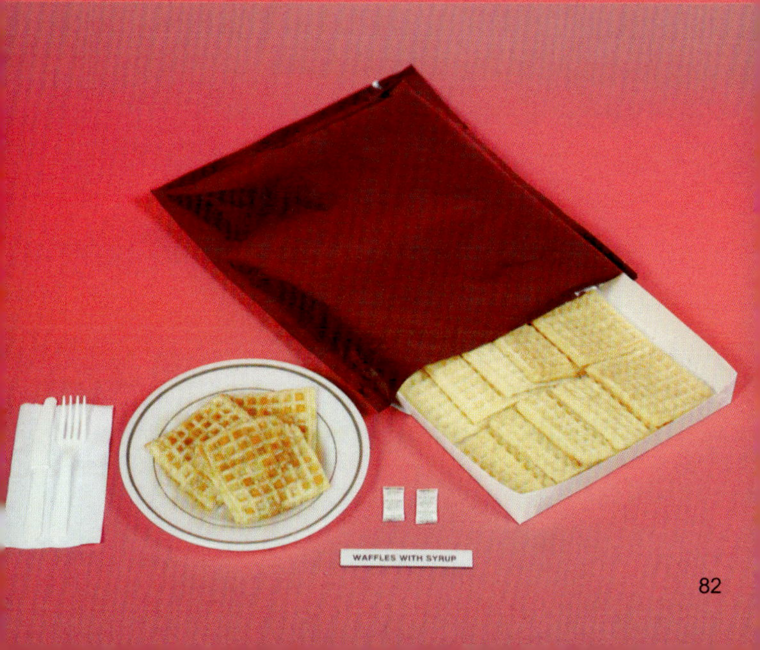

WAFFLES WITH SYRUP

82

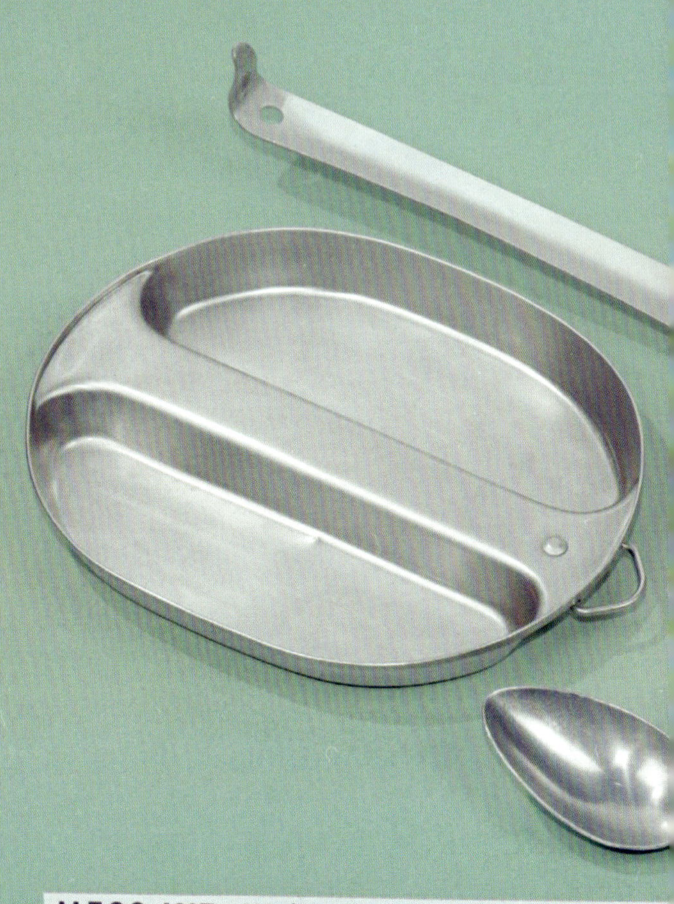

MESS KIT, W/FORK, KNIFE AND S

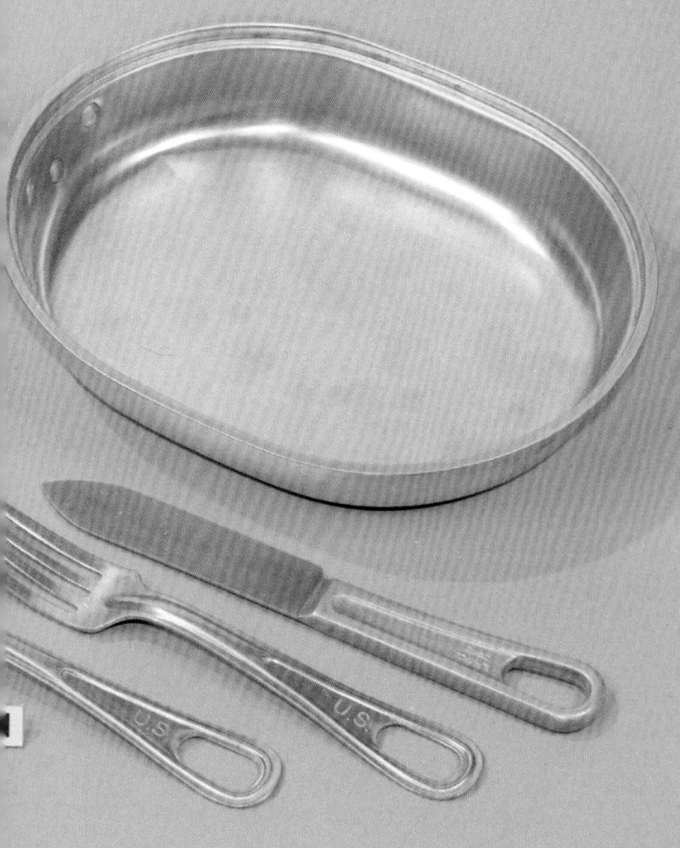
U.S.
U.S.

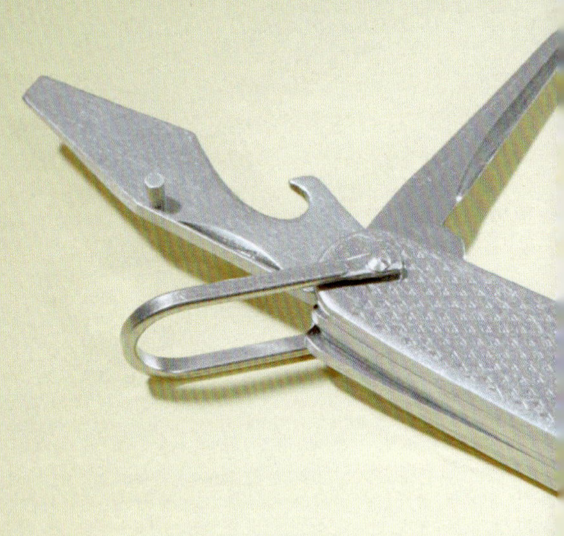

KNIFE, SURVIVA

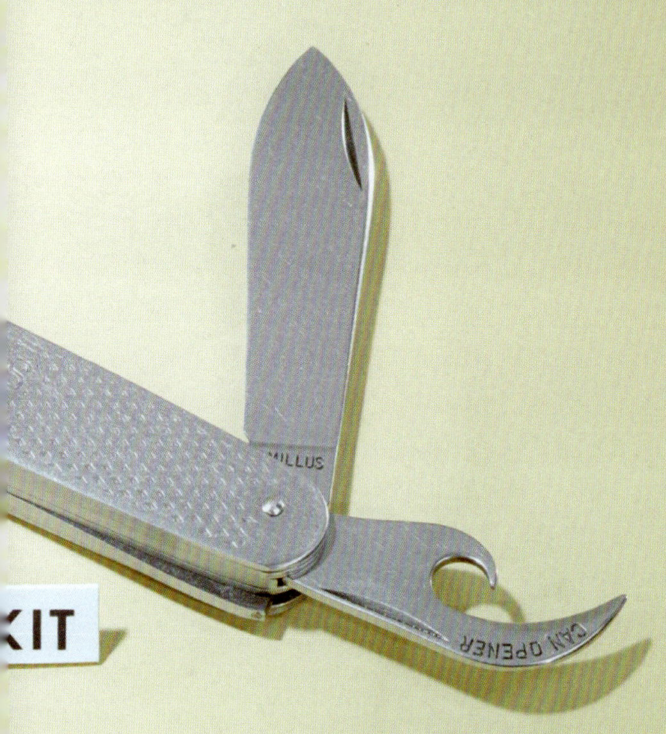
MILLUS
CAN OPENER

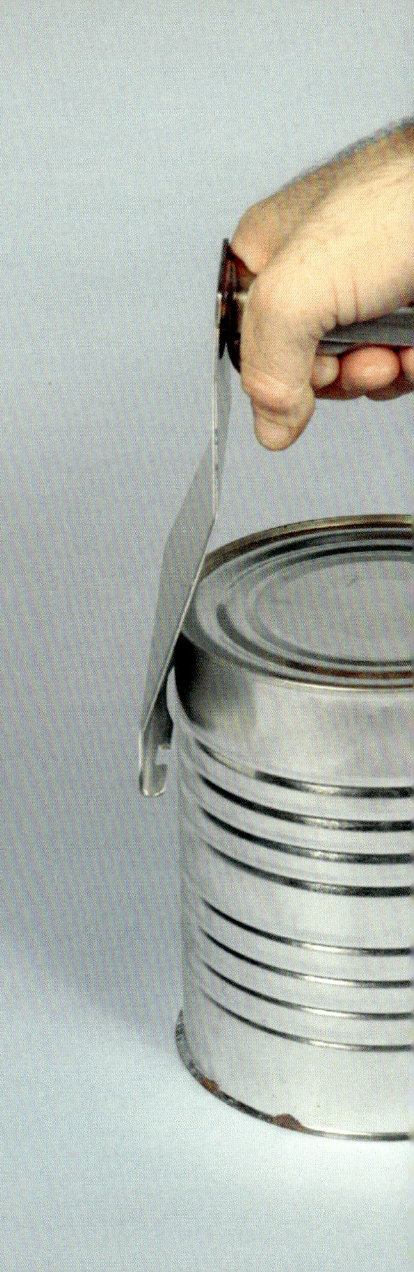

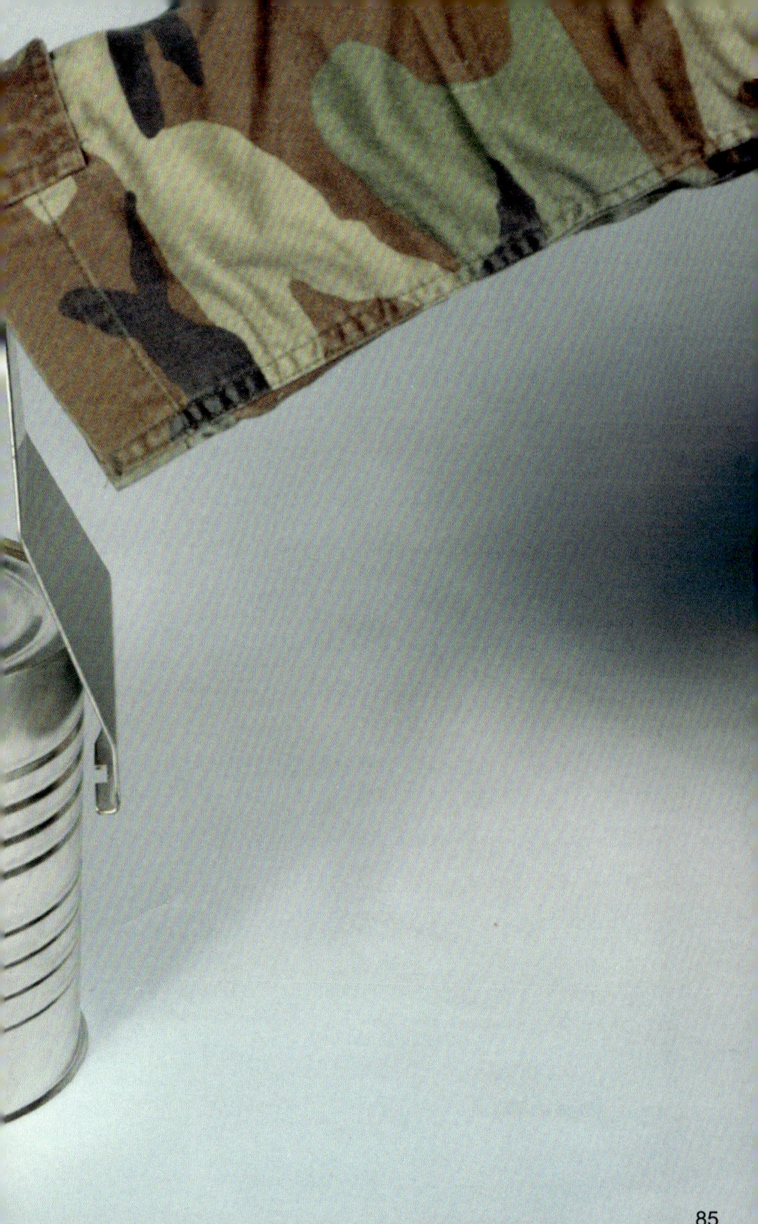

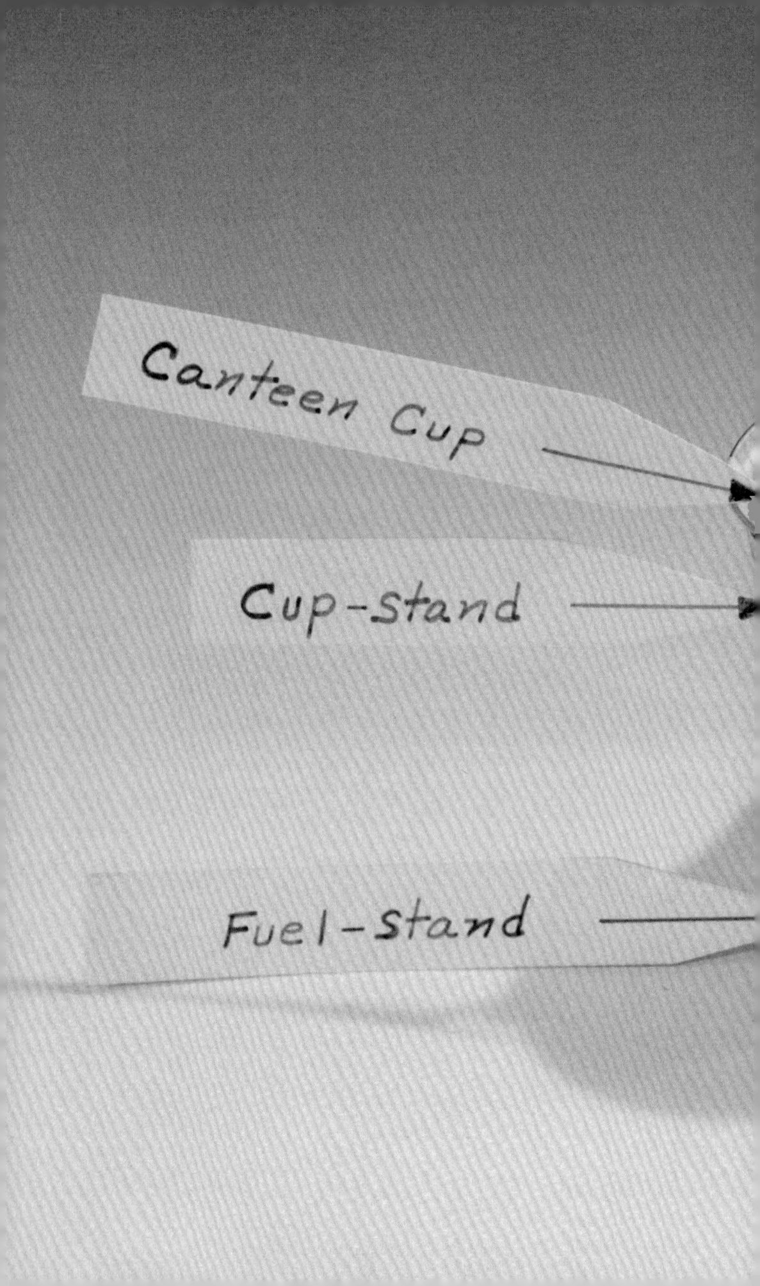

Canteen Cup

Cup-Stand

Fuel-Stand

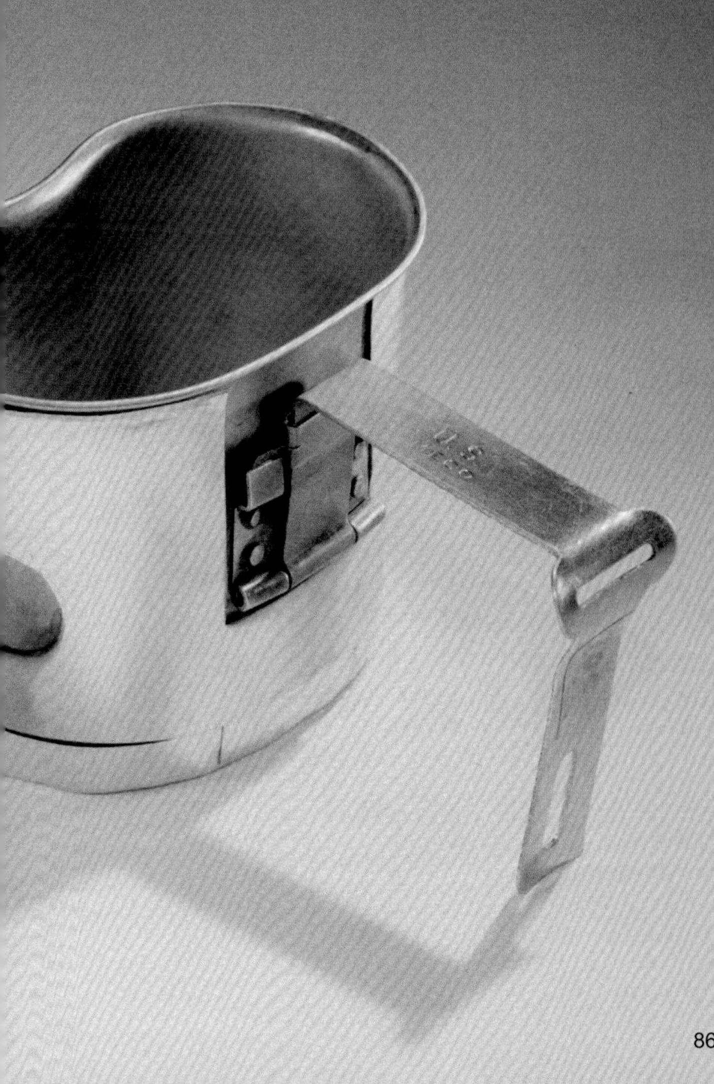
U.S.

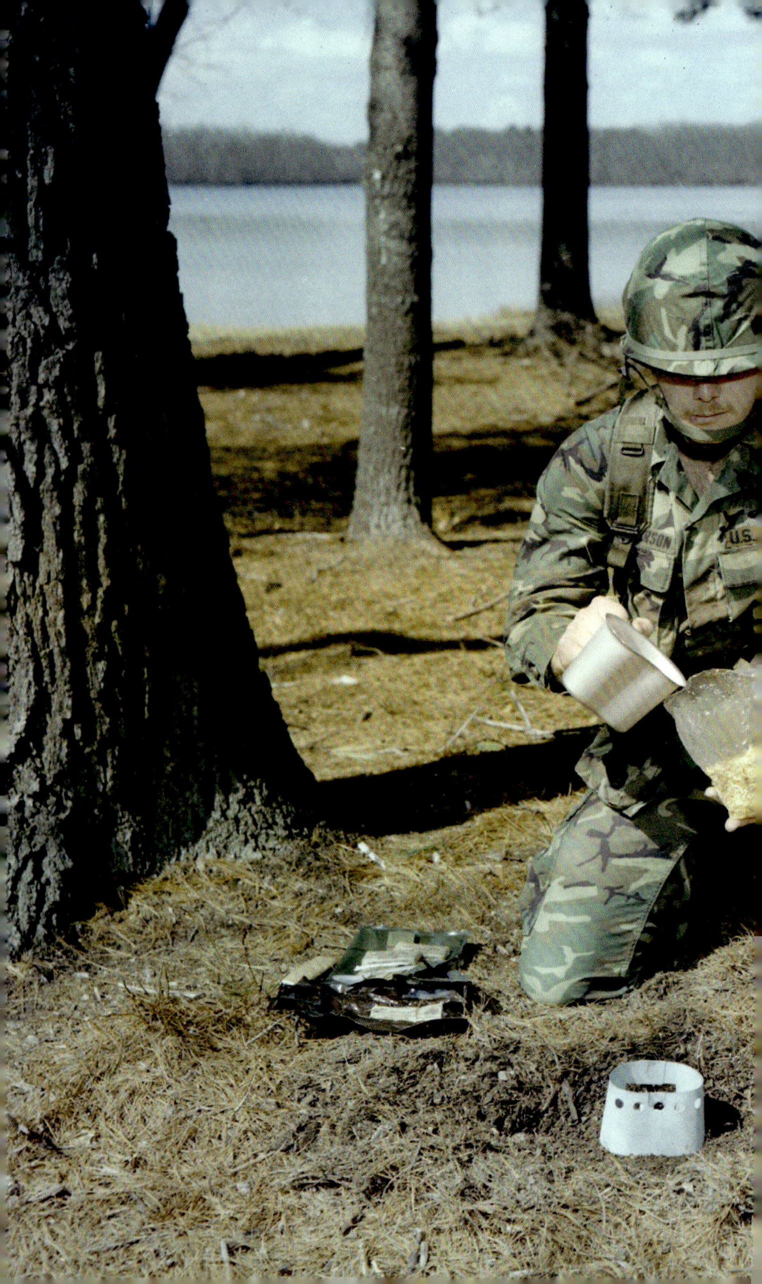
U.S.

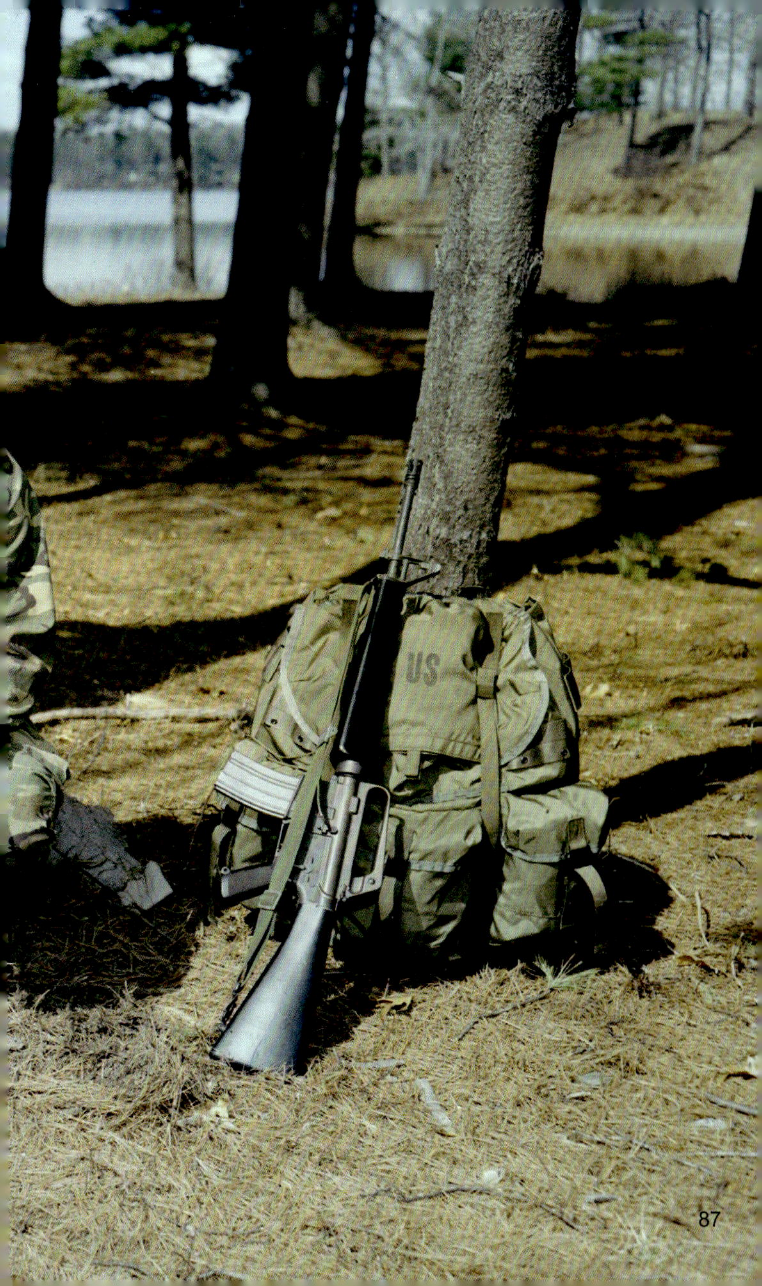
US

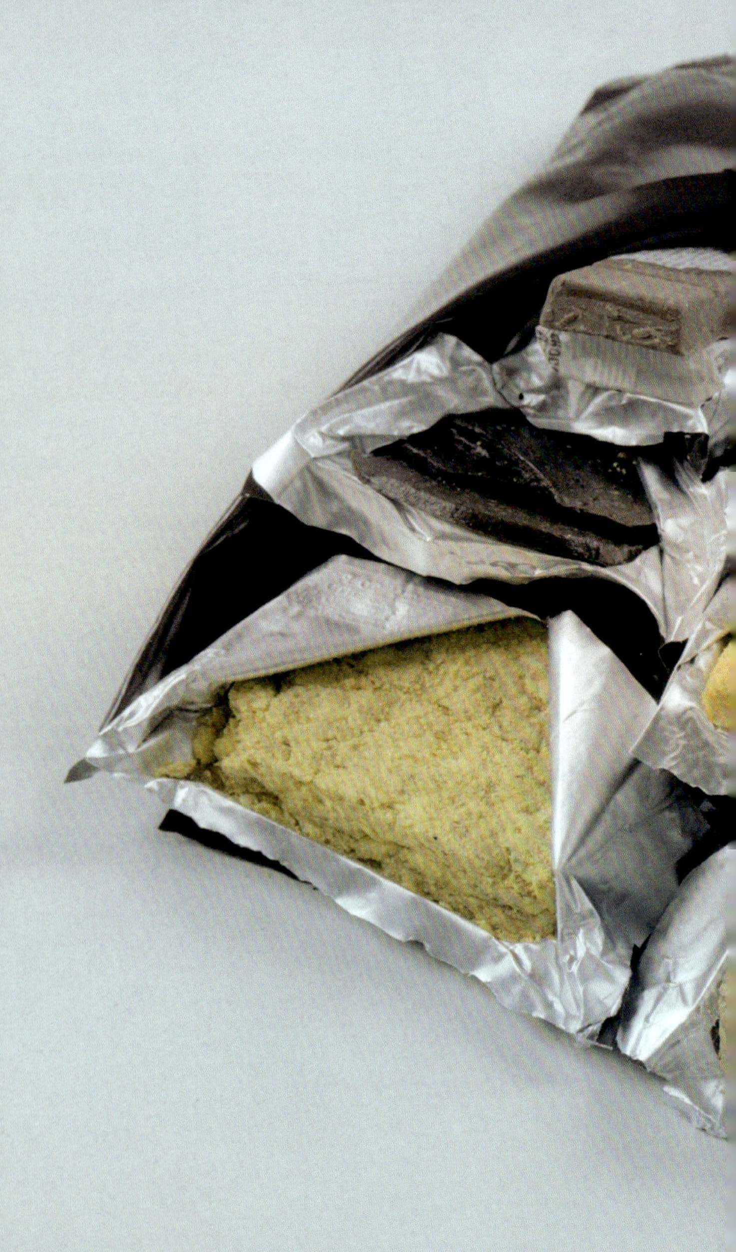

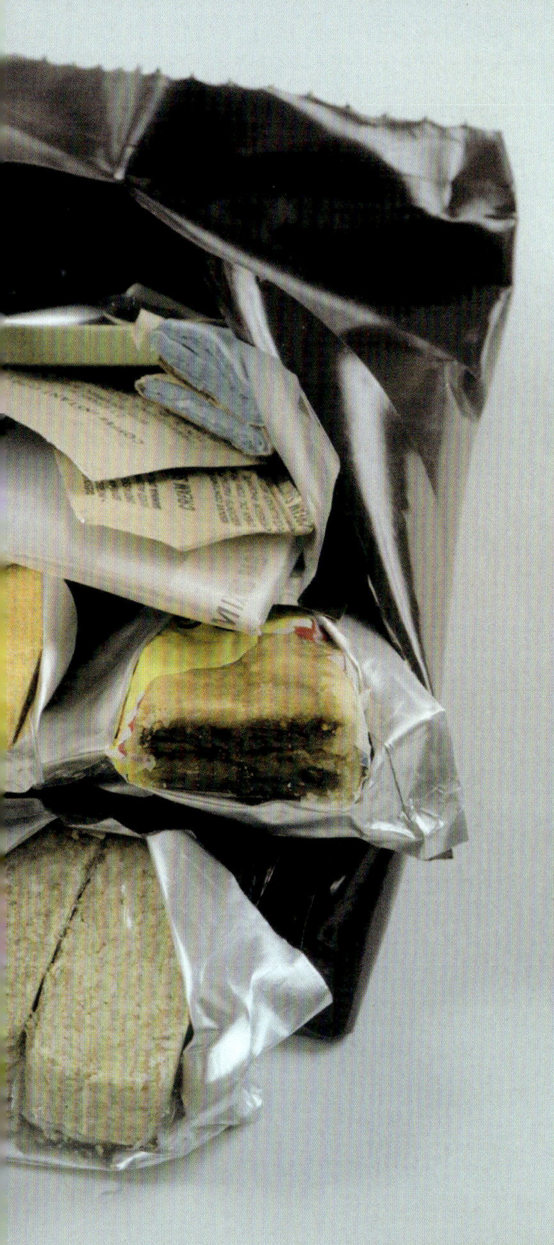

FOOD ACCEPTA

1. FOOD ITEMS DEVELOPED AT NLA
2. QUALITY CONTROL OF FOODS BEIN
3. RESEARCH ON ACCEPTANCE METH

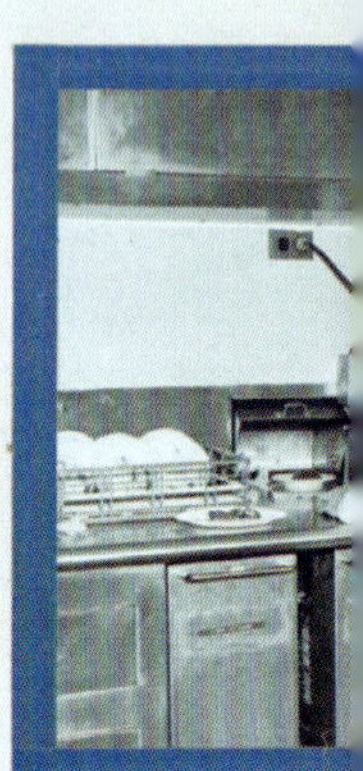

S

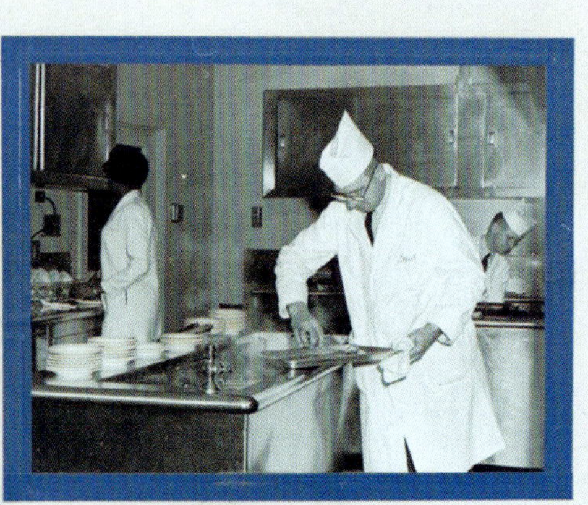

PREPARATION OF SAMPLES

HEDO

RESULT: BETTER FO

E LABORATORY

RED FOR RATIONS AND MESS HALLS

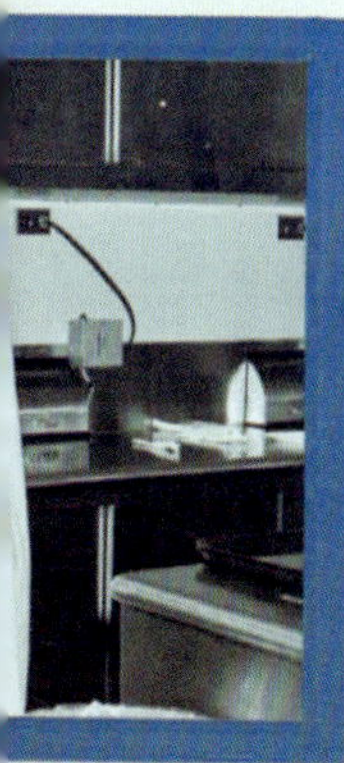

G

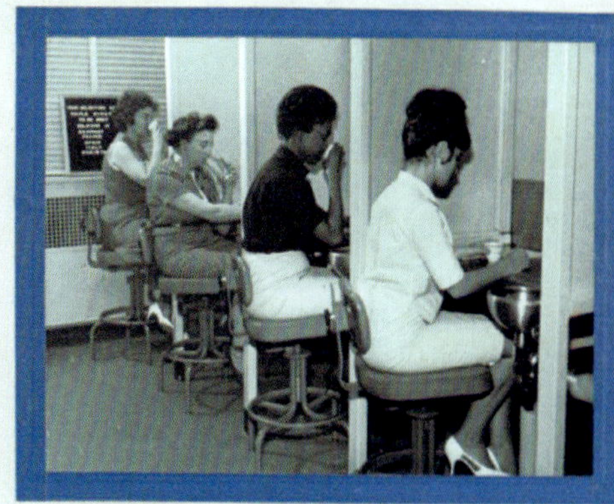

EVALUATION BY CONSUMER PANEL

ATING

OUR FIGHTING MEN

BETTER FOOD FOR OUR FIGHTING MEN

This book contains a selection of images, produced mostly in the 1970s and 1980s, from the archives of the U.S. Army's Natick Soldier Research, Development and Engineering Center near Boston, Massachusetts. The center is still operational today, and employs both military personnel and civilian contractors in its mission to improve the daily lives—and diets—of American soldiers.

For the world's most formidable army, feeding the troops is fraught with logistical, psychological and food safety challenges. Bacteria is an enemy; supply chains are vital, intricate delivery systems. The goal is to provide sustenance and boost morale across the full range of terrain and troop configurations, from mess halls for the officers and self-service buffets for the rank-and-file to battlefield canteens and survival rations for commandos behind enemy lines.

Solving this logistical puzzle is like trying to stuff a square peg into a round hole: once you have devised ways to optimize the daily nutritional requirements of the bodies in question, you need to work out the best solutions for preserving and transporting the food, and still guarantee a minimum level of flavor to keep the soldiers happy.

Irradiate, dehydrate, thermostabilize, compress, preserve, rehydrate, heat up, dish out... These images document the experiments developed by nutrition and logistics experts in the Army's "food science laboratories," their taste tests and focus groups, their stylized pack shots of the meals they designed.

A glossary with 24 entries explains some of the acronyms used in the image captions, describes the staples of a typical soldier's diet and traces the new technologies that enabled the food industry to manufacture and supply those rations. As is often the case, the innovations developed by the U.S. military had multiple applications in civilian life, many of which are manifest on the shelves of supermarkets today.

Bon appétit.

GLOSSARY

01 ARMED FORCES RECIPE SERVICE (AFRS)
02 CANNING
03 CONVENIENCE FOOD
04 DESERT BAR
05 FIELD KITCHEN
06 FIELD RATION
07 FIRST STRIKE RATION (FSR)
08 FOOD IRRADIATION
09 FOOD SAFETY
10 FOOD SERVICE
11 FREEZE-DRYING

12 FREEZING
13 GARRISON RATION
14 LONG RANGE
PATROL RATION (LRP)
15 MEAL,COMBAT,
INDIVIDUAL RATION
(MCI)
16 MEAL,READY-TO-EAT
(MRE)
17 MESS
18 PASTEURIZATION
19 RETORT POUCH
20 SHELF-STABLE
FOOD
21 SLOPPY JOE
22 SOLDIER SYSTEMS
CENTER
23 THERMOSTABILITY
24 VACUUM-PACKING

01 ARMED FORCES RECIPE SERVICE

The Armed Forces Recipe Service manual is a compendium of high-volume food service recipes written and updated regularly by the U.S. Department of Defense Natick Laboratories. Used by military cooks, institutional and catering operations, the compendium was first published in 1969 as a consolidation of the cooking manuals of the four main branches of the armed services. The current AFRS manual includes recipes from military publications dating all the way back to 1896, when the U.S. Army first began to standardize its culinary offerings. Most of the AFRS recipes are based on traditional American cooking, but they have been updated to include vegetarian, kosher and halal recipes to meet the evolving needs of the troops being fed. Each recipe card in the AFRS has a standardized format; each is calibrated to feed one hundred people, and each lists the basic nutritional values of the recipe across the top. Historically, the AFRS manual was available only in print; the compendium is now a digital database maintained by the Joint Culinary Center of Excellence, a division of the U.S. Army Quartermaster School in Fort Lee, Virginia.

02 CANNING

Canning is the process of cooking food, sealing it in sterilized cans or jars, and boiling the containers to kill or weaken any remaining bacteria. Invented by the French confectioner Nicolas Appert, this process was used by the French Navy in 1806 to preserve meat, fruit, vegetables and even milk. Although Appert had discovered a new and effective means of preserving food, the science behind it was not fully understood until 1864, when Louis Pasteur studied and then demonstrated the correlation between microorganisms, food spoilage and illness.

03 CONVENIENCE FOOD

Convenience food—also called tertiary processed food—refers to food that is commercially prepared to optimize ease of consumption. Such food is usually ready to eat as soon as it is removed from its packaging, without any further preparation. Convenience food may also be easily portable, have a long shelf life or offer any combination of consumer-friendly characteristics. Many of these products can trace their origins to military research and development laboratories, where their packaging and processing were designed for storage longevity and ease of preparation on the battlefield. At the end of World War II, a number of commercial food companies that had worked as contractors for the military began to manufacture and sell freeze-dried and canned foods for civilian use. As is often the case with new product launches, relatively few of these were successful. For every successful launch of a convenience food staple like fish sticks or canned peaches, there were a score of failures, like ham sticks and cheeseburgers-in-a-can.

04 DESERT BAR

In the late 1980s, the U.S. Army's Natick Laboratories created a new high-temperature chocolate snack—dubbed the "Congo Bar" by researchers—that could withstand heat in excess of 140°F (60°C) and used egg whites to create a fudge-like texture. During Operation Desert Shield and Operation Desert Storm, The Hershey Company was the primary manufacturer of these chocolate bars, shipping 144,000 units to American troops. While Army spokesmen indicated that the bar's taste was good, troop reactions were mixed and the snack was never put into full production. The war ended before Hershey's stocks of the experimental bar had been shipped, so the company packaged the remainder of the production run in a "desert camo" wrapper and sold it to civilians as the Desert Bar. It proved a brief novelty, but Hershey's declined to make more once supplies ran out.

---

05 FIELD KITCHEN

A field kitchen is a mobile kitchen, a mobile canteen or food truck used by militaries to provide warm food to the troops in temporary encampments, often near the front lines.

---

06 FIELD RATION

A field ration—also known as a combat ration, ration pack or food packet—is a type of pre-packaged or canned military ration. Field rations are distinguished from garrison rations by virtue of being designed for minimal preparation and long shelf life. They often include canned, vacuum-sealed, pre-cooked or freeze-dried foods, as well as powdered beverage mixes and concentrated food bars. The acronym MRE—a "meal, ready to eat"—is sometimes used synonymously with field ration, but it more accurately describes a specific type of field ration used by the U.S. military. Today, most of the world's militaries use some form of pre-packaged combat ration, often tailored to national or regional tastes. Field rations have proved invaluable in emergency or disaster relief efforts, when large stocks of pre-packaged meals need to be delivered quickly and easily to meet the basic nutritional needs of victims before field kitchens can be deployed. Rations intended for disaster relief are often called "survival rations."

07 FIRST STRIKE RATION

A First Strike Ration (FSR) is a compact, eat-on-the-move food pack intended for use during highly intense, highly mobile combat assaults. A single FSR provides the equivalent of 24 hours of rations and is only about half the size and weight of three MREs. Each FSR—roughly 15% protein, 53% carbohydrates and 34% fat—delivers 2,900 kcal (12,000 kJ), compared to the 3,800 kcal (16,000 kJ) that three MREs provide. FSRs have a two-year shelf life if stored below 80°F (27°C), and the food they contain is packed into a single, trilaminate bag with a myriad of pockets, one containing a chicken or tuna sandwich, another with 2 cereal bars, one dairy-based calcium-enriched dessert bar, 2 packets of a high-energy drink mix, 2 packets of beef jerky (BBQ or Teriyaki flavored), a pouch of fortified applesauce, a nut-and-fruit mix, caffeinated gum and an accessory pack with salt, matches, tissues, a plastic spoon and moist towelettes.

08 FOOD IRRADIATION

Food irradiation is the process of exposing food and food packaging to ionizing radiation, such as from gamma rays, x-rays or electron beams. Food irradiation improves food safety and extends product shelf life by effectively destroying the organisms responsible for spoilage and foodborne illness. It inhibits sprouting or ripening, and is an effective means of controlling insects and invasive pests. Consumer perception of foods treated with irradiation is more negative than that of foods processed by other means. The U.S. Food and Drug Administration (FDA), the World Health Organization (WHO), the Centers for Disease Control and Prevention (CDC) and U.S. Department of Agriculture (USDA) have performed studies that confirm irradiation to be safe. Food irradiation is permitted in over 60 countries, and about 500,000 metric tons of food are processed annually worldwide.

---

09 FOOD SAFETY

Food safety, or food hygiene, refers to routines in the preparation, handling and storage of food in ways that prevent foodborne illness and injury. A “foodborne disease outbreak” is defined as the occurrence of two or more cases of a similar illness resulting from the ingestion of a common food. The principles of food safety, according to the World Health Organization (WHO), are based in five simple routines:

— Storing food at the proper temperature
— Using clean water and safe raw ingredients
— Cooking foods for the appropriate length of time and at the appropriate temperature in an effort to reduce pathogens
— Separating raw and cooked foods to prevent contamination of the cooked foods
— Preventing the contamination of food by pathogens that spread from people, pets and pests.

---

10 FOOD SERVICE

The food service industry comprises all the companies and institutions which prepare meals outside the home, including restaurants, school and hospital cafeterias and catering operations. Suppliers to food service operators are known as food service distributors, which provide small wares like kitchen utensils and a wide variety of food. Some manufacturers offer food products in both consumer and food service versions. The consumer version, intended for retail sales, often comes in individual-sized packages with elaborate label designs. The food service version of the same product is generally packaged in larger industrial-sized containers and lacks the colorful labelling of its counterpart.

11 FREEZE-DRYING

Freeze-drying, also known as lyophilization or cryodesiccation, is a low-temperature dehydration process that involves freezing a food product, lowering pressure, then removing the ice by sublimation. By contrast, conventional dehydration evaporates water from food products using heat. Because of the low temperatures associated with freeze-drying, the quality of the food, when rehydrated, tends to be very good. When solid foods like strawberries are freeze-dried, the original shape of the product is maintained. When a liquid is freeze-dried, the properties of the final product are optimized by the addition of so-called excipients, often inactive ingredients. Other than food processing and preservation, freeze-drying is commonly applied to biological and biomedical products, including bacteria and yeasts, and in the preparation and storage of surgical transplants.

12 FREEZING

Freezing is one of the most commonly used processes, both commercially and domestically, for preserving a very wide range of foods, including prepared foods that would not have required freezing in their original, unprepared state. Potato waffles, for example, are meant to be stored in a freezer, yet potatoes themselves require only a cool, dark place for proper storage. In many countries, cold stores provide large-volume, long-term storage for strategic food stocks held in case of national emergency.

13 GARRISON RATION

A garrison ration is a type of military ration defined as the quantity and type of food served to a soldier when they are stationed in a town, fort or other permanent encampment. Garrison rations are not the same as the rations fed to troops in combat or transit—usually referred to as combat rations, field rations or marching rations. The term is relatively anachronistic and is mostly used with respect to historic militaries, or in reference to the logistics of armed forces in underdeveloped countries.

14 LONG RANGE PATROL RATION

The Food Packet, Long Range Patrol, commonly known as an LRP (pronounced "lurp"), was a freeze-dried field ration used by the U.S. Army during the Vietnam War (1955-75). It was developed in 1964 for use by Special Operations troops, small but heavily armed, long-range reconnaissance teams that patrolled deep inside enemy-held territory. Standard MCI rations—canned and rather bulky—proved too heavy for extended missions on foot. Since it was a freeze-dried ration, the LRP required 1.5 U.S. pints (700 ml) of water to reconstitute and to cook the food inside the packet. This was not a problem where water supplies were plentiful. But in Vietnam, water sources were often teeming with viruses and parasites like blood flukes and tapeworms, and the water had to be boiled or mixed with iodine tablets, the latter resulting in an unwanted flavor in the food. Rainwater could also be used as a fresh water source and, in an emergency, an LRP could be consumed "dry," but the soldier doing so had to consume copious amounts of extra water to prevent dehydration. Some soldiers mixed the contents of LRPs with canned MCI rations to reduce monotony and to supply an extra dietary charge, since they considered a standard ration insufficient for an active soldier. However, this defeated the purpose of deploying the LRP ration in the first place. Another complaint was the absence of cigarettes found in standard MCI rations.

---

15 MEAL, COMBAT, INDIVIDUAL RATION

The Meal, Combat, Individual (MCI) was the name of canned wet combat rations issued by the U.S. Armed Forces from 1958 until 1980, when it was replaced by the Meal, Ready-to-Eat (MRE). MCIs were also commonly known as C-rations.

---

16 MEAL, READY-TO-EAT

The Meal, Ready-to-Eat (MRE) is a self-contained, individual field ration in lightweight packaging developed by the U.S. Department of Defense for its service members for use in combat or field conditions where other food is not available. While MREs should be kept cool, they do not need to be refrigerated. The MRE replaced the canned MCI in 1981 and is the intended successor to the lighter LRP ration developed by the U.S. Army for Special Force and Range patrol units in Vietnam. MREs have also been distributed to civilians during natural disasters.

---

17 MESS

The mess—also called a mess deck aboard ships—is an area where military personnel eat, socialize and, in some cases, live. The term is also used to indicate the groups of military personnel who belong to separate messes, such as the officers' mess, the chief petty officer mess and the enlisted mess. The root of the word *mess* is the Old French *mes*, "portion of food" (cf. modern French *mets*), drawn from the Latin verb *mittere*, meaning "to send" and "to put," the original sense being "a course of a meal put on the table."

18 PASTEURIZATION

Pasteurization is a process for the preservation of liquid food. The process was named after French microbiologist Louis Pasteur, whose research in the 1860s demonstrated that thermal processing would deactivate undesirable microorganisms in wine. Spoilage enzymes are also rendered inactive during pasteurization. Today, pasteurization is used widely in the dairy industry and other food processing industries to guarantee food safety and preservation.

19 RETORT POUCH

A retort pouch, or retortable pouch, is a type of food packaging made from a laminate of flexible plastic and metal foil. It allows for the sterile packaging of a wide variety of food and drink handled by aseptic processing, and is considered an efficient alternative to traditional industrial canning techniques. The foods packaged in retort pouches range from mineral water to fully cooked, thermostabilized, high-caloric meals (1,300 kcal on average) like MREs. Food packaged in retort pouches can be eaten cold, or warmed by submersing the pouch in hot water or heating it with a flameless ration heater, a handy component introduced by the U.S. Army in 1992. Retort pouches are used in field rations, space food, fish products, camping food and instant noodles, in brands such as *Capri Sun* and *Tasty Bite*.

20 SHELF-STABLE FOOD

Shelf-stable food, sometimes called ambient food, is food of a type that can be safely stored at room temperature in a sealed container. The term includes foods that would normally be stored in a refrigerator but which have been processed so that they can be safely stored at room temperature for a particularly long period of time. A number of different preservation and packaging techniques are used to extend a food's shelf life: decreasing the amount of available water in the product, increasing its acidity, irradiating or otherwise sterilizing the food and then sealing it in an airtight container. All of these methods deprive bacteria of the conditions they need in order to thrive, and all serve to extend the shelf life of a food product—often without significantly changing its taste or texture. For some foods, alternative ingredients can be used. Common oils and fats become rancid relatively quickly if not refrigerated; replacing them with hydrogenated oils delays the onset of rancidity, increasing shelf life. This approach is frequently used in food production, but recent concerns about health hazards associated with trans fats have led to their strict control in a number of different countries.

21 SLOPPY JOE

A sloppy joe is a sandwich consisting of ground beef, onions, tomato sauce or ketchup, Worcestershire sauce and other seasonings, served on a hamburger bun. The dish originated in the United States in the early 20th century. Mid-20th-century American cookbooks provide plenty of sloppy joe recipes, though they go by different names: Toasted Deviled Hamburgers, Chopped Meat Sandwiches, Spanish Hamburgers, Hamburg a la Creole, Beef Mironton and Minced Beef Spanish Style. Marilyn Brown, director of the consumer test kitchen at H.J. Heinz in Pittsburgh, Pennsylvania, says their research at the Carnegie Library suggests that the sloppy joe's origins lie with "loose meat sandwiches" sold in Sioux City, Iowa, in the 1930s and were the creation of a cook named Joe. References to sloppy joe sandwiches proliferated in the 1940s. One example from Ohio is an advertisement in the 1944 *Coshocton Tribune* that reads "'Good Things to Eat: 'Sloppy Joes'—10¢—Originated in Cuba—You'll ask for more —The Hamburg Shop" and further down the same page, "Hap is introducing that new sandwich at The Hamburg Shop—Sloppy Joes—10¢." Early on, the term sloppy joe also was used to identify a restaurant or lunch counter that served cheap food quickly. In the 1960s, food companies began producing packaged sloppy joes, in cans with meat or with just the sauce, the most popular of which was branded *Manwich*.

---

22 SOLDIER SYSTEMS CENTER

The Combat Capabilities Development Command Soldier Center (CCDC SC) was formerly the United States Army Natick Soldier Research, Development and Engineering Center. Today, it is a tenant unit of the U.S. Army Natick Soldier Systems Center (SSC), or Soldier Systems Center Natick. The CCDC SC is a military research complex and installation in Natick, Massachusetts, charged by the Department of Defense with the development, including the fielding and sustainment, of food and other service member support items for the U.S. military.

The installation includes facilities from all branches of the armed forces, not just the Army, and is configured to facilitate cross-service cooperation within the facility as well as collaboration with the many academic, industrial and governmental institutions in the Greater Boston area.

The SSC's efforts to improve combat rations have led to a number of groundbreaking developments in food irradiation and freeze-drying.

23 THERMOSTABILITY

Thermostability is the quality of a substance to resist irreversible change in its chemical or physical structure, often by resisting decomposition or polymerization, at a high relative temperature.

24 VACUUM-PACKING

Vacuum-packing is a process by which food is stored in a vacuum environment, usually in an airtight bag or bottle. The vacuum environment strips bacteria of the oxygen it needs for survival. Vacuum-packing is commonly used for packaging nuts because it reduces a loss of flavor due to oxidization. One major drawback to vacuum-packing, on the consumer level, is its tendency to deform the contents and form of foods during sealing and can rob certain foods, such as cheese, of their flavor. Delicate food items, like potato chips, that might be crushed in the process of vacuum-packing, avoid the problem by replacing the oxygen inside the package with nitrogen gas. This has the same effect of inhibiting deterioration or the loss of flavor associated with oxidization.

(Source: Wikipedia, June 2022)

IMAGE NOTES

1 Tear notch for opening, 1972
2 Food taste kitchen, taste test, volunteer sampling food, 1977
3 Formal test panel dental liquids, 1978
4 Food Science Lab, telemetric utensile system, 1976
5 Foreign food bar, 1978
6 Overbaked (burnt), optimum, underbaked, 1987
7 A typical tray pack, canned white bread, 1982
8 Proposed bread alternative, cheese-flavored bar 1984
9 Proposed bread alternative, coconut bar, 1984
10 Proposed bread alternative, orange nut bar, 1984
11 Proposed bread alternative, pizza bar, 1984
12 Lamb chops, 1977
13 Meat grinder, 1977
14 Slices of ground meat, 1977
15 Sipping containers being packed, 1978
16 Irradiated ham, 1972
17 Irradiated ham (for Skylab) in flex-pack, showing excess moisture absorption material, 1972
18 Taste-testing ready-to-eat meal, 1978
19 Meat loaf, soy protein added, 1979
20 Textured beef roast, oven-cooked and water-cooked, 1976
21 Canned corned beef log plus slices, 1982
22 Equipment, packaging polyester wrap (after heating), 1973

23 Freeze-dried blueberries, compressed, 1969
24 Freeze-dried carrots, compressed, 1969
25 Food lab dehydrated disks, 1983
26 Freeze-dried, compressed; moistening freeze-dried peas, 1975
27 Food lab, AUSA exhibit, compressed F.D. peas and spinach bars before and after rehydration, 1975
28 Assault bar production, 1981
29 Freeze-dried compressed, beef and vegetable bar (1 oz.), 1971
30 Freeze-dried, rehydrated food in plastic bag (as eaten by G.I.), 1973
31 Freeze-dried, pork pattie and flex pack (as eaten by G.I.), 1973
32 Tray pack insulator, 1989
33 Vending machine food, 1979 (9 views)
34 Vending machine with Air Force officer, 1977
35 Speed kitchen, 1969
36 Equipment, kitchen, mobile, field (partly assembled), 1973
37 Goulash in can, 1976
38 Display, pecan cake can, 1976
39 Food lab, dental liquid meal to solid meal, 1988
40 Freeze-dehydrated ground beef, freeze-dehydrated ground beef pulverized, 1978
41 Dental liquid ration, 1988
42 Aladdin trays, 5 trays & cover & bottom, 1977
43 Field kitchen, 1982
44 Single serving, egg, 1989
45 Thermally processed eggs, 1993
46 AFRS, tacos, rice + salad, 1973
47 AFRS, submarine sandwich (roast beef), 1973
48 Tray pack, hamburgers with rolls and condiments, 1988
49 Frozen convenience foods, individual serving modules, 1970
50 Chicken chow mein, 1991

51 Beef stroganoff, beef in BBQ sauce, beef stew, mushroom gravy with braised beef tips, sliced beef in Italian sauce, 1978
52 Cooked roast beef dipped & ladled with au jus, 1976
53 Food science lab, eating chamber with test subjects, 1978
54 Irradiated foods: chicken, potato, 1978
55 Irradiated foods: shrimp, potato, 1978
56 Pie filling, 1981
57 Cakes, 1979
58 Hi-energy meal, 1989
59 Fruit chew bars, 1991
60 Desert Shield, candy bar on sand with flag, 1991
61 Meal, ready-to-eat, individual, menu #11, 1970
62 Food packet, survival, abandon aircraft, 1970
63 Food packet, survival, abandon ship, 1970
64 Emergency assault pack, menu #6, 1980
65 MRE, 1982
66 Food packet, life raft, aircraft, 1982
67 Chicken a la king, freeze dehydration and compression, preconcentration, 1987
68 Chicken a la king institutional pouch, 1989
69 Foreign technology, shelf-stable sandwich, 1994
70 Spoon and bowl feeder (spaghetti with meat sauce), 1969
71 Thermostabilized wet meat products, 1969
72 Thermostabilized wet meat product, turkey & gravy, 1969
73 Smokey frankfurters, potato sticks, 1991
74 Tube food processing, 1980
75 Tube food processing, 1980
76 Peach puree, apple sauce, sloppy joe, beef and gravy, toffee pudding, butterscotch pudding, 1977
77 Tube feeding through mask, 1985
78 Thermostabilized salads (sandwich fillings), ham, tuna, chicken, 1969
79 Peach puree, 1977

80 Sloppy Joe, 1977
81 Pancakes with syrup, 1989
82 Waffles with syrup, 1989
83 Equipment, mess kit with fork, knife and spoon, 1971
84 Equipment, knife, survival kit, 1971
85 Can lifter, 1990
86 Canteen cup, cup stand, fuel stand, 1970
87 G.I. in new helmet eating thermo-processed food, command briefing, 1970-93
88 Assault pack with open portions, 1983
89 Food acceptance laboratory, 1972
90 Food lab, B ration study, 1981
91 MRE, beef stew, opened, 1983

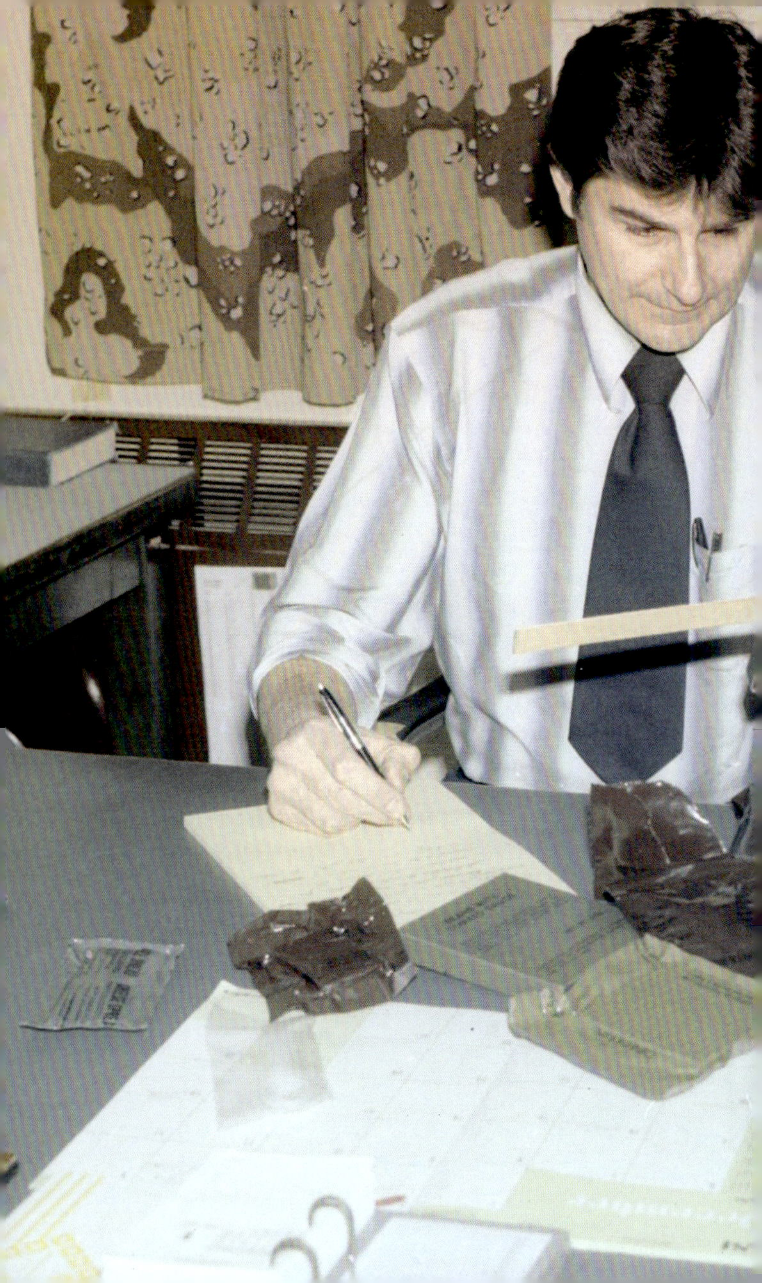

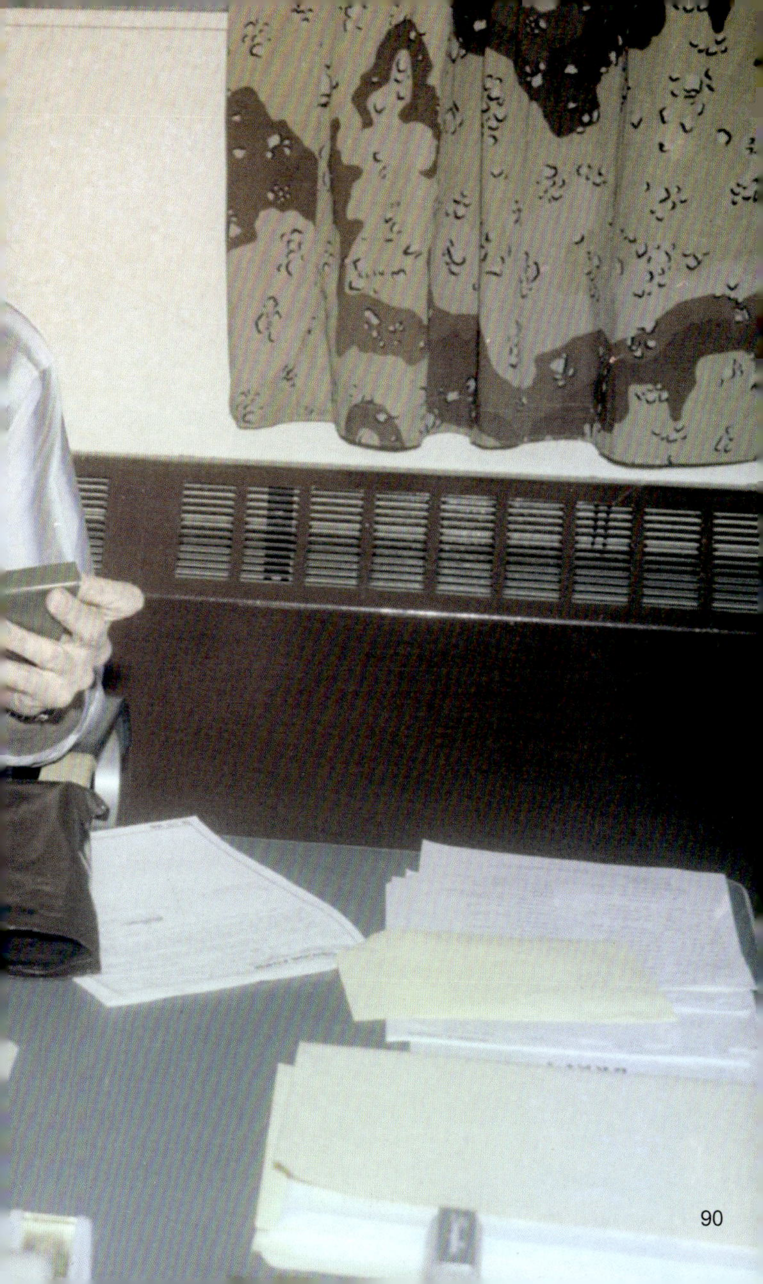

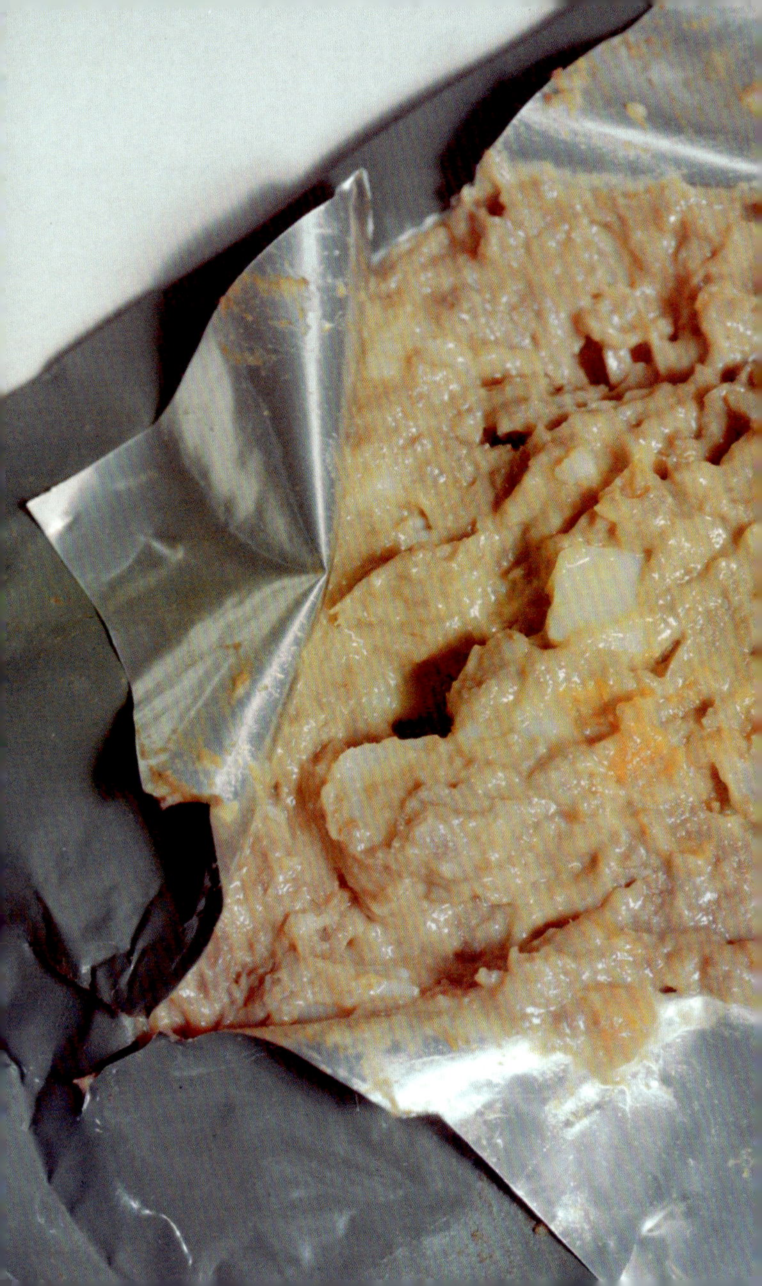

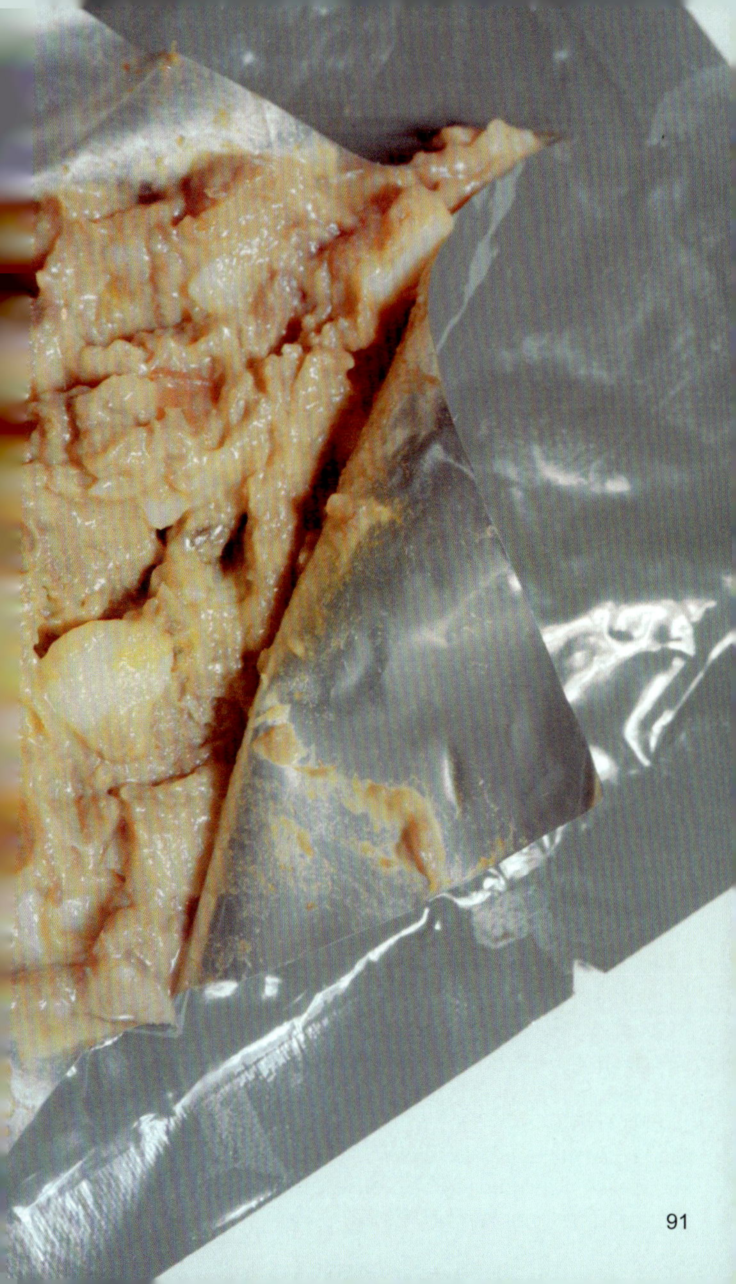

Better Food for Our Fighting Men
Edited by Matthieu Nicol

Graphic design: Catherine Barluet
Color separation: Fotimprim
Proofreading: James Eric Jones
Publisher: RVB BOOKS, Matthieu Charon, Rémi Faucheux
in collaboration with Too Many Pictures

ISBN 978-2-492175-22-0

Achevé d'imprimer en septembre 2022 en Italie.
Dépôt légal : septembre 2022.